Blue-Collar Broadway

Blue-Collar Broadway

The Craft and Industry of American Theater

Timothy R. White

PENN

UNIVERSITY OF PENNSYLVANIA PRESS

PHILADELPHIA

Copyright © 2015 University of Pennsylvania Press

Published by
University of Pennsylvania Press
Philadelphia, Pennsylvania 19104-4112
www.upenn.edu/pennpress

Printed in the United States of America
on acid-free paper

1 3 5 7 9 10 8 6 4 2

A Cataloging-in-Publication record is available from the Library of Congress
ISBN 978-0-8122-4662-9

To my parents
Jean A. and James D. White

Contents

Introduction

IT IS SAID that good magicians never reveal their secrets. This has certainly been true on Broadway, where the virtuosos of stagecraft have built scenery, costumes, lights, and other components for decades but left few clues about their work. Theater historians have gathered some information about these physical components and the stagecraft of putting them together, but most studies of scenery, costumes, or lights focus on design rather than construction or implementation. Despite a rich scholarship of theater history, there exists scant published information about how and where American craftspeople actually built such products.[1] Perhaps this is because no party is sufficiently interested in knowing such details. Why investigate the sources of lumber or the carpenter pay scales for *Death of a Salesman* when one could discuss Jo Mielziner's clever scenic design? When Jule Styne's rousing score, Jerome Robbins's brilliant staging, or Ethel Merman's clarion voice is available for study, why would anyone care about the costume fabric sources used for *Gypsy*? Such questions of craft often pale in comparison to more exciting questions of artistry.

Another reason not to dissect the construction and craft of Broadway is that this strips the Great White Way[2] of its mystery and magic. As any good magician will explain, details of a hat or sleeve can ruin the allure of an elegant trick. So it goes on Broadway, where stage lighting is said to be best when not noticed, where scene shop foremen have held their secrets close for decades at a time, and where costume designers rarely discuss the small armies of seamstresses who bring their designs to fruition. Design has reigned supreme in most histories, and craftspeople have generally stayed out of the spotlight.[3]

Had anyone developed a special curiosity about the people who hammered, painted, and sewed behind the scenes in the commercial theater, they would have been easy to find. Especially prior to the 1970s, such skilled workers were overwhelmingly clustered in one district: Times Square. Despite their ubiquity for many decades, previous histories of this quintessential urban space give short shrift to the carpenters, seamstresses, and other craft experts who brought stage shows to fruition. They often operated major supply shops and theater-related contract businesses but have yet to factor significantly into any history of Times Square.[4]

From a single vantage point, Broadway between 48th and 49th Streets, one can easily trace the prominence of such shops throughout the twentieth century. In August 1936, for example, the visitor to this stretch of Broadway would have quickly encountered theater-related buildings, businesses, and workers. At midday he or she might have seen actors from the Federal Theatre Project's *We Live and Laugh* on their way to rehearsal at Ringle Studios, 1607 Broadway.[5] Directly across the avenue, he or she may have spotted the proprietor Morris Orange or one of his seamstresses on lunch break from their costume rental store at 1600 Broadway.[6] Immediately to the north, the visitor may have seen the cast and craftspeople of the play *Stork Mad* as they walked to the Ambassador Theatre next door.[7]

Twenty years later a 1956 visitor would have been surrounded by the highest concentration of theater-related businesses and employees in the block's history. On the northeast corner of 49th and Broadway, one of the several local Capezio stores offered dance shoes and clothing for hoofers and ballerinas. The Morris Orange costume shop had left 1600 Broadway, but the Broadway Music Soundtrack Service had moved in. Across the street Ringle Studios still operated at 1607 Broadway and was joined by Selva & Sons, suppliers of dance clothing.[8] Just around the corner, at 209 West 48th Street, the Carroll Musical shop offered music publishing and orchestral arrangements, while on the southeast corner of 49th and Broadway, one store sold "novelty costumes" and another "shoes for dancers."[9] The Brill Building housed singers, songwriters, and music publishers, and though the DuMont Television Network had colonized the Ambassador Theatre in 1950, the Shubert Organization would quickly reclaim the space for theater by October 1956.[10]

Beyond this one intersection, a 1956 New Yorker could walk for twenty minutes in any direction and easily find the following: talented scenic designers; lumber, canvas, plywood, and paint; skilled costume beaders; wild varieties of fabric, of every texture and color imaginable; prima ballerinas; finely crafted toe shoes; violin strings; world-class musicians; the union

offices of stagehands, carpenters, and actors; technologically advanced spotlights; skilled spotlight operators; baritones, tenors, and sopranos; method
actresses; Shakespearean actors; composers of beautiful melodies; writers
of witty lyrics; and of course actors of many heights, sizes, shapes, and
personalities. It was an age when the theater district was thoroughly theatrical.

At the same spot in 1976, a visitor would have encountered an entirely
different mix of stores and people. Many more nontheatrical workers
would have sauntered on city sidewalks, from the topless dancers of the
Pussycat Lounge and Cinema to the peep show and massage parlor employees of 1609, 1601, and 1591 Broadway. Although massage parlor prostitutes
plied their trade at 1591 and peep show patrons brought their quarters to
1601, Ingerid's Hair Salon of 1595 Broadway survived right between them,
with a full stock of wigs for Broadway hoofers and pole dancers alike.
Across the street the Music Soundtrack Service had fallen by the wayside,
but a veteran costumer, Madame Bertha, had moved her rental business
into its former workspace at 1600 Broadway. The Brill Building languished,
with a full third of its rental space vacant, but the Ambassador Theatre next
door hosted three legitimate plays throughout 1976.[11] Adult establishments
had certainly invaded the block by the 1970s, but they were not so dominant that theater-related businesses were invisible.

After another twenty years, however, by 1996, anyone visiting Broadway
between 49th and 48th Streets would be hard-pressed to find a single site
of theatrical craft or construction nearby. Real estate development had radi-
cally transformed the block, first with a massive Holiday Inn at 49th and
Broadway in 1986 and then with an office tower at 1585 Broadway.[12] The
closest this block got to theater craft was the sheet music at Colony Records
and the Broadway Video Company, both in the Brill Building. At the
Ambassador Theatre, a popular tap show, Bring in 'da Noise, Bring in 'da
Funk, opened in April 1996, and the new Holiday Inn across the street
undoubtedly facilitated attendance. Broadway consumption was robust,
and city leaders had made considerable progress in reducing adult establishments, but in so doing they had left little to no room for theater craft.

As profound as it was for the Broadway craft economy to be pushed
out of this district by one more global, white collar, and tourist oriented,
the displacement of Broadway's craft and construction activities was not
the only major force at work here. During the same decades that theater-
related shops such as Morris Orange costumes were being squeezed out of

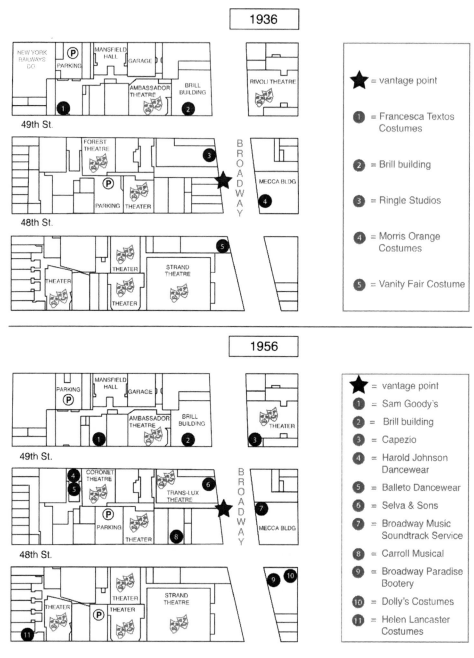

Figure 1. Maps showing that theater-related businesses and activities were numerous and would have been noticeable from the vantage point of Broadway between 48th and 49th Streets. The maps use *Business Listings* and fire insurance information from 1936 and 1956. Conceived by the author and illustrated by Manuel Barreiro.

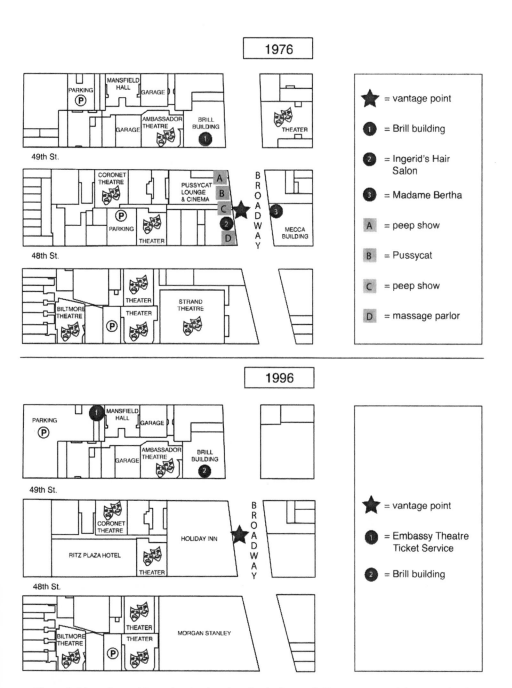

Figure 2. Maps from 1976 and 1996 showing the decline and disappearance of theater-related businesses over time, based on *Yellow Pages* and fire insurance information. In addition, they chronicle the proliferation of adult entertainment in the 1970s near the vantage point of Broadway between 48th and 49th Streets. Illustrated by Manuel Barreiro.

midtown, their proprietors and unionized workers were also pulled out of the region, toward jobs in regional theaters and performing arts centers. Especially in the 1960s and 1970s, American theater craft shifted away from Gotham and into the basement scene shops and costume workrooms of countless regional theaters and performing arts centers nationwide.

With no small amount of local pride, cities that had enjoyed first-rate commercial theater in the late nineteenth century, before New York City's Broadway brand became predominant, stole back control over production by investing in state-of-the-art theaters. Having been ensnared in the awesome power of the Broadway brand from the turn of the twentieth century to the 1960s, cities such as Seattle, San Francisco, and Dallas began to manufacture their own costumes, scenery, and other components in these buildings, engaging in substantial theater craft for the first time in decades.

For these reasons *Blue-Collar Broadway* begins in the late nineteenth century, back when theater-related work was relatively multinodal and spread liberally across a national economic landscape. Before the Broadway age, stock and repertory theatrical companies often recycled and reused old costumes and scenery with abandon. From the 1870s to the 1890s, when most lighting was not bright enough to reveal flaws in well-worn costumes or scenery, resident and traveling theater troupes had almost no incentive to pay for new, professionally constructed components. Audiences' expectations for scenery, costumes, wigs, and other items were generally low, enabling a small market for finished components to emerge, but nothing on the scale of Broadway many decades later. This market and those who manufactured for it were well dispersed nationally, as there was no dominant Broadway brand demanding that specialty components be hammered and sewn on the streets surrounding Times Square.

By the turn of the twentieth century, this brand began to shape America's commercial theater with considerable force. Through the "production photos" used to advertise Broadway tours, featuring costumes, scenery, and backdrops that audiences would now expect to see, along with changes in playwriting and production styles, New York City gained more control than ever over commercial theater. As Manhattan-based shows and the national tours they spawned began to tour aggressively, the number of components needed in Manhattan grew by leaps and bounds. To keep pace with this expansive industry, enterprising New Yorkers founded a wide array of theatrical supply companies and shops. Throughout the 1910s and 1920s, such theater-related businesses and their employees grew increasingly specialized and unionized. By the end of the 1920s, there were so many people and buildings dedicated to these activities in and around Times Square that it was a veritable factory for making plays.

Though the 1929 stock market crash was devastating for Broadway, the years between 1929 and World War II were not as lean in the theater district as one might expect. Theater-related craft work in the 1930s and 1940s was highly fluid, with theater-related businesses moving between stage work, radio broadcasting, and eventually television. Because the shops, suppliers, and skilled workers in and around Times Square succeeded in contracting with alternative forms of media, they stayed relevant and solvent in a rapidly changing economy. Even as they did so, the seeds to Times Square's precipitous decline took root. As sites of radio or television broadcasting, many of Broadway's playhouses suffered from deferred maintenance, neglect, and structural damage.

By the 1940s and 1950s theater-related trades revived along with the national economy through hits such as the famous musical *Oklahoma!* As the costumers, designers, actors, and other individuals working on this musical tromped across the sidewalks of Times Square en route to rehearsals, fittings, design meetings, and other work sessions in 1942 and 1943, they infused the neighborhood with law-abiding pedestrian traffic. These individuals made western midtown a theater district, not just when curtains went up at 8:00 P.M., but every morning, afternoon, and evening. They crafted *Oklahoma!* during the day from workrooms and rehearsal studios tightly concentrated within one district of midtown; yet most of the buildings where they did this work were at least twenty if not forty years old. As vital as it was through the 1950s, the Broadway industry would soon suffer the consequences of its aging stock of buildings.

In the 1960s the centripetal forces that had piled so much theatrical craft work onto the island of Manhattan in earlier decades dissipated. Though some of this enervation had to do with the shift of American freight transport from rail to roadways, most of it stemmed from the decentralizing power of the regional theater movement and the construction of many dozens of performing arts centers nationwide. Each time civic leaders and local philanthropists joined forces to concoct a self-sustaining theatrical production center in a city such as Minneapolis, Dallas, or Seattle, complete with new costume workrooms and scene shops, they weakened Broadway's grip on the national market for specialized theatrical goods.

Compared to the newly built work spaces of the regional theater, the walk-up buildings and dilapidated lofts near Times Square in the 1970s and 1980s were a sad excuse for theatrical production infrastructure. Too small and run-down to merit refurbishment, those buildings that were not torn down tended to be underutilized. This legendary midtown district was dealt a double blow after the 1960s. It lost jobs and businesses to the Sunbelt while also playing host to a shocking new mix of drug peddlers, prostitutes, and criminals. The underutilized, abandoned buildings of Broadway's former production infrastructure became fervent petri dishes for the proliferation of crime and adults-only entertainment in Times Square after 1960. The fact that Times Square lost a sizable part of its theatrical craft and construction economy was certainly not the only cause of this notorious flowering of all things adult and criminal in the 1970s and 1980s, but it did play a strong role.

In the late 1970s, Broadway industry leaders navigated new problems of localized crime, rising costs, rapid globalization, and insufficient local work spaces for craft, rehearsal, and component construction. As anyone familiar with the multimillion-dollar shows of the 1980s knows, America's commercial theater was transformed but not crushed by forces of decentralization and deindustrialization. Much to the contrary, Broadway tourism grew more profitable than ever for the producers of international hits such as *Evita, Cats, Les Misérables, The Phantom of the Opera,* and *Miss Saigon.* But in this era, traditional theater-related craft work played an increasingly smaller role, as breathtaking new technologies began to whisk scenery around at the touch of a button.

Through these narratives of growth, transformation, and loss, *Blue-Collar Broadway* pushes against the design-oriented boundaries of theater history. As an alternative, this book invites readers to consider the very real and well-documented history of the Great White Way as an industry, in the full blue-collar sense of the word.[13] After gaining profound cultural power over the national market for theater, largely through the Broadway brand, New York City producers got to work in the early and mid-twentieth century, paying professional craftspeople to make shows. Through all of these decades, more individuals got paid to sew costumes than to design them or wear them onstage. There were more people standing on ladders painting than there were actors emoting in front of finished backdrops, before audiences. Even when jobs began to bleed out to other states and regions, these craftspeople and proprietors were still a crucial, if diminished, part of the New York City economy. Wedged between the fifty-story office tower next door and the drug pusher on the sidewalk, they continued to do craft work against all odds. This book is their story.

Chapter 1

"Second-Hand Rose"

The Stage Before the Broadway Brand

IT WAS 1875, and Mathias Armbruster did not know any better. He did not know that scenery shops should be in New York City, nor did he know that painted backdrops for the commercial stage were supposed to be crafted with a "Broadway" pedigree. He did not know these truisms of the commercial stage because they were not yet true—not in Columbus, Ohio, and not in 1875. It was in this city and this year that Armbruster founded his scenic studio, which grew into a major national supplier of theatrical components, especially painted backdrops. By the turn of the twentieth century, Armbruster boasted that his was the second-largest scenery firm in the United States. If the reality of his shop fell a bit short of this claim, it was not by much. A German immigrant trained in landscapes, perspective painting, and feather-brush strokes, Armbruster made good in the business by crafting the "wing, drop and border type of setting" used by minstrel and vaudeville shows. Ordering via mailed letters and sketches from across the nation, countless stock theater impresarios and minstrel managers bought components from the firm over its impressive seventy-five-year history.[1]

Armbruster first made his mark during an era that can be described as pre-Broadway, when a concentrated swath of New York City was not yet synonymous with most commercial theater in the United States. Especially during the 1870s, when Armbruster opened for business, the theatrical craft and construction trades were notably free of the cultural and economic monopolies that would tie them so tightly to New York City within a few short decades. This city was already America's uncontested theater capital, and the play agents and brokers of Union Square certainly wielded awesome power nationally. New York City shops, however, were not yet building theatrical components for national consumption. Manhattan *Business Listings* from the 1870s, 1880s, and 1890s consistently name fewer than fifty theater-related firms or craftspeople, most in costuming or costume supply. There were only one or two scenery contractors listed in this entire era, and none stands out as a notable supplier for Broadway shows or national tours. Compared to the amount of theatrical activity happening in New York City, and especially compared to the number of national touring companies launching from that city, the number of firms working in costuming, scenery, painting, and other theater-related trades seems paltry.[2]

In a Gilded Age nation of tremendous economic and theatrical dynamism, why were there so few third-party contractors? Also, if New York City was the uncontested theatrical capital of the nation beginning in the 1870s, and most theater historians agree that it was, why were proprietors such as Armbruster not opening in Manhattan rather than in Columbus?

The answers to these and other questions lay in the limited craft and construction demands of nineteenth-century theater. Prior to the 1880s, commercial shows, both within New York City and without, succeeded with far fewer crafted components than did their twentieth-century counterparts.[3] Stock theater troupes stayed put within their home playhouses for entire seasons at a time, sometimes touring in the summers. Peppering the American landscape prior to 1870, these troupes met most of their component needs through a surprisingly simple strategy: storage. With many dozens of painted backdrops and costumes stored in-house and with audiences expecting familiar "classics" each season, it was relatively easy for the actor-managers who ran these institutions to fill their stages with components they already owned.[4]

Even after the Civil War, when a new business model called the "combination company" gradually supplanted stock as the primary vehicle for commercial theater in the United States, demands for crafted components remained comparatively limited. Combination companies did not stay in residence at home theaters as stock players did, performing a repertory or mix of plays. On occasion after the 1820s and with greater frequency after 1860, combination shows came together for one play or musical only. Combination companies were a temporary fusion of performers, costumes, scenery, and stage crew, hastily pulled together by producers during rehearsals and then disbanded just as quickly when the show closed. The historian Alfred Bernheim said it best when contrasting stock to combination companies, writing that "where the stock company is a continuous producing organization, the combination company is ephemeral. It is created for a specific purpose and it vanishes into nothingness when that purpose is fulfilled."[5] Despite the obvious similarities between these more modern vehicles for commercial theater and the union-crafted, laboriously constructed productions of the twentieth century, combination companies did not kick U.S. demand for crafted components into high gear, at least not initially.

As they first existed in the mid-nineteenth century, combination companies were still part of a preindustrialized commercial theater. Craftspeople in scenic painting and costuming were more likely to be on the payroll of a leading producer than to be a union member, and actors routinely supplied their own costumes. Gas-lamp lighting kept even the most well-worn or dog-eared scenery and costumes safe from the harsh glare of audience scrutiny, and the culture of theatrical classics and revivals made it possible for stages and actors to be dressed in the same old components year after year.[6] Through all of this history, neither markets nor culture mandated that mass quantities of Manhattan-built components travel with combination companies.

During the last twenty years of the nineteenth century, however, this was precisely what craftspeople began to supply and what audiences began to demand. For myriad reasons, finely crafted stage components, especially those built in Manhattan, became de rigueur for touring shows to be successful. Much of this had to do with the advent of electrified stage lighting, which rapidly raised the bar on the quality of stage components during the 1880s. These were also the years when the Broadway brand grew stronger within the theatergoing economy, enabling producers to advertise their shows not as "direct from New York"[7] but as "direct from Broadway." The aggressive business strategies of the Theatrical Syndicate and the Shubert brothers at the turn of the twentieth century were another major part of this equation. So too was realist playwriting, a significant contributing factor in the rising monopoly of Manhattan's theater-related firms over most of American stagecraft. Last but certainly not least, photography modernized in ways that raised the value of the components seen, and photographed, on New York stages.

By the early twentieth century, theatergoers from across the nation demanded and received lavish "Broadway" productions during their visits to New York City and also through elaborate national tours arriving in their hometowns. These productions were a far cry from the charming muslin backdrops of Armbruster's studio in Columbus, Ohio. Their components were far more elaborate than any painted drop to have ever emerged from Mathias Armbruster's cavernous, sun-lit painting room. Most important, these productions came from and were defined as "Broadway." Though it was culture that bound so many American theatergoers to the Broadway brand, it was craft that made this brand possible on a national scale. Crafted components were also a defining feature of the new Times Square neighborhood, which developed rapidly after 1900 as a theatrical district. In these ways, even though Broadway producers ascended to the throne of America's commercial theater through the ephemeral power of culture, it was ultimately craft that enabled them to stay there.

Stock Theater Components

It is no exaggeration to say that the theatrical components of the stock era, when measured by the standards of modern Broadway, were a hot mess. They ranged from new construction to threadbare and from exacting specificity to dubious relevance. They were sewn, painted, and hammered by expert professionals in some cases but more often by rank amateurs. Measured by the expectations for the nineteenth-century theater, however, the components of the stock era were wonderfully efficient. They were only as fine and as specific as they needed to be and not a stitch more. Most were worn, hung, displayed, and utilized time and again until the end of their life cycle, well used and well loved like a toddler's blanket.

Guiding this subculture of storage and reuse were three defining features of crafted stage components in the age of stock theater, prior to the 1880s. First, the prevalence of repertory, melodrama, and oft-performed classics on American stages made the patterns of component reuse eminently practical and sensible. These patterns were so efficient, in fact, that many actor-managers could get a show up on its feet without making any payments whatsoever to third-party contractors or the proprietors of rehearsal studios. The second defining feature of the stock era was its limited stage lighting, which kept the bar relatively low on component quality and craftsmanship for most of the nineteenth century. Third, the disparate geography of commercial theater in this era made patterns of storage and reuse far more attractive than they would be at the turn of the twentieth century. By that time much more of America's commercial theater had been crammed onto the island of Manhattan, where storage space came at a premium.

It is a well-established fact of nineteenth-century theater that stock stages were dominated by repertory, "classics" such as Shakespeare, and melodramas with plots and characters nearly indistinguishable from one to the other. New shows did appear on stages nationwide every season, but few of them strayed far from familiar plotlines, characters, and settings. Whether one paid to see Augustin Daly's stock company as it toured in Denver or Laura Keene in stock in San Francisco, the shows available were quite similar. Scholars and enthusiasts alike have chronicled this history well, mapping out a landscape of distinguished stock houses, traveling minstrels, and touring "stars," both English and American-born. All of these varied vehicles for theater served up melodrama or classics in one form or another. The minstrels may have been parodying Shakespeare, with shows such as *Hamlet & Egglet*, but as the scholar Lawrence Levine has cleverly pointed out, "people cannot parody what is not familiar."[8]

Whatever their muse, theatrical companies of all stripes performed the same or similar shows with such frequency that their use of recycled and stored costumes was a given. By definition, a costume acquired for repertory would be saved for the following season, unless it was entirely specific to some horrible flop of a play. Most costumes were not specific at all, however, so they tended to go right into storage. If Juliet's dress was good enough for *Romeo and Juliet* audiences in 1869, it was certainly good enough for the same actress in the same part in 1870.

Similar incentives existed for saving melodrama costumes, which were tailored to "types" or "lines" within a group of actors. Character lines such as "ingenue, female," "juvenile, male," "aging comic, male," and "comic old hag" pigeonholed actors into the well-worn slots of melodrama and enabled actor-managers to costume them with relative ease. Since most melodramas featured precisely these types of broad, recognizable characters, costumes could be stored and accumulated according to characters rather than plays.

Character lines made costuming such a cinch that it was an afterthought of theatrical decision making and mostly the responsibility of actors themselves. It was the actor who had to cobble together or rustle up an appropriate costume when a new show went into rehearsal, and it was the actor who had to dive into storage racks when cast in a part from the company's repertory. Given that actors, not producers or third-party contractors, bore most of the responsibility for concocting costumes in the 1860s and 1870s, it is not surprising that these costumes were notoriously inconsistent. One newspaper wag in New Orleans, complaining about glaring costume anachronisms of an 1873 production of *Macbeth*, suggested that they were "of every age and nation except the right ones."[9] Other examples from the shabby end of the costuming spectrum include the antics of Otis Skinner as a young actor.

At least as he explains it in his memoir, Skinner was a bit of a costuming shirker during his early career in the 1870s. Skinner wrote, "I was taught how to . . . transform a frock coat into a military uniform by pasting disks of gilt paper on the buttons, and pinning strips of yellow braid on the shoulders for epaulets." He also related a story of a "dress shirt famine" backstage when he had to use a paper cuff to create a makeshift collar. On another occasion Skinner needed a "whiskered face" to play "an Irish cutthroat" and had to make do with "fine-cut tobacco pasted to my jowls, [which] formed convincing looking mutton chop whiskers." Skinner went on to explain, however, that "the only trouble was that they slowly disintegrated during the evening, and I was left, after a scene of assault upon the heroine, with nothing on either jaw but a dark brown smear."[10] If these were the costuming behaviors of a celebrated performer, later picked up by the decorated Augustin Daly Players, one can easily imagine the makeshift tawdriness of the costumes for lesser actors, bit performers, and one-line members of the ensemble.

On the opposite end of the spectrum, there is evidence of lavishly crafted costumes, custom-built couture gowns, and even batches of costumes sent over from the finest fashion houses of London and Paris. Such grandeur in costuming, however, was the exception rather than the rule. It tended to be available only in America's leading theatrical cities, such as Chicago and New York, and was always advertised prominently. No matter of course, such costumes were championed and advertised in ways that speak to their rarity. For Imre Kiralfy's 1888 "spectacular" at the Academy of Music in New York, the impresario advertised "costumes specially designed by Wilhelm of London, manufactured by Mons. Landolft, of Paris, Mr. Fischer of London, and Messrs. Eaves and Madame Cranna, of New York."[11] While Mr. Kiralfy's show demonstrates that costumes could get star billing on occasion, it is safe to say that in the age of stock theater, the number of polished, finely crafted, or lavish costumes was trifling compared to those that were tattered, dog-eared, and just sad, tired little things in general. There is little evidence that this bothered most actors, who worked in an industry for which secondhand costumes were the norm, before newly crafted pieces became standard issue for each new show. Fanny Brice, singing "Second-Hand Rose," may have famously lamented her secondhand clothes decades later, but most late nineteenth-century performers did not seem to have been perturbed by their hand-me-downs.

During decades of repertory, melodrama, minstrelsy, and other theatrical forms that painted time and place in broad strokes, backdrops and other stage scenery were almost as makeshift as costumes were. The dictum "the play's the thing" rang true, and scenic components were, more often than not, the bastard stepchildren of the theater. When they could get away with it, the actor-managers in charge of stock theater companies ordered the same tired, old backdrops to be dusted off and unfurled. They rarely portrayed the settings of plays with any sort of precision. Audiences seem to have tolerated the sort of glaring period inaccuracies and anachronisms that make twenty-first-century reviewers seethe. While these practices may seem to have been rather mundane details of an age when theater buildings had copious storage spaces, they were far more profound than this.

Stored and reused backdrops kept stock theater companies in the black. If new costumes became necessary, an actor-manager could lean on his actors to go get them on their own time and their own dime. If a new backdrop was necessary, however, even the most enterprising member of the team could not produce one on his or her own. It would need to be painted by skilled craftspeople, perhaps at Armbruster Scenic Studio in Columbus, Ohio. If stock companies had been forced to pay for a new backdrop for each of their new shows, most would have sunk faster than a stock portfolio on Black Tuesday. Thankfully the more affordable reused backdrop was widely accepted. The expectations for what would appear behind the actors were so low that many actor-managers skipped backdrops altogether, paying only for simple landscapes to be painted on the brick walls at the back of their stages.[12]

When the managers of stock companies did order new backdrops from a firm such as Armbruster Scenic Studio, they tended to be smart about it. Their most frequent purchases were versatile ones that could be jiggered up to support a broad spectrum of places and plots. Among the choices in Armbruster catalog, "Hotel lobby" was a best seller not because it evoked any particular hotel or city but "because it was a good neutral setting for vaudeville acts."[13] Notions of theater artistry during these years were many steps removed from the expectations of the twentieth century, and back-drops were expected only to hint at the setting, such as "southern porch" or "Japanese garden." Although such practices would not fly today, it was entirely possible for actors playing nineteenth-century Georgians to erupt onstage in front of a Mount Vesuvius backdrop and still have themselves a hit show.[14]

Because most scenery was vague and unimpressive, perhaps even thread-bare or damaged, any theater company featuring new and elaborate scenery tended to score major headlines for its efforts. Back in 1854, when New York City's wealthiest theater-loving families pooled money to build an Academy of Music intended to rival the theaters of Europe, they nabbed headlines by securing the talents of an Italian-trained scenic designer named Signor Allegri. In an effort to turn their 14th Street venue for opera and other enter-tainments into something truly special, they not only hired Allegri and his European-trained assistants as "designers" but also built them an "immense scene room" to execute their designs.[15] It was unusual for any mid-nineteenth-century theater to have a designer, let alone an ample space for this type of work. Allegri's scenic setup was an anomaly also because the Academy of Music had separate designers in costuming and scenery. Most designers from the 1850s through the 1880s had to earn their keep by design-ing everything, including scenery, backdrops, and costumes.[16]

Another institution to enjoy headlines for building new scenery was the stock company at Niblo's Garden, also based in New York City. When the Niblo's company revived a hit 1870 melodrama in 1878 and did not pull any old pieces from storage, critics saw fit to note this prominently within their reviews.[17] Clearly, if all new shows featured all new scenery as a matter of course, the Niblo's development would hardly have been newsworthy. They did not, making the Niblo's strategy in 1878 a notable exception. As a general rule, only the most successful of America's stock theaters could afford to bypass the dominant patterns of storage and reuse for something more grand.

Outside of New York, there were other mavericks who decided to buck the secondhand trend in scenery, especially among companies that focused only on touring, without residing in a stock theater. Some of the most famous theater troupes of this type were the Hanington Brothers and the Kiralfy Brothers, both specializing in "extravaganza" tours during the 1870s and 1880s. These two operations raised the bar for backdrops and scenery because they were selling visual "spectaculars" rather than classics or melodramas.[18] Instead of relying mostly on stored components, troupes such as Hanington's and Kiralfy's routinely purchase them anew for each new production.

Though most stock theaters utilized storage as their primary method of dressing up a show with components, there was enough business in new backdrops to support the operations of firms such as Armbruster Scenic Studio in Columbus, Ohio. Mathias Armbruster was the painter who "didn't know any better" in 1875, featured at the start of this chapter because his business had so little to do with "Broadway." There was far more to this firm's story than the simple fact of its location in the Midwest. Armbruster also stands out because of his use of a catalog, which listed and displayed the backdrops and scenery pieces that he and his crew could craft, paint, and mail to stock and touring customers nationwide. There is archival evidence that the managers of touring minstrels and vaudeville companies also ordered custom pieces not in this catalog by sketching out their requested designs and then mailing them to Columbus.[19]

For theater troupes opting out of the stock system and spending all their time on "the road," Ohio was a surprisingly natural and efficient location for a scenery supplier. Many dozens of melodrama, minstrel, and vaudeville acts crisscrossed the country in all directions after the Civil War, and if the need arose, they could easily pass through Ohio to grab a heavy, rolled-up scenic backdrop. For traveling troubadours not planning to pass through Ohio anytime soon, Armbruster Scenic Studio also had a lightweight option that was a godsend to troupes on the go. It was a backdrop wide enough to span the stage but also thin enough to fold inside a traveling "property box," normally used to store anything from properties to smaller costume pieces. Mathias Armbruster succeeded in crafting this highly mobile product by using ultrathin and lightweight fabrics, which were dyed and brushed with pigment rather than slathered with opaque paint.

Had they stayed put for any length of time, Armbruster's gypsylike customers would have probably stockpiled a wide mix of backdrops within their home theaters, as so many stock companies did. Through the 1860s and 1870s this was the dominant business model for stage components of all types, from costumes and backdrops to smaller items such as wigs, shoes, lighting equipment, and stage props. Most stock playhouses therefore had a dynamic functionality, and their components had a long-lived utility.

From "Page to Stage" in the Stock Age

The use of space during the stock era was so multifunctional and pragmatic that most actor-managers were able to get new shows up on their feet, from "page to stage" so to speak, without paying for any external rehearsal halls, dance studios, scene shops, or music rooms. Their use of components was equally efficient, keeping design, craft, and construction costs for new costumes, backdrops, and scenery to a bare minimum. Because the American stage was so dominated by institutions rather than external markets, the managers of these institutions had to use every tool at their disposal to create shows almost entirely in-house. Within backstage painting rooms and basement storage rooms, theater companies from New York and Boston to San Francisco and Seattle found ways to craft fully realized shows without hiring outside experts.

Performance halls usually contained a main stage for shows; backstage rooms for music, rehearsal, and dance; basement workrooms for carpenters, electricians, and seamstresses; and occasionally sun-lit drafting rooms upstairs for scenic designers.[20] Perhaps most important of all, any available basement room, backstage hallway, or wing space on the side of the stage was devoted to the storage of backdrops, scenery, and costumes whenever possible. It was quite valuable to operate within a theater building that had spaces for painting, sewing, and hammering. It was even more valuable to be able to grab preexisting components from storage and dust them off for a new show.

To get a show from page to stage prior to the 1880s, an actor-manager such as Lester Wallack or Augustin Daly would first acquire a script, often without paying any royalties. Next the stock of actors under this manager's tutelage would assemble for a reading of the play, performed either by the actors in their assigned roles or sometimes by the actor-manager himself. Available photographs of these readings suggest that they often happened on the main stages, perhaps because rehearsal rooms were not large enough to fit the whole flock of players at once. After the reading of the chosen play, rehearsals began in earnest, in every available room. Given that most stock theater companies had to start work on a new show while the old one was still in performances, it was entirely likely for an actor to be working on a read-through or a rehearsal of *Romeo and Juliet* by day while performing *Hamlet* by night.

It is a notorious truth of the stock age that actors had to rustle up their own costumes and wigs, but some were even put to work on scenery and

Figure 3. Augustin Daly reading a new play to his company in 1884. Courtesy of the Rare Book & Manuscript Library, University of Illinois at Urbana-Champaign, Theatrical Print Collection.

backdrops in between rehearsals.[21] Granted, many of the crafted pieces appearing on nineteenth-century stages were simply pulled from storage, but there were also plenty of occasions when performers had to stitch, paint, or hammer specialty items from scratch. As actors scrambled by day to find their costumes for a new show and evening attendance for the current show flagged, the actor-manager would make the call about the new opening night, and rehearsals would accelerate. Actors could rehearse independently or with cast mates, but it was actually quite rare in this period for a show to be "directed." Directing as it is known on Broadway came later.

These were days when actors were burdened with tremendous responsibility in return for their weekly or monthly paychecks. They kept up their performance in current shows, memorized lines for future shows, strived to make their acting interesting without the aid of a director, and also found themselves elbow deep within in-house racks and storage rooms, digging for costumes, hats, or wigs appropriate to their characters. Actors who had no luck in a stock theater's existing collection faced the prospect of shelling out their own hard-earned money at a costume rental facility, millinery shop, or dress shop.

After the previous show had finally closed, any scenery pieces or backdrops that did not fit the new play would be "struck" from the stage, and new components would be hung or staged in their place. This step enabled the actors to perform a final series of dress rehearsals on the main stage, with full costumes, scenery, and lights. A new play was then whipped into shape, to the satisfaction of the actor-manager, just in time for the curtain on opening night. When the play was already part of a stock theater's repertoire, this entire page-to-stage process was streamlined, assuming that the actor-manager had had the presence of mind to store the necessary components of his hit play and assuming that crucial backdrops, costumes, wigs, or bonnets had not been not lost in the shuffle.

It is fascinating that as businesspeople, the maestros of these operations were able to meet so many of their theatrical needs without incurring unnecessary operating costs. Before there were any notable theatrical unions to speak of, the only real limitation placed on the daily hullabaloo of development work within theaters was square footage. If an actor-manager squeezed as many developmental steps as possible into a multipurpose building, this person could limit payments to third-party contractors. If he or she squeezed more labor out of the performers already on the payroll, as so many did, this would limit payments to in-house craft workers. This was true, of course, only until the rise of theatrical unions, which pushed back against the exploitation of actors and painters alike in the late nineteenth and early twentieth centuries.

Another major aspect of theater during this era that made all of this dizzying in-house craft work possible was, of course, the type of shows being presented. Stored bonnets and hastily repainted backdrops were all well and good for vaudeville or melodrama, but such shenanigans would certainly not do for the searingly realistic Henrik Ibsen plays of the 1880s. Gradually from the 1880s to the 1890s profound changes in playwriting and the aesthetics of scenery and costumes chipped away at the old habits of the stock age. These changes certainly cramped the style of star-manager types fond of running the same old ragged costumes and backdrops in show after show. But for the decades immediately following the Civil War, at least, the dominant practices in component construction remained a fascinating hybrid of executive fiat and communal effort, taking place within multipurpose performance halls and storage spaces named after famous actor-managers.

Although efficient, the practice of constructing and storing all manner of theatrical items in the same building where performances took place proved deadly in 1876, when a deadly fire tore through Conway's Theatre in Brooklyn, New York. During the investigation of the tragedy, which killed 238 people, it was discovered that the conflagration burned more rapidly because so many of the theater's nooks and crannies had been crammed full of stored scenery. As the theater historian Mary C. Henderson has explained, this single incident dramatically altered the patterns of theater craft in New York State, provoking a state law banning scene shops, painting rooms, and stored scenery from performance halls.[22] On a national level, the Conway's fire was just one of several important catalysts stoking the winds of change and moving production patterns away from their in-house roots.

Lightbulbs and Stage Realism

Also looming large as a force of change, as a bridge from the stock to the Broadway era, was a tiny but powerful invention: the lightbulb. Though available in major cities as of the 1880s, lightbulbs did not become a standard feature of theaters until the next decade. For many years prior to this, theater companies of all types had to rely on the less bright, more mercurial gas lamp. These lighting devices were the second defining feature of the stock era, the other side of melodrama's coin.

Though gas lamps were a vast improvement over the candles of the seventeenth century or the oil lamps of the eighteenth century, the simple truth was that gas lamps were bloody dangerous and still not all that bright. In stock theaters from coast to coast, they had been jerry-rigged onto theater walls, balconies, stages, prosceniums, and boxes. Those who worked on costumes and scenery at this time had good reason to be cavalier about their makeshift quality; few people could see them well, despite efforts to cast light from every available perch. Given these limitations, the lack of specificity in crafted stage components during the 1860s and 1870s made perfect sense. Why work to convert a cookie-cutter "southern porch" from Armbruster's into a more exacting backdrop portraying the house of the family described in the play when few in the audience could see it well anyway? Under the glow of gas lamps, few actors went to great lengths to stitch fine brocade to their military jackets or lovely lace to their ingenues' dresses.

Granted, these were not entirely dark ages in production value. Actor-managers could fire up an unusually large number of gas lamps to illuminate especially lavish components, though they did increase the risk that they would burn their houses to the ground. Most were content to offer their audiences melodramas, minstrel shows, and classics in poorly lit theaters. In order to be seen and understood in these shows, actors such as Ada Rehan and Otis Skinner utilized larger-than-life mannerisms, facial expressions, and gestures. Performing was so consistently melodramatic that actors often trained in the rote repetition of over-the-top, formulaic gestures that would be legible from the back of the house. Given that the American appetite for melodramas was steady, these gestures were useful for years on end. Actor-managers such as Augustin Daly could keep a star actress such as Ada Rehan on his payroll, as he did through the 1880s, and feature her under the gas lamps with the same gestures in play after melodramatic play.

The much brighter limelight was available relatively early in the nineteenth century, but it was tricky to operate, and only the best of technicians could mask the sickly green tint of its bright glow.[23] When the incandescent lightbulb became available in 1879, everything changed. These bulbs were so much brighter than all previous lights that they literally transformed what actor-managers could sell to audiences. They became an integral component of a massive but gradual sea change in stage presentations from roughly 1880 to 1900. These were the years when the well-oiled machinery of melodramatic plays, overblown acting styles, and recycled stage components fell out of fashion and a sleek new Broadway business model muscled into the spotlight, complete with lightbulbs, stage realism, and newly crafted components.

At first, when the "age of electricity . . . exposed patched-up costumes relentlessly,"[24] garments and other components were decidedly *not* ready for their close-ups. Despite this, actor-managers had little choice but to irradiate shows as brightly as their competitors did, with all the complications and pitfalls that this entailed. Tattered costumes, makeshift moustaches, and fading, anachronistic backdrops were only part of the problem. The lightbulb also exposed aging ingenues and leading men equally long in the tooth. Though they were not as unforgiving as high-definition television would be in the twenty-first century, it is reasonable to assume that electric lighting inspired panic among some of the more aged performers of the late nineteenth century.

Before electric lighting, ingenues could stay ingenues for as long as actor-managers dare present them as blushing Juliets. Male juvenile characters could conceivably keep their roles, and their jobs, even if they carried the "spare tire" of a thirty-something man. Under the gas lamps, if a performer's acting was strong and inflections were true, she or he could keep on keeping on in the same role, or the same character line, for years at a time.[25] Under the harsh glare of modern new lights, such longevity in the same role or character line was possible only for those who happened to have decrepit portraits of themselves hidden away in attics and were named Dorian Gray. In other words, the jig was up.

Stage shows of all stripes moved in a more realistic direction, because for the first time in the history of commercial theater, just about everyone in the audience could see just about everything onstage. Stage realism began to appear on American stages at the end of the nineteenth century, through the playwriting of Anton Chekhov, Henrik Ibsen, and George Bernard Shaw. Simply put, realism was a theatrical trend in which playwrights, scenic designers, and producers reached out to audiences through true-to-life dialogue, scenarios, scenery, and costumes. When producers combined playwriting and stagecraft for realist plays, it was therefore important to choose or construct components with care. Should any piece of a realist play appear too slapdash under the unforgiving shine of lightbulbs, the overall play would have little chance of achieving the playwright's intended "naturalness."

In the realism trend of the late nineteenth century, no figure towers quite as tall as the playwright Henrik Ibsen. A native of Norway, Ibsen has been named the first major realist playwright because of the quick popularity of his iconic plays *A Doll's House* (1879) and *Hedda Gabler* (1890).[26] Anton Chekhov was certainly close on Ibsen's heels, writing *The Seagull*, *Uncle Vanya*, *Three Sisters*, and *The Cherry Orchard* in the late 1890s, but these plays took longer than Ibsen's to become mainstays of the American stage. Similar timing unfolded for the British realist George Bernard Shaw, whose work began to appear regularly in the United States only after 1900.

Ibsen's play *A Doll's House*, however, debuted in New York as early as 1889, after having played Europe to great acclaim throughout the 1880s. When this play arrived in New York at Palmer's Theatre near Herald Square and at Broad Street Theater in Philadelphia, these productions were islands of realism in a sea of melodrama. Audiences were reportedly stunned by the play's jarring, modern, and decidedly *not* happy ending, especially in Philadelphia. Having seen the title of *A Doll's House* advertised in 1889, apparently more than a few mothers brought their children in the expectation that it would be especially enjoyable for little ones. It was not.[27]

It did not take long for theatergoers to warm to Ibsen's cold, emotional realism, however, and by 1908 American producers had mounted *A Doll's House* seven times in the city of New York alone. For reasons having to do with the lightbulb, the realism concept, and the trends of Broadway business history, each of these seven stagings required a new batch of costumes, scenery, lights, and other components to be gathered and assembled.[28]

These new components were necessary because of the vast gulf between *A Doll's House* and the run-of-the-mill melodramas, such as *The Drunkard*, that had previously played Palmer's. Unlike *The Drunkard* and its ilk, *A Doll's House* occurred in a highly specific place. According to Ibsen, it occurred within "The Helmers' Living Room; a small Norwegian town, 1879."[29] Ibsen does not send his characters to any of the settings of nineteenth-century melodrama, such as the intimate boudoir, the formal dining room, or the off-limits servants' quarters. These places were infused with meaning and familiar to audiences. Had the lead character of *A Doll's House*, Nora Helmer, traversed any of this well-trod theatrical territory, producers could have easily pulled less specific backdrops or preexisting scenery pieces from storage. The play does not slot into any of these melodramatic ruts, however, evolving instead within one and only one drawing room, which the central character of Nora leaves only at the play's famous ending.

The constricted setting of A Doll's House meant that existing backdrops or stock scenery depicting New England, Georgia, or even Vienna were entirely unacceptable. The stage needed to suggest a "small Norwegian town" in no uncertain terms. Rented costumes appropriate to a slightly different time or place were equally unwelcome, especially considering that lightbulbs had indeed been installed at Palmer's by 1889. Ibsen had no intention for Nora's plight to be presented onstage in broad, melodramatic strokes. For the play to work properly as a realist piece, the Helmer drawing room needed to be built from scratch, as the Helmer drawing room.

Why could the producers of A Doll's House at the turn of the century not track down the drawing room from the most recent staging, rather than building anew? First, each production of the play between 1889 and 1908 was financed by a different, competing producer. This created a huge disincentive for sharing or lending scenery, lights, draperies, and costumes. Second, even if competing producers were feeling magnanimous, most were adopting the new business practices of the 1880s, disassembling, destroying, or selling components after closing night rather than storing them. After about the 1880s, the cost of storing scenery or assembled lighting trusses, in the hope that they might become useful later, became prohibitive, especially in Manhattan.[30] Available evidence strongly suggests, therefore, that Broadway craftspeople did craft seven separate batches of components for A Doll's House between 1889 and 1908.

Hedda Gabler, another famous Ibsen play, tapped the well-illuminated potential of stage realism in much the same fashion. After succeeding in Europe in 1890, it too inspired seven distinct Broadway productions from the early 1890s to 1908.[31] In 1904 there were even two productions of Hedda running simultaneously on Broadway, at the Daly's and Manhattan Theaters.[32] Hedda's setting is as confined as is that of Doll's House, with the entire play occurring within "the home of George and Hedda Tesman, Christiania, Norway, near the turn of the twentieth century."[33] Ibsen does briefly send his players into a small side room off the drawing room, but the play's realist restrictions are basically the same. Hedda does not leave her original setting until the play's conclusion, in an exit even more dramatic than Nora's.[34] The cramped setting of *Hedda Gabler* requires that the passage of time as well as changes in tenor and mood be indicated by highly specific costumes and lighting. At nightfall in a straightforward, realist production of *Hedda*, the light coming through the drawing room windows would change and diminish. The scenery also had to be extremely specific to Christiania, Norway, as audiences were being asked to follow a story about "real" characters rather than melodramatic ones.

Everything in a realist play had to be custom built, unless a designer was lucky enough to find preexisting scenery pieces or costumes that were a perfect match. This meant that for *A Doll's House* and *Hedda Gabler* combined, the craft work of scenic construction, drapery hanging, lighting design, and costume construction occurred roughly fourteen times between 1890 and 1910.

As one of several prominent realists, Henrik Ibsen was only a part of a much larger trend that reshaped what commercial stage shows looked like after 1880. The currents of change in lighting and playwriting ran strong in ways that would make scenery, costumes, and backdrops virtually unrecognizable by the turn of the twentieth century. Lighting and realism were only two parts of a much broader set of changes, all of which repositioned New York City as an uncontested giant in the crafting and manufacturing of stage components.

Geographic Dispersal

A third defining feature of the stock era was its wide-ranging geographic dispersal. From the 1850s to the 1870s, stock theaters existed in just about every major city in America and also in more than a few Podunk towns. At the peak of their influence, they probably totaled approximately five hundred in number from sea to shining sea. Each of these institutions had an in-house stable of actors, racks of costumes ready to be pulled, stored lighting equipment, and at least a few backdrops on hand, all ready for their next big scene. All of these stock companies, even those that happened to be on Broadway in New York City, lived and died according to the reputations of their actors, especially their actor-managers. Their success depended on people rather than on any mythical New York boulevard or district they might call home.

Touring routes in the stock era were equally disparate, spanning all regions and many corners of the vast United States of America. These were years when the best of America's commercial theater came to you, at least eventually. This was especially true when the "star system" developed as a variation on regular stock patterns. The theater historians William Zucchero and Mary C. Henderson locate the birth of the star system in 1820, when the British actor Edmund Kean made his epic, well-publicized sojourn through America. Regular stock theater sustained local "stars" in cities such as Buffalo, New York, or Winston-Salem, North Carolina, but no one on the scale of Kean or successors such as Charles Macready or Henry Irving. After the telegraph and the railroad had transformed America, culturally, into a much smaller nation, it became easier for popular actors to rocket to national recognition. The first wave of "stars" was mostly British, but as the nineteenth century progressed, Americans began to worship at the altars of homegrown heroes such as Edwin Forrest and Joseph Jefferson. These true "stars," whether British or American, did not reside in stock, at least not for long. They toured.

Especially after the mid-nineteenth-century boom in railroad construction, theatrical stars from England and the United States toured frequently. Looking at the breathlessly excited announcements, headlines, and reviews for these tours, it would appear that many theatergoers in distant corners of the United States were beside themselves that a star had come from London or New York to visit their humble hometowns. There was a catch to all this excitement, however. It was the hangover of becoming drunk with excitement over a visiting star. After the hubbub died down, actors who had been playing in town for years suddenly paled in comparison to the memory of the recently departed luminary. Evidence suggests that in the wake of a passing tour, stock audiences found their regular players to be a bit too regular.[35]

They responded to this malaise by demanding more tours and more stars. If a second-rate talent from England or New York could pass for a star in Peoria, as many did, she or he answered this call. Most stars toured, however, with only their personal assistants, their costumes, and perhaps a wig or two. Those who traveled light counted on stock companies to supply all other trappings of the shows they had agreed to perform. Most arrived just a few days before the opening of their engagements, gracing the existing companies with their presence for only a few quick "put-in" rehearsals, if that. As soon as the visiting stars had established some semblance of rapport with the ensembles, actor-managers, probably chomping at the bit, rushed to raise the curtains, usually to adoring audiences and windfall profits. In some of the more notorious cases of star mania, curtains went up on stars and ensembles that had not rehearsed together even once.[36]

One might ask why star performers would tour the provinces so relentlessly in the 1840s and 1850s when more urbane settings awaited them in New York or London. They were shunted to America's provinces and periphery simply because that is where most of the market for commercial theater was located. That is where most of the backdrops, wigs, lighting trusses, scenery pieces, and costumes were, and that is, in essence, where most commercial theater resided. For decades it resided in stock theaters, dotting the landscape nationwide. Stars who had not surrounded themselves with some sort of finished, traveling production had to connect those dots on their tours. Many did travel with their own costumes, of course; the most celebrated of nineteenth-century actors could easily afford to do this. They carted a collection of fine costumes around with them for all of their well-known roles. Unfortunately many larger, more unwieldy components were out of their control.

When star actors agreed to be plunked into the center of preexisting stock theaters, they were stuck with whatever actors, backdrops, or stage components lay waiting for them. Some were undoubtedly a lovely, well-crafted surprise, while others were, not surprisingly, appallingly bad. Quickly after the rise of the star system, touring performers got smart about components, the unpredictable Achilles heel in their touring shows. They figured that if they could bring an entire production along with them, complete with fellow players and components, they could stop sharing the stage with sub-par scene partners and a shabby mishmash of stock components. They could, in essence, control the artistic quality of their entire tour.

Thus the combination company was born. Unlike stock, these companies were mobile, rootless, temporary compilations of all the necessary scripts, performers, costumes, wigs, lights, sets, backdrops, scores, and musicians needed for one particular play, melodrama, operetta, or "big-time" vaudeville show. After being combined into a salable product within a major U.S. city such as Baltimore or Boston and performing locally for a few weeks, or at most a few months, the whole kit and caboodle was packed up and sent on tour via railroad. With increasing frequency after 1850, combination companies arrived in towns and cities across America with several train cars of physical components in tow. These companies did not supplement, enhance, or mesh with stock theater troupes, as touring stars had. They supplanted stock, transforming playhouses from sites of apprenticeship, craft, and performance to more limited sites of performances only, available to the highest bidder.

Most theater historians agree that combination companies chipped away at the stock system until the financial crash of 1873, when a massive number of stock companies folded and combinations became the dominant vehicle for theater in the United States. This is the consensus among theater historians from the 1930s to the present day.[37] What is not as clear is the impact that this shift had on components. It is tempting to think that the ascendance of combination companies was the real birth of the Broadway business model, and that after 1880, most American stage components must have been built in New York. This is certainly the position taken by Alfred Bernheim in 1931 when he wrote in *The Business of the Theatre*, "[W]here decentralization was the keynote of the stock system, centralization became an outstanding feature of the combination system. This centralization had two manifestations. In the first place it made New York City the producing center for the entire country. . . . it actually became the feeder for virtually all the theaters that adopted the combination system, for New York . . . was the only city where all the plays could be cast and mounted that were needed to supply the theaters throughout the country."[38] It is undoubtedly true that by the 1870s and 1880s, combination companies were running roughshod over stock theaters and that more of these companies launched from the city by the Hudson River than any other.

Yet the *Business Listings* for theater-related trades in Gilded Age New York do not support the idea that the city was quite as dominant as Bernheim suggests. In the Manhattan *Business Listings* for 1879, only thirty-one suppliers appear in all theater-related trades, such as costumes, stage armor, masks, and calcium lights. This in a city that already had more than a dozen playhouses and would quickly get many more. By 1888 the total number of theater-related suppliers had grown from twenty-seven to forty-seven, but this total would drop to only forty-three in the 1896 *Business Listings*.[39] New York City certainly had more theater-related businesses than cities such as Chicago or San Francisco, but not that many more. Even after the turn of the twentieth century, about two-thirds of combination companies still launched from cities other than New York.[40] The reality of the late nineteenth century, even after the ascendance of the combination company, was that theatrical craft was still multinodal. Even old Armbruster's, the distinguished backdrop manufacturer in Columbus, Ohio, continued to do brisk business with vaudeville and minstrel shows well into the twentieth century, without even bothering to open a New York City branch office.

Additional evidence of this multinodal, geographic dispersal is available in the advertisements for combination or stock companies on tour. Boosters and "advance men" did not advertise either form as "direct from Broadway" in the 1870s or 1880s. They did not boast of components built by Broadway contractors. Instead they packaged and sold incoming productions by the names of their famous actor-managers or sometimes their cities of origin. The actor-manager Augustin Daly, who in one advertisement was touted because he "personally, directs every performance" of a show on tour, was more of a brand than Broadway. It was Daly and famous players, such as Ada Rehan, that audiences wanted, or at least that is what the advance men and advertisers believed. In some cases the name of the theater was the hook, such as in 1888 when the Chicago Opera House got the A. M. Palmer's company "Direct from the Madison Square Theatre, New York." Stock companies could play to packed houses on tour without being advertised as Broadway shows, just as the Hanington or Kiralfy brothers succeeded with their spectaculars without even playing New York. When an impresario such as Lester Wallack was the brand, the actor-manager and the players of a stock theater were an attraction regardless of whether they launched from Baltimore, San Francisco, New York, or any other major city.[41]

Even in the 1890s, when the Broadway brand was beginning to take shape, high-profile tours launching from Gotham City continued to be advertised as "direct from New York" rather than "direct from Broadway."[42] Most New York theaters were located on Manhattan's oldest and most famous boulevard, which just so happened to be named "Broadway," but they did not yet promote themselves as Broadway houses. Short of going back in time to ask 1880s Denver or San Francisco theatergoers whether they would pay more for a show arriving "direct from Broadway," it is hard to know how much weight this verbiage carried at the time. What we can say, with certainly, is that combination companies were *not* Broadway shows, at least not necessarily and not yet. They were getting close, however. Consider the advertisements run by the managers of the Chicago Opera House for their 1888–89 season, after they had convinced Lester Wallack to send his latest hit play directly to Chicago upon its closure in New York. They proudly described their coup as follows: "[T]he first piece will be *The Lady and the Tiger*[,] which made such a hit at Wallack's. It will be produced with all the original scenery and costumes."[43] While this promotional copy did not tout Broadway per se, it came mighty close.

The Rialto at Union Square

During the last few decades of the nineteenth century, as stock theaters sank and combination companies flooded the nation, New York City elites may not have hammered, painted, or sewn most American stage productions, but they certainly booked them. Booking agents in New York, particularly Union Square, became a crucial part of the burgeoning Broadway brand. Beginning in the 1870s, the Union Square district became a bustling hotbed of theatrical booking activity, and was also home to most of the city's theater-related specialists and third-party contractors. Within this mix of publishers, portrait studios, and restaurateurs catering to theater industry insiders, it was the booking agents who held the most power.

These agents had gained control because of the chaos of the 1850s and 1860s, when an expanded rail network launched theatrical touring into hyperdrive. Stars caused a stir in many a medium-sized American city after pledging to appear there onstage, only to cause a bigger, probably angrier stir when they skipped out on the engagement. Countless theatergoers from the mid-nineteenth century counted the days until their star would finally arrive, not knowing that they were waiting for a Guffman or a Godot who would never come.

Those who owned theaters, and who had promised these deadbeats and no-shows, were hardly angels in this chaotic, unregulated hodgepodge of a system. Through the 1850s and 1860s theatrical touring was a dizzying and bewildering crisscross of broken promises in all directions. To protect themselves financially, and perhaps to allay their fears of disappointed, star-obsessed mobs, theater owners routinely double-booked two acts into the same playhouse for the same week or weekend. Touring groups that kept their promises would show up in town only to find themselves stranded without a playhouse because a rival company was already there, in the thick of performances. Considerable evidence indicates that this era was truly first-come, first-served when it came to bookings.

To counteract this chaos, booking agents nationwide, but especially in Union Square, began to organize theaters into touring circuits, following sensible geographic patterns. They did this with the best of intentions, and with no small amount of self-interest. Circuits arose for all flavors of theatrical entertainment, but they were especially dominant in the here-today, gone-tomorrow world of vaudeville.[44] Even as New York–based booking agents rose into positions of tremendous national power, components were still crafted and discovered all across the country.

As the theater's circuits grew stronger and more predominant, they did much to solidify the Broadway brand. The circuit to end all circuits was the Theatrical Syndicate, founded in 1896 in New York by six leading theatrical managers. Because these six titans of the theater agreed to freeze out other producers, and because they owned most of the theaters into which they would all book their shows, their syndicate became an awesome, oligarchic force to be reckoned with. It also became a target.

Reading the newspapers of the day, especially Harrison Grey Fiske's antisyndicate circular, the *Dramatic Mirror*, one might suspect that the "big six" of the Syndicate were the first to have ever frozen rival producers out of their circuits or the first to have baldly placed bottom-line concerns at the forefront of their theatrical enterprise. They were not, of course, but all six of them did happen to be Jewish. Recent scholarship on the battles between the Syndicate and its rivals has suggested, quite convincingly, that the protests hurled at this oligarchy were laced with, and grounded in, anti-Semitism.[45] Whatever their motivations may have been, eventually the Syndicate's enemies prevailed. The brothers Shubert staged a successful challenge to this trust soon after the turn of the twentieth century, toppling it to become a monopoly in their own right by the 1910s. In this drama the Shuberts have often been cast as David to the Syndicate's Goliath. This story has been told before and told well. It has not yet been told, however, as a story of components.

In terms of stage component history, the location of both David and Goliath in New York City had profound and long-lasting implications. Neither the Syndicate nor the Shuberts had any interest in developing stock theaters. They produced only combination shows, and they happened to do so within New York City. The melding of these two factors would directly lead to the mighty and long-lasting monopoly that New York City firms gained in the national market for stage components. Perhaps more than the lightbulb, more than playwriting, and more than any other catalysts for change, New York City's combination companies became the building blocks of the Broadway show.

This is fascinating because the power wielded by New York's combination companies was as much cultural as it was economic. Profits did flow disproportionately back to New York City, giving New York operations an unfair leg up in the commercial theater game. Equally important in the bizarre alchemy of the "Broadway show," however, was the ever-changing culture of theatergoing. Audiences from the 1850s to the 1880s clamored for star performers and directors but did not seem to have paid more for a show arriving "direct from Broadway."

By the 1900s and 1910s, however, "Broadway shows" were everywhere. Audiences yearned for them, and advertisers promoted them relentlessly. "Direct from Broadway" language was no longer the occasional tagline but the standard centerpiece of most advertising. Whenever shows from New York City arrived in any other city, "direct from Broadway" advertisements were an absolute must. There is even evidence suggesting that in the 1920s, the Shuberts would mount shows on Broadway for brief spells, as short as one night, just so they could cash in on the lucrative legitimacy of the mighty brand when the show toured.[46]

When theatergoers across the country paid to see a show "direct from Broadway," they held many common assumptions about what this claim entailed. Among the assumptions: all costumes, backdrops, scenery pieces, shoes, wigs, lights, technologies, and other components had come from Broadway, meaning New York City. Even more powerful was the assumption that all of these components were somehow, in some way, inherently better for having come from Broadway.

Photography played a major role in the spread of widely held assumptions about New York–built components. Through the 1880s pictorial advertisements for stage shows routinely featured portraits of leading players, often taken at the legendary Sarony's portrait studio at Union Square. Such portraits operated as enablers of makeshift, lackluster costumes, because there was no connection between what an actor wore for his or her portrait and what he or she wore onstage. With improvements in camera technology and portability in the 1890s, however, a new photographic style known as "production stills" took over.

Unlike portraits, production stills actually showed an actor onstage and in costume. Cameras had been liberated from the confines of the studio, and "stills" began to appear routinely in posters, advertisements, and magazines. They created entirely new expectations among audiences. New Jersey readers of *Stage Chat* magazine in 1914, for example, saw photographs of the celebrated actress Maxine Elliott in full costume onstage in the New York run of *Hearts Aflame*.[47] The producers of this hit play had little choice but to present Elliott in those very same costumes and in front of the very same scenery when the show toured in New Jersey. Even if producers were willing to foist makeshift components on the touring production, saving their more beautiful pieces for an upcoming Manhattan play, they ran the risk that critics in New York would recognize them. These critics would see from old production stills that producers had cut corners instead of using new costumes or backdrops. As production stills began to dominate advertising in the 1890s, the American market for components was transformed. Components had shorter life cycles and were expected to come directly from the New York stage if they had been part of a hit show.

Another example, this time from 1903, illustrates in no uncertain terms that national audiences were both demanding and expecting New York City components. Just as Elliott's play had, a play called *Favor of the Queen*, helmed by the star actress Percy Haswell, went on tour. While stationed in Baltimore, the production lost something even more rare and precious, perhaps, than its leading lady. A fire destroyed every last piece of the scenery and costumes, and the tour came to an abrupt end.[48] The surprising decision of the manager to scrap the tour altogether is a telling example of the awesome new power of the Broadway brand.

In the nineteenth century, no conflagration of mere stage components could derail the tour of a great star. Audiences who flocked to see stars on tour cared little for backdrops and costumes, and they were hard to see by gas lamp anyway. While they were occasionally important for "spectaculars," it was rare for components to dictate the success of a show. By 1903, however, a fire in a crowded costume or scenery storage space could actually stop a national tour in its tracks. For Percy Haswell's play, it was apparently not an option for Baltimore dressmakers and painters to create replacement components, because these pieces would not have been "Broadway." Broadway had developed into far more than an industry or a place; it was a national brand. New York City's "Broadway" rose into prominence and would not share center stage with anyone or anything for over fifty years. Over the course of its fascinating reign in commercial theater, the practices of Broadway producers ranged from ruthlessly monopolistic to inspiringly artistic. Broadway simultaneously functioned as a vast, productive national industry and a sweeping, sordid swindle.

Chapter 2

"A Factory for Making Plays"

Broadway's Industrial District

IN 1902, twelve years before Henry Ford introduced his revolutionary automobile assembly line in Michigan, the Broadway producer Henry W. Savage built a theatrical assembly line, of a sort, on the island of Manhattan. At West 27th Street and 10th Avenue, Savage hired carpenters, scenic painters, costumers, electricians, and property makers to work in a single building. As the *New York Times* noted in its 1906 feature on the facility, entitled "A Factory for Making Plays," "so complete is the factory in every detail that raw material is taken in through one door, while one month later the finished play, from scenery to flashlights, leaves by the opposite."[1]

Although innovative, Savage's amalgamated facility was hardly the stuff of magazine covers, as Ford's would become after 1914. Stock companies had already been crafting costumes, scenery, and other components within the same buildings for most of the nineteenth century. In one aspect, though, Savage's structure was unique: it was not adjacent to a theater. Far from it, the plant was about ten blocks, and a good three to four avenues, from the nearest 1902 playhouse. It stood amid the gas plants and foundries of the far west side, on a parcel of land much larger and more affordable than anything near Times Square. As an independent site of show construction physically removed from theaters and devoted completely to the assembly of theatrical products, the Savage plant heralded the modern age of industrialized Broadway.[2]

Though Ford would easily outdo them in efficiency, mass production, and notoriety, Savage's stable of costume, property, and scenery crafts-people did manage to pull off an impressive seamlessness, despite the fact that there were no conveyor belts on the premises. According to the *New York Times* feature, "[T]he property man . . . places any little thing, such as a vase, table, or picture that is to be used in the scene near the canvas, in position . . . to get the proper effects in color and height, so that it will look right when in actual use. The electrician is also called in and receives directions as to light effects. The costumer must likewise consult him to assure the harmonizing of the costumes and scenery. . . . Everything must be in keeping with the general scheme of the whole."[3] None of Savage's employees was the proprietor of his or her own independent theater-related business, but their work in specialized theatrical show building did move the industry one step closer toward its fully industrialized future. A generation later, as Savage lay dying in 1927, the efficiency he birthed on 10th Avenue had grown exponentially in and around Times Square, having been writ large upon a sprawling, productive, industrial district.[4]

Producers, property owners, and Broadway craftspeople built up this dynamic, interconnected district in midtown Manhattan during the first three decades of the twentieth century. In this era theatrical leaders abandoned nineteenth-century modes of in-house production, opting instead to purchase and rent their components from third-party contractors. Broadway's craftspeople gained power within this modern system by removing their skilled labor in costuming, carpentry, painting, and lighting to specialized locations and by opening their own businesses and hiring themselves out on a contract basis. By the 1910s Broadway was well supplied by these businesses, but many craftspeople still had little control over their working conditions. To rectify this, musicians, scenic artists, costume workers, and actors founded or joined unions. Together with the long-influential stagehands' union, these newly organized workers built a dazzling array of commercially viable, artistically compelling, and well-crafted works of stage art in the early twentieth century.

At the same time, because producers exported these works to other cities, the Times Square industrial district was more than just the supplier of products to Gotham; it was the "factory for making plays" of the entire nation. This was especially true after 1914, when the American film industry expanded rapidly, killing off many of the surviving stock or local theaters outside of New York City. In the age of affordable moving pictures,

Figure 4. Times Square ca. 1908, looking south toward the Times Building (in the center) and the Astor Hotel (on the right, with the flag). Courtesy of Detroit Publishing Company Collection, Prints and Photographs Division, Library of Congress.

stage troupes and vaudevillians across the country all but disappeared, save for the touring companies launching from Broadway.[5]

As Times Square and the far west side matured, filling to the brim with businesses and highly skilled laborers, the occupants there began to enjoy the economies of scale that so often define industrial districts.[6] These economies of scale enabled firms, even rival firms, to benefit from intense concentration and proximity. Companies contracted out excess workloads, benefited from each other's specialties, and purchased raw lumber, paint, and fabric through bulk suppliers. The economic benefits of this dense concentration of talent, skill, and knowledge brewed even among the most mercurial and idiosyncratic of Broadway's painters, performers, dancers, choreographers, and designers. Though hard-nosed producers sometimes complained that Broadway's bohemians had made Times Square "chock full o' nuts," each provided a unique and economically valuable flavor to the overall artistic capacity of the district.

As competing firms and producers unwittingly aided each other and as artists made positive economic contributions whether they intended to or not, building after midtown building was put to productive theatrical use. Some of them were preexisting and converted for use as sites of theater craft, while others were built anew by the new masters of the midtown universe. These individuals included the usual suspects such as producers, agents, and theatrical financiers but also the proprietors of craft firms, such as Charles Geoly of Eaves Costumes. Geoly was more than just the skipper of one of the district's largest costume firms; he also became a mover and shaker in Times Square real estate, purchasing several expensive, well-located buildings in 1921.[7]

From roughly 1900 to 1930 these captains of America's theater industry built up an impressive construction district within many dozens of buildings in and around Times Square. This de facto "factory," churning out shows for national consumption, has yet to be given its due in history books and is little understood as the mighty industrial district it truly was. Within this district scenery, lighting, costumes, properties, and other components moved out of their tattered, secondhand, nationally dispersed past into an era of incredible Broadway concentration and dominance. Firms, craftspeople, and buildings all helped to solidify this unbalanced geography, and theatrical businesses in New York City enjoyed staggering power. In the years leading up to 1929, midtown's component suppliers helped to turn Broadway into more of a national monopoly than it had ever been before or ever would be again.

Industrialization in Scenery

Scenic design had certainly been transformed by the lightbulb, which rendered so many of the nineteenth century's threadbare backdrops obsolete. As craftspeople built new shows in the early twentieth century, they changed scenic design yet again, in ways even more profound. Scenery, in essence, became art. This is not to say that the elegant brushstrokes and the carefully painted perspectives of Signor Allegri or Mathias Armbruster had not been art. Of course they had been, but only within the two-dimensional confines of a backdrop. Armbruster and his nineteenth-century ilk had manufactured some three-dimensional, freestanding scenery pieces, framing the stage or the actors, but only on occasion.

The new, artistic scenic designers and builders of the early twentieth century played more aggressively with shape, light, color, and scale in all three dimensions. Producers such as David Belasco began to order fully realized, inhabitable playing spaces from their scenery builders, bending the realism trend of the 1880s in a far more literal, fleshed-out direction. Belasco was the producer who famously demanded that his craftspeople build a working kitchen onstage, complete with a working griddle where actors could cook their "wheatcakes" before the eyes of spellbound audiences.[8]

Simultaneously designers such as Robert Edmund Jones played more with abstraction, concocting towering buildings, bridges, rooms, ceilings, doorways, and stairways of every conceivable three-dimensional shape and size. Frequently hired to design for Broadway in the 1910s, Jones and the other leaders of what would soon be called the "New American Stagecraft" could hardly expect to execute these visions on their own, as Armbruster had done. Their designs were simply too monumental and often too unusual to complete without the aid of specialized scenery firms, which were rapidly multiplying on the far west side of Manhattan. There, expert craftspeople brought the experimental designs of the new century to fruition using wood, iron, canvas, lights, and paint.

These transformations played out slowly. Beginning in the 1880s, scenic painters and carpenters had already come to terms with the rather important fact that audiences could now see more of their craft work in close detail, and they had adjusted accordingly. Some had taken the tack of David Belasco, offering painstaking, even literal portrayals of onstage playing spaces, while others had opted for art and abstraction in painted backdrops. No matter which strategy one took, all of this work took more space and more time. Many painters, carpenters, and electricians completed these tasks while still working in-house at a particular theater or for a particular producer.

A handful of entrepreneurs, however, such as a 1902 supplier of scenery named C. L. Hagen, began to operate independent businesses, which were available on a contract basis. By the 1910s these businesses had become the exception rather than the rule in scenery construction. By 1915 a total of twenty-six independent theatrical supply businesses had appeared in the Manhattan *Business Listings*, all available as providers of scenery, lights, scrims, or other scenery-related products. By 1929, just before the great stock market crash, there were a whopping seventy suppliers of specialized theatrical goods in Manhattan. Of the seventy, a full twenty-five of them were devoted exclusively to the construction of scenery, and all but one (the Standard Asbestos Co. office at 69 Beekman) were located on the west side of midtown, between 14th and 53rd Streets.[9]

What accounts for this exponential growth in scenery and scenery-related companies in New York City? The solidification and proliferation of the Broadway brand, in the minds and consumption habits of thousands upon thousands of American theatergoers nationwide, certainly did not hurt. This trend funneled contract after contract in scenic construction directly to New York City, fostering an unprecedented wave of industrialization in the trade.

The details of David Belasco's scenery building and his ever-changing relationships with local craftspeople are an excellent example of the burgeoning industrialization of the era. After beginning as a stage manager and playwright in the 1890s, Belasco began featuring "photographic realism" at the turn of the century, to great fanfare and acclaim. When he first unveiled his realistic scenic designs, he did so within a rented theater on 42nd Street, relying on the skills of the painter Alexander Grinanger, the designers Wilfred Buckland and Ernest Gros, the electrician Mitchell Cirker, and the lighting designer Louis Hartmann.[10] All were frequent Belasco collaborators who worked extensively but not exclusively for the impresario over many years.[11] A New York Times feature on their work in 1904 praised the team's leader as "head and shoulders above other stage managers in creating 'atmosphere,'" referring to the stage settings they had created for a play called The Music Master.[12]

Scenic details of The Music Master reveal just how much the "master of stagecraft" and his team had leapfrogged the incipient realism of people such as the playwright Henrik Ibsen. Rather than simply demanding that the living room of The Music Master be appropriate to the lead character, as the living room in A Doll's House was to Nora Helmer, Belasco and his team fleshed out their character's life in exacting detail. In the living room of their leading man, an impoverished German musician, they had randomly scattered piles of sheet music. Low-lying, easily reached furniture was meticulously polished, but globes on a high mantle were caked with dirt because the musician's housekeeper was "too old to climb up there." As a finishing touch, the team created a prominent "clean spot" in the shape of a cuckoo clock on the wall, signaling to the audience that the musician was forced to remove the cherished relic from its perch on the wall and sell it for cash.[13]

Belasco pushed the realism envelope even further in 1907 when he constructed a brand new theater on 44th Street. After many years of collecting lucrative Broadway bounty from adoring audiences, the "bishop of Broadway"[14] finally had the coin to build his own playhouse, and he really went for it. Belasco not only built an elevator to switch in scenery quickly at the pull of a lever, but he also invested in a "complex lighting switchboard," developed by his designer Louis Hartmann. At the cutting edge of electrification at the time, the switchboard facilitated photographic realism in two key ways. It delivered the overall brightness necessary for even the finest details of dust, dirt, and a clean spot in the shape of a cuckoo clock, while at the same time its sixty-five dimmers provided the fluidity to shift quickly between the lighting conditions of morning, noon, and night along with indoor and outdoor scenes. As an added bonus, Belasco's dimmer board significantly reduced the number of electricians needed to adjust lighting during performances, therefore reducing weekly operating costs.[15]

Organizationally, Belasco's efforts bridged the in-house show building of the nineteenth century with the independent contracting of the twentieth, because some of his experts, especially Alexander Grinanger, worked for other producers on occasion.[16] The fierce in-house loyalties of the nineteenth century grew muddled in the twentieth. Back in the days of Signor Allegri at the Academy of Music (1854) or Albie McDonald at the Grand Opera House (1890; see below), no designer would dare work for a rival producer in a rival house—not, that is, if he wanted to continue enjoying the perks of his "immense scene room" or his sun-lit drafting work space. The more modern understanding between Belasco and his experts may have been something akin to "save the last dance for me," but even this arrangement buckled under the pressure of the rapidly modernizing and expanding industry. In 1913 Belasco lost his head electrician Cirker for good when Cirker cofounded an independent scenery firm with R. N. Robbins. Their Cirker and Robbins Scenic Studio, ensconced within a 29th Street shop on the far west side, tallied up scores of Broadway credits between 1913 and 1953, when Cirker passed.[17]

Mitchell Cirker was hardly the only designer to blaze this trail. Many left a cozy drafting room above a theater and a coveted salaried position for the riskier, yet roomier life of an independent proprietor. John H.

Figure 5. Lighting panel box in the Belasco Theatre, ca. 1900–1920.
Courtesy of White Studio. © The New York Public Library.

Young, for example, had an upstairs work space complete with bookshelves
and a comfortable drafting table in 1903 as the in-house designer for the
Broadway Theatre at 41st Street, but he gave it all up around 1904 to found
Young Bros. and Boss Scenic Studio with his two sons.[18] These three muske-
teers of scenic backdrops had room to grow in their new space on West
29th Street and 11th Avenue in 1905, which had both skylights and soaring
ceilings, ideal for backdrop painting.[19]

   Albie McDonald Sr. made a similar move from a drafting space to a
spacious and well-equipped workshop. After beginning his career in a space
above the Grand Opera House at 23rd Street in the 1890s, McDonald
moved on to found the T. B. McDonald construction company with his
sons in 1921. Partnering with a stage rigger named Peter Clark, the McDon-
alds were able to buy themselves an expansive building at 534 West 30th

Street. Using this lofty work space, the McDonald firm built scenery for many notable Broadway shows, including a famous 1936 production of *Saint Joan* starring Katherine Cornell.[20]

When experts such as Young and McDonald jumped ship to found independent businesses, producers such as Belasco were not left in the lurch. Theater craft was a growth industry in the 1910s and 1920s, making replacement talent readily available, and some craftspeople stayed put, preferring salaried positions over independent contracting. After Cirker decamped for a proprietor's life, for example, Belasco still had the designers Louis Hartmann and Ernest Gros on his payroll.[21] Rolling with the punches of a modernizing Broadway, producers also had the option to contract temporarily with the increasing number of third-party artisans in their midtown midst. As Belasco continued to experiment with stage lighting through the 1920s, his eponymous theater on 44th Street was joined by the Display Stage Lighting Co., which opened just down the block at 334 West 44th Street.[22]

It is not known exactly how many local businesses were employed by the bishop of Broadway in this era, but the fact that they appeared and proliferated in close proximity to his theaters is indisputable. Wolf Dazian, for example, a major supplier of scenic fabrics, had beaten Belasco to the block, relocating his Dazian's firm to 142 West 44th in 1902. We know that Wolf's son Henry, who took over the scenic drapery firm after his father's passing, was at least friends with Belasco (if not business partners) because of the following tidbit from his father's 1941 obituary: "When Wolf Dazian's son Henry was running the store on 44th street, he used to hold card games with David Belasco in an apartment that he maintained above the shop."[23] As Belasco played cards with young Henry after 1907 and continued to produce impressive works of photographic realism onstage at 44th Street, he was surrounded by an increasing number of specialists to work with offstage.

The lasting legacy of David Belasco was not realism per se but rather the "box set," an enclosed playing space for actors simulating one or two rooms of interior space, which could be rolled on and off the stage. Belasco rolled such scenery onstage so regularly on Broadway and with such success that he is credited with launching the "box set" into national popularity as a device for stage scenery.[24]

Belasco's realism and famous box sets were hardly the only trends in scenic design to fuel the fires of industrialization on Broadway after 1900.

Equally catalytic were the abstracted designs of theater artists such as Joseph Urban, Livingston Platt, Norman Bel Geddes, Donald Oenslager, Aline Bernstein, and Robert Edmund Jones. Among this illustrious group of celebrated scenic designers, Jones stands especially tall. Mary C. Henderson, in her exhaustive and compelling *Theater in America*, goes so far as to call Jones the "high priest and principal spokesman of the new stagecraft, or New Movement, in America."[25]

What were these designers, especially Jones, doing so differently from their counterparts from the late nineteenth century or even so differently from Belasco? For starters, they adhered only loosely to the literal playing spaces envisioned by most playwrights, often substituting aspects of light and color for more tangible, three-dimensional pieces of scenery. They played with space through their designs. When a 1914 playwright suggested doors and windows, Robert Edmund Jones designed little more than striking silver rectangles. When Shakespeare called for Hamlet to brood and bellow within the rooms of the castle, Jones served up only a vast, sprawling sweep of stairs in 1922.[26]

The designs of Jones and the other leading abstractionists in scenic design, such as Joseph Urban, were hardly a letdown to theatergoers. Although they may have taken a bit of getting used to, especially for audiences fond of Belasco's sizzling onstage wheatcakes, these designs quickly became widely celebrated on Broadway. When John Barrymore ranged, roamed, and emoted all over Jones's stairs, under a carefully orchestrated mix of lighting and special effects, his 1922 production of *Hamlet* became a monster hit. Though Jones's abstracted stairs were on the opposite end of the tangibility spectrum from Belasco's design work, the antithesis of photographic realism, they were equally effective in sparking and sustaining construction work in scenery.

This was true because the stairs had to be built anew but also because they were bathed in experimental lighting, requiring a whole additional batch of equipment, experts, and contractors. In the work of artists such as Jones, Urban, Oenslager, and Bel Geddes, lighting became far more than just a brighter version of nineteenth-century oil lamps. In the 1910s and 1920s designers folded aspects of abstraction, design, and artistic expression into the lighting itself. After the turn of the century, new technologies had made possible a new slew of "special effects," and the practitioners of the new stagecraft relished them. Mary C. Henderson describes the lighting of Robert Edmund Jones by saying that "his sets were washed in constantly moving and shifting lights, which gave them a special luster."[27] As a specific example of his use of lighting, she explains how Jones was able to bring the ghost of Hamlet's father onstage using nothing more than a dance of lights on "rippling curtains."[28] As Henderson's descriptions indicate, it was difficult to separate scenery and lighting in the earliest decades of the twentieth century; more often than not, and quite literally in the case of the 1922 production of *Hamlet*, they moved together.

All of these interwoven trends of scenery and lighting from 1900 to 1930 fed into and promoted the rapid specialization and industrialization of Broadway craft. The designs of Belasco and other purveyors of realist stagecraft generated work, so much in fact that craftspeople such as Mitchell Cirker were able to branch off as independent proprietors. Abstracted designs did just as much to promote the growth of small scenery and lighting businesses on the far west side. The work of Robert Edmund Jones on the legendary 1922 production of *Hamlet* is a case in point. His stairs were certainly no ordinary stairs. Every step, span, and width of them had to be crafted anew to exacting specifications. This work certainly could not have occurred at the Sam H. Harris Theater on 42nd Street, where *Hamlet* opened, nor could it have taken place way off at Armbruster Scenic Studio in Columbus, Ohio. Because of the inflexible strictures of the Broadway brand and because of the industrial direction in which Broadway was moving, this work occurred precisely where so many thousands of Americans expected it to: "on Broadway."

Never mind that the actual construction location was on the far west side, closer to the Hudson River than to New York's Great White Way. As long as this construction took place on the island of Manhattan, or at least within a nearby borough, it still counted as made on Broadway and was sold and consumed as such. The wheels of industrialization began to turn more rapidly every year after the turn of the century, as more and more skilled craftspeople were dislodged from salaried positions and spun into more risky careers as contractors for hire. When this external market for skilled theatrical labor arose on the island of Manhattan, the unions that would organize and regulate it were not far behind.

Laboring over Scenery

No matter how many craftspeople in scenery, painting, or lighting may have left in-house positions for third-party proprietorship, there would have been no "industrialization" to discuss without craft unions. At the turn of the twentieth century, Broadway had several such unions and was set to get many more. Scenic painters were among the first to organize, forming the American Society of Scene Painters in 1892 as a local branch of the International Brotherhood of Painters, Decorators and Paperhangers (IBPAP). After New York City's stagehands[29] formed the notoriously tough and unified American Alliance of Theatrical Stage Employees in 1893, however, New York City's scenic painters decided to hop on their coattails, leaving the IBPAP behind for a rival union. Playing second fiddle to stagehands was apparently not all it was cracked up to be, however, and by 1918 the scenic painters had come back to the IBPAP, presumably with their painter's hats in hand.

It was at this moment, when the scenery workers of New York City reconnected to the IBPAP in 1918, that labor organizing and jurisdiction policing in scenery really began in earnest. Calling themselves the United Scenic Artists, Broadway's painters, designers, and carpenters finally abandoned the in-house employment of the nineteenth century for good, making their bed in the far more industrialized option of a trade union. They bypassed older notions of apprenticeship and loyalty to a mentoring actor-manager or producer and took a rotating series of regulated gigs on a contract basis.

Having made this bed, scenery workers had to lie in it, of course, and their working arrangements on Broadway did not always go smoothly. The new IBPAP local quickly became a strong advocate for its workers at a time when their industry was in flux. Precious few scenery workers now had salaries, so every job counted. One of the problems was the overlap between the stagehands' union, renamed the International Alliance of Theatrical Stage Employees (IATSE) in 1902, and the new United Scenic Artists (USA). Although the USA had earned the right to speak on behalf of many craftspeople as of 1918, the stagehands' union still spoke for more of them. This New York local of IATSE, number 644, was notoriously territorial and did not necessarily welcome the USA, with a jurisdiction so uncomfortably close to its own.[30]

To illustrate this awkwardness, consider a piece of scenery constructed for the original 1922 production of *Abie's Irish Rose*.[31] The craftspeople who hammered, painted, and assembled the scenery and then carted it to the Fulton Theatre would have all been card-carrying members of the USA. Upon its arrival at the Fulton, however, the scenery would have become

Figure 6. An IATSE sticker for scenery from Nolan Bros. on the far west side.
Courtesy of IATSE stagehand Michael Corbett.

the property of IATSE stagehands in charge of rigging it up and managing it during the famous long run of the show. Once a piece of scenery had been certified as union-built, IATSE would slap a sticker on it, which stagehands could look for as they unloaded scenery at any theater in America.

Even more uncomfortable were incidents when members from one union blatantly violated the work rules of another. In a 1921 letter from the USA to the IATSE, the leaders of the young union explained that they had to shut down a scene shop because its proprietor, Joseph Physioc, was "having stuff built by the I.A. members and is painting it himself." According to union rules, Physioc was supposed to secure a contract for scenery, file it at the USA office on West 46th Street, and then hire a team of USA's painters to do the work. He had done none of this. Even worse, he had hired members of the rival IATSE to help him cheat USA members out of painting gigs. Physioc was fined for his transgression but was allowed to keep his shop within the USA's union orbit.[32]

Despite the occasional flare-up in hostility along these lines, the two unions hammered out a working relationship as best they could during the 1920s. Available evidence in the minutes and correspondence of the USA suggest that more often than not, the twenty-plus proprietors of New York City's scene shops played by the rules. By 1924, when the United Scenic Artists was firmly established, its members raised the stakes on their work by voting to convert to a closed shop. This meant that all new members had to take an entrance exam to join, and the union would be under more pressure to guarantee quality work from all of its artists and painters.

After the establishment of the closed-shop policy, IATSE stagehands worked with increasing doggedness to confirm that each piece of scenery

they loaded into a Broadway house was certified as union-built. Officially
they were strictly forbidden from mounting, hanging, or working on non-
union scenery, and most of the time this closed jurisdiction seemed to hold
reasonably well. Unlike the wild, unregulated days of the late nineteenth
century, producers in the 1920s who wanted their shows to have scenery
simply had to hire Broadway's unionized designers and craftspeople. Scenery built by others would be ferreted out by IATSE stagehands once it
arrived at a Broadway house. Anything confirmed to be nonunion would
be promptly torn up and thrown onto the street as garbage.

As scenic painting and construction became rigorously unionized
trades, they opened up fascinating possibilities of free agency among stagecraft specialists. The most talented of designers, once jealously guarded by
proprietary producers, kept on salary, and hidden away in garreted drafting
rooms like so many Rapunzels, were now available for hire on a union wage
scale to anyone willing to pay. Any 1920s producer in search of a particular
effect in scenic painting or lighting design could hire an expert in that style.
Producers could learn of the many talents on the USA's menu by attending
shows by other producers and looking in the backs of their playbills for the
now-mandated credits listed for all third-party contractors on Broadway
shows. This was all happening in a decade when Broadway had its greatest
number of new shows per year, so it was highly likely that producers would
see a wide variety of scenic designs over the course of a theatrical season.
In the 1920s, when most shows did not run long and Broadway producers
churned out an impressive number of new shows per year, it is therefore
not surprising that the dance cards for most of New York City's scene shops
stayed full.

Getting far more than ten cents a dance for contract scenery, some of
these shops were even profitable enough for their proprietors to buy entire
buildings rather than renting spaces. Nolan Bros., named on the IATSE
sticker in Figure 6, was one such firm. The Nolans purchased a six-story
building on West 24th Street in 1926, just a few years before the frenzied
bubble in Broadway show building was set to burst. In what must have been
a costly renovation, the Nolans went so far as to have the fifth and sixth
floors of this building combined into a tall, lofting work space and to have
oversized elevators and doors installed for the smooth transfer of scenery
and backdrops. Despite having sunk considerable sums into this fifty-seven-
foot-wide building, Nolan Bros. did not succumb to the economic chaos of
the 1930s. Like most of their colleagues, the shop's painters, builders, and

proprietors scraped by on a reduced diet of available contracts for stage and screen. It also appears that they divvied up their ample space at 533 West 24th Street so that they could rent to other scenery builders. In the 1940 *Business Listings*, both the Jules Laurents Studio and Manhattan Scenic and Decorating crop up at the Nolans' address. Since Nolan Bros. owned the building well into the 1950s, it stands to reason that these two firms were tenants.[33]

Another scenery proprietor who went all in during the economic boom of the 1920s was George M. Vail, founder and president of the Vail Scenic Construction Company. When Vail bought his building near 10th Avenue in 1923, he got far more than six stories, an oversized basement, and a location proximate to Broadway's theaters. His structure, at 530–32 West 47th Street, had been fused together as the scenery construction site for the legendary Hippodrome Theatre and had been reconfigured specifically for that purpose around 1903 or 1905.[34] With this real estate deal, Vail was getting all the advantages of the Nolan facility without having to install them himself.

Scenery proprietors not lucky enough to be the Nolan brothers or George M. Vail, operating shops only blocks away from America's most active theaters, were not completely cut off from the amazing hustle and bustle of 1920s Broadway. Though the United Scenic Artists' main membership was in Manhattan after its 1918 founding, it did not leave its wider ranging brethren totally high and dry. Not all stock theaters, of course, had been snuffed out by the relentless success of Broadway's touring combination companies, and those left standing tended to have in-house scenic designers who needed union protection. There were actually fifty-three small-time stock theaters of this ilk operating across the nation in 1927, all brought into the USA union fold. It is important to note that these were only a faint echo of the robust and profitable stock theaters from the 1860s and 1870s. The Irene Summerly Players in Amarillo, Texas, for example, listed by the USA as a unionized theater group, were hardly in a position to brand themselves as Broadway or as a rival to Broadway. Most of these theaters sprang into action only in the summers, giving rise to the still-extant concept of "summer stock."[35] Though the USA union had invited fifty-three stock scenic artists, many from distant corners of the nation, into its fold, most would lose their jobs when the economy collapsed in 1929. More often than not, the institutions where they had worked in-house simply disappeared.

Rising up to fill the void as an entertainment option, of course, was film, and not just film but talking pictures. The efforts of the USA to expand its jurisdiction beyond New York City had partly been prompted by the union's stray designers who happened to be located outside of New York City, but these efforts also had a great deal to do with the scofflaw film producers of Hollywood, who had made it clear early on that they had no interest in complying with the USA's pay scales or work rules. By 1927 a USA publication called *The Scenic Artist*, printed in New York City of course, had the following to say about the shenanigans of Hollywood producers: "[O]ur professional is migratory and therefore national in character . . . the natural law of just compensation can not be amended or abridged. It is not a matter of geography."[36] This bold statement would foreshadow later efforts of the USA to expand its jurisdiction beyond the Empire State, but it also reveals the inherent tension of a locally defined jurisdiction for an industry with jobs that could be so migratory.

Despite the impending stock market crash of 1929, which would challenge the United Scenic Artists union severely, it is clear that the scenery piece of Broadway's industrialization puzzle was firmly established by the mid-1920s. Tightly concentrated between several avenues on the westerly side of the island, New York's robust scenery sector would weather the storms of the Great Depression with surprisingly effective adaptations. Even after the Depression had wracked the industry, the *New York Times* was able to strike a positive note about the state of scenery in 1936, comparing its construction process to that in the 1890s: "[B]uilding stage scenery today is a whole lot different than it was then. With such complicated settings as are at present designed, using revolving stages, acting levels and particularly emphasizing realism, the job of the scene builder is comparable to that of contractor on a more permanent structure, with the designer standing in the place of the architect."[37] Such three-dimensional construction was indeed a far cry from the simple, charming backdrops of the nineteenth century.

Industrialization in Costuming

In costuming, the progression from in-house employees to unionized contractors unfolded differently, with much of the external market for costumes emerging earlier. Costuming work in the stock era, detailed in

Chapter 1, fell on the shoulders of actors far more than work on scenery or backdrops. As lighting intensified and more precise costumes became necessary, actor-managers and theater owners were not well equipped to supply them because they had been leaning so heavily on their actors, such as Otis Skinner, to do the work. It therefore makes sense that an external market for used costumes emerged relatively early. In the mid-nineteenth century, a hodgepodge of secondhand costume dealers sprang up to supply this market in dozens of U.S. cities, with several more substantial costuming houses arising on the East Coast. At the end of the nineteenth century, when lighting got brighter and realist and spectacle shows created bumper crops of work, commercial costume craft expanded all over the United States. By one estimation, "every major city in America that could boast a theater or two also had a costume house."[38]

The distribution of this craft work across the nation was always more wide-ranging than that of scenery, for good reason. Backdrops and scenery pieces were fitted to prosceniums and fly spaces with only the most basic of measurements, and theater owners could easily conquer any issues of fit by cutting, shaping, cramming, or otherwise manipulating them. The same could hardly be said for costumes, however, as they intersected with the infinitely varied buttocks and bosoms of America's actors.

Fit in costuming has always been more intimate, requiring costume craft to stay much closer to the theaters where shows were set to open for most of the nineteenth century. It did not take long, however, for the revolutionary combination company and almighty Broadway brand to snuff out costumers outside of New York City. When these two change agents combined, they came to rule costuming with a cultural iron fist, smashing any and all competitors through the subtleties of branding. Producers such as Charles Frohman, Henry Savage, and Klaw and Erlanger did not have to go marauding through the countryside like a crazed bunch of stage Stalins, burning piles of non-Broadway costumes in an orgy of monopolistic destruction. Culture and reputation did this work for them, castrating non-Broadway components and rendering them worthless because their sites of construction or cities of origin were not "Broadway."

This is why poor Percy Haswell's tour was canceled in 1903 after the untimely fire burned up all of her touring show's costumes. Local replacement costumes sewn, purchased, or rented in Baltimore would have been lacking in Broadway lineage. This section of Chapter 2 is about the consequences of this lineage on the people, buildings, and economy of the Times

Square district. Within this district, with even more density than their counterparts in scenery building, an astonishing number of costume shops and suppliers germinated in the years leading up to 1929.

As early as 1896 there were already forty-three "costumer" listings in the city directories of New York. Granted, many of these listings were for nothing more than individual costume makers or secondhand dealers, but the total is still impressive. Only six years later, in 1902, the number of listed Manhattan costumers had jumped to seventy-four, a 70 percent increase.[39] This growth was partly the result of the increasing number of playhouses in New York City, but it also reflected a booming business in national tours, which peaked in the first decade of the twentieth century.[40]

As impressive and seemingly industrialized as these seventy-four entries may seem, in a city boasting just one listed scenery builder, it is important to note that few of these listings were linked to a major operation. Of the seventy-four, only a few firms could claim copious workrooms, a large number of employees, or a fine collection of period rentals. These houses, namely Dazian's, Eaves, and Brooks, would be the quickest to expand when the all-powerful Broadway brand launched New York City into its monopolistic position in national stagecraft.

As Broadway took over the reins of a ruthlessly organized commercial theater in America, the top costume houses were even more impressive than the sheer number of costumers opening in New York City.[41] These were the powerhouse firms securing lucrative contracts for the top shows on Broadway and also exporting finished garments to the hinterlands by the trainload. The oldest among them was the aforementioned Dazian's Theatricals, a great-grandfather of costuming firms with roots reaching all the way back to Union Square in 1842. Throughout the latter half of the nineteenth century, when Times Square was still a déclassé mix of stables and horse exchanges, Wolf Dazian's venerated shop at 26 Union Square was already costuming and draping productions up and down Broadway.

When the proprietor Wolf Dazian moved his shop up to West 44th Street in 1902, he landed smack in the heart of a theatrical building boom. Yes, this relocation did bring Dazian's son Henry to the same block as his gambling buddy David Belasco, but of course there was much more at stake here. The new building was just off the newly christened "Times Square," it was newer and more spacious than the old Union Square digs, and it put the entire Dazian's team within close walking distance of most of the action in Broadway rehearsals and show construction. From 1902 to 1919, when

Figure 7. Portrait of Wolf Dazian, founder of Dazian's, Inc., no date. Courtesy
of the Billy Rose Theatre Division, The New York Public Library for
the Performing Arts, Astor, Lenox, and Tilden Foundations.

the firm finally dropped out of costuming to focus on specialty fabrics, it
was perfectly situated among the city's most active playhouses. Under the
stewardship of Wolf Dazian and later his son Henry, Dazian's Theatricals
was also poised to supply crates and racks of costumes to both the Pennsylvania and Grand Central railroad stations.

Though not quite as old as Dazian's, Eaves Costumes also had a long-standing presence within the New York City economy, dating back to the nineteenth century. The firm kicked off at Union Square in the 1860s, under the stewardship of the actor-turned-costumer Albert G. Eaves. After costuming an abundance of shows for several decades, including the spectaculars of the Kiralfy brothers, Eaves sold the operation to an employee named Charles Geoly around the turn of the century. By 1902 the firm had jumped uptown to 586 7th Avenue, at the intersection with 42nd Street, which is about as "Times Square" as one can get. Theatrical business was positively booming in the district when the Eaves firm arrived, and by 1914 Geoly was doing so well that he succeeded in buying an entire building for his robust costuming concern, on West 46th Street just east of Times Square. Five years later this errand-boy-turned-proprietor purchased an additional four buildings on the same block, becoming a landlord in addition to a leading costumer.[42]

It is important to note how dramatically the costuming business changed between its Union Square infancy and its Times Square adulthood. These changes were far more than a simple expansion of business as usual. When Wolf Dazian and Albert G. Eaves had been key players down at 14th Street, they dealt with a dizzying array of producers, actor-managers, and performers. They sold, rented, and crafted custom pieces for minstrel shows, vaudeville, musical comedies, ballets, traveling extravaganzas, and the occasional Ibsen or Belasco experiment in early stage realism. By the time Wolf Dazian, Charles Geoly, and other industry heavyweights had moved up to Times Square, they spent much less time dilly-dallying with small-time rentals or construction contracts.

The costuming of the 1900s, 1910s, and 1920s grew increasingly organized, streamlined, profitable, and unionized with each passing year; in a word, it was becoming industrialized. Through these changes, business began to overpower craft as raison d'être in the biggest of Broadway's costume shops, with the solo customers having to wait their turn until bigger hitters had ordered garments for choruses of fifty or even a hundred. Though costuming was well on its way to full-scale industrialization by the turn of the twentieth century, these dramatic transformations did not unfurl overnight, like some fabulous new backdrop. During the last decade of the nineteenth century and the first of the twentieth, several leading producers of the commercial stage pushed stagecraft into its adolescence.

The first well-documented producer to push Broadway in an industrialized direction appears to have been the aforementioned Henry W. Savage, who by 1902 was paying seamstresses to craft costumes within his "factory for making plays" on West 27th Street. According to the *New York Times* in 1906, Savage had built "a costume department with fifty women busily at work."[43] Close on his heels, the famous backers of the Hippodrome, Fred Thompson and Elmer Dundy, took a page out of the Savage playbook when they opened their gargantuan complex in 1903. Several avenues to the west and just a few blocks uptown from their Hippodrome, Dundy and Thompson bought additional buildings on West 47th Street, which they would combine into a complex for off-site craft work, especially costuming.[44]

Also in 1903 their colleague and competitor Daniel Frohman built a seven-story tower for stagecraft as an extension of his New Lyceum Theatre, complete with an ample costuming workroom. A *New York Times* feature on the facility describes a "costumers' hall, in which fifty seamstresses may ply their needles together, aided by as many cutters as necessary."[45] The exact match between the "fifty women" of the Savage facility and the "fifty seamstresses" suggests that *Times* journalists were maybe not taking an exact count so much as they were estimating the number, or perhaps taking the boasts of the producer at face value. Even at only thirty-five or forty workers each, however, both facilities constituted a striking departure from the makeshift shabbiness of the nineteenth century.

These three off-site craft buildings represented a fascinating middle ground between preindustrial and industrialized Broadway, and they certainly stood as milestones in costume craft. None was a totally independent contractor in the mold of Dazian's or Eaves, however, because ultimately the costumes and other components crafted within their walls were for the exclusive use of one theatrical producer. There is no evidence that Savage or Dundy and Thompson were willing to rent out their skilled teams to other producers, and while they stayed active as producers, there was little incentive for them to do so.

Frohman, on the other hand, pushed his facility and his crews as far as they would go, milking his capital outlaws for all they were worth. Rather than monopolizing craftspeople for his own shows exclusively, Frohman wisely organized them into independent units, available to contract with other producers or supply for tours.[46] His scene shop, costume shop, and rehearsal studios could therefore generate income whether or not the impresario himself had a show in development. Writing about this setup, the theater historian Mary C. Henderson suggests that Frohman had "one foot in the nineteenth century and the other in the twentieth."[47]

Figure 8. Daniel Frohman in his office, no date. Courtesy of the Billy Rose Theatre
Division, The New York Public Library for the Performing Arts,
Astor, Lenox, and Tilden Foundations.

Although he eventually backed away from producing shows and disbanded his company, Frohman's impressive collection of period costumes lived on when they were purchased by a uniform supplier named Ely Stroock in 1919. Upon this foundation Stroock built one of the most successful costuming businesses in the history of Broadway.[48] In many ways the sale of the Frohman collection to Stroock was a symbolic moment of transition from costuming adolescence to industrial maturity. Stroock represented the new, fully fledged industrialization of the twentieth century, because here was a proprietor who never aspired to produce anything other than costumes. His son James did occasionally invest in Broadway shows after he took over the firm in 1933, but he did not aspire to be an impresario. Both father and son were costume proprietors first and foremost, running a major theater-oriented business in the heart of the bustling Times Square industrial district.

The Brooks operation, reportedly named Brooks because Ely Stroock thought it sounded "very British," actually began as a uniform supplier in 1906. The elder Stroock had never intended to be a costumer, but then someone ordered a small army's worth of uniforms for a massive spectacle show at the Hippodrome. Next, none other than Florenz Ziegfeld proposed a business partnership in the 1910s for *Ziegfeld Follies* costumes costing as much as one thousand dollars per "show girl." Ely Stroock was no fool. With so much lucrative work cropping up in theatrical garments, he made his play for the Frohman collection in 1919, setting himself up with capacities in both made-to-order costuming and period rentals.[49]

Rather than dropping the already bustling uniform component of his company, Stroock simply expanded, squeezing both wings of his expansive business into the available space at 1437 Broadway throughout the 1920s. At some point in the 1930s, Brooks relocated to a much larger space at 1150 6th Avenue, just south of 46th Street. The 1930s were also when Ely Stroock handed over the costuming division to his son James. Given that James was reportedly doing this so his father could return to uniforms full-time, perhaps Ely's heart was never really in costumes after all.

James, on the other hand, enjoyed saying that he "kept Broadway in stitches" and seemed to have relished his role as one of the city's top costumers. This "dapper man with wavy hair" had the good fortune of becoming the costumer of choice for producers such as Rodgers and Hammerstein, the Theatre Guild, and Robert Whitehead, and he would routinely costume the likes of John Raitt, Rosalind Russell, and Audrey

Hepburn. His 1940s advertisements suggest a proprietor confident about his place in the industry, boasting of "the largest collection of the world's finest costumes . . . the kind Broadway stars wear."[50] During its heyday at midcentury, Brooks chalked up more Broadway credits than perhaps any other costumer, from *Glass Menagerie* to *Gypsy*.[51]

Ely Stroock had fielded major requests from the "great Ziegfeld" in the 1910s, and James was able to handle most of the requests made by Broadway and Hollywood producers after 1933. Despite the vast workforces and work spaces of midtown shops such as Brooks, Dazian's, and Eaves, however, even these facilities could fall short of the seemingly inexorable demand for custom-made costumes in Manhattan. This was especially true when it came to customized and couture gowns for Broadway's leading ladies.

Into the breach stepped New York City's department stores and fashion houses, such as Lord & Taylor and R. H. Macy. Their involvement in costuming was so substantial that by the early twentieth century, according to Marlis Schweitzer's recent book on the subject, more than a few had established "special departments or 'annexes' exclusively devoted to stage costuming and staffed by individuals whose primary responsibility was liaising with Broadway." For the purposes of this project, these annexes represented yet another layer in the multifaceted, theatrical production district that flourished in midtown after 1900. No census counter or city planner would ever have considered shops such as Wanamaker's to be theatrical satellite businesses, and yet their skilled employees went about their business making costume after costume throughout the 1900s, 1910s, and 1920s.[52]

The glamour and cachet of department stores and their fashionable dress-making operations gave an additional shot in the arm to the already illustrious Broadway brand. Americans in this era were already ascribing meaning to their clothes with guidance from magazines and other forms of popular culture, and few forms of entertainment loomed as large in this culture as Broadway. When a Lord & Taylor or R. H. Macy gown glimmered under the bright lights of Broadway, hanging from the body of a beguiling actress, this reinforced assumptions that Broadway costumes were somehow inherently superior to costumes stitched elsewhere.

After 1900 a vast majority of American theatergoers nationwide came to believe that these costumes, sewn and cut at places such as Eaves or Dazian's in New York City, had some sort of automatic edge over any homespun concoctions crafted in other cities. Even if seamstresses in Des

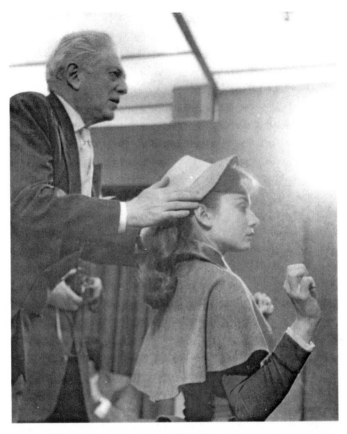

Figure 9. Jimmy Stroock fitting Audrey Hepburn at Brooks Costume, ca. 1958.
Courtesy of the Billy Rose Theatre Division, The New York Public Library
for the Performing Arts, Astor, Lenox, and Tilden Foundations.

Moines or Duluth were to marshal the loveliest fabrics west of the Missis-
sippi and lavish countless hours of design and craft on them, they still faced
an uphill battle. They could advertise their creations as the "finest costumes
to have ever been sewn in Des Moines" or the "best in the history of
Duluth," but in the early twentieth century there was still one tagline that
always had them beat: "the costumes come direct from Broadway."

With all of these varied workshops producing costumes, even in department stores, and with aggressive unionization occurring among stagehands,
scenic designers, painters, and carpenters, it makes sense that unions for

costume workers would emerge too. The problem was that costume workers came in many forms. Designers gained union protection under the United Scenic Artists umbrella as of 1918, but the people who actually sewed, cut, beaded, and fitted costumes did not. To rectify this, the massive International Ladies' Garment Workers' Union (ILGWU) founded a Costume Workers Local, number 124, in 1924.[53] For many decades costume designers remained members of the USA, while their workers and seamstresses joined the ILGWU. When costumes were completed, the lines of jurisdiction were similar to those in scenery construction. After the designers of the USA and costume workers of the ILGWU had completed their work, they sent their components to a Broadway house for dress rehearsals. They were received by IATSE, whose "costume mistresses" were responsible for maintaining all garments once they crossed the threshold of a Broadway theater.

With most costuming craftspeople covered by one union or another by 1924 and with at least seventy or more costumers active throughout the 1910s and 1920s, this was a trade undergoing an unequivocal wave of industrialization.[54] The density and close proximity of New York's industrialized costumers had a twofold impact on the local environment after 1900, especially during the 1920s.

First, the streets of midtown surrounding Times Square benefited from the presence of stable, law-abiding, and productive daytime businesses. Many city leaders took the stability, safety, and legality of western midtown for granted, and for several decades this swath of the city did function smoothly as a theatrical production center for the United States. It is easy to assume that such stable, daytime shops were unflaggingly strong in twentieth-century midtown, what with its impressive real estate values, convenient transit, and the high-profile nature of its streets. This was not the case.

After World War II, when this production center shrank precipitously and costume shops, fabric supply stores, and other costume-related businesses dwindled, merged, and disappeared, western midtown was thrown into relative chaos. It seems that the mayors, urban planners, and other city leaders who presided over midtown during the 1910s and 1920s, when its lofts were filled cheek to jowl with commuting, outer-borough seamstresses and when its sidewalks were filled with a steady stream of costume racks, never knew just how good they had it.

A second benefit of the rising industrialization in Broadway costuming was closely related to the first; administrators and performers could easily and quickly use local sidewalks to go see, feel, and try on garments as they were being made. Even headliners such as John Barrymore took advantage of the density and walkability of the industrial district to help make his costumes the best they could be. The producer Arthur Hopkins, a contemporary of Barrymore, described him as follows in 1937: "[O]f all the actors I have ever known, [John Barrymore] was the most conscientious and untiring in preparation. Nothing was too much trouble. He would go to the costumer, the bootmaker, the wig maker, the armor maker, twenty times each, if necessary to get everything right."[55] Barrymore's doggedness was replicated by many dozens of performers, designers, and producers throughout the Broadway boom years of 1900 to 1929. With the industry firing on all pistons, work opportunities for actors, singers, and dancers were ample, at least for those living in New York City.

Industrialization Among Performers

Even earlier than their colleagues in painting and costuming, performers had been shaken loose from salaried, in-house, guildlike jobs during the 1860s and 1870s. They navigated the treacherous waters of the combination system as best they could, booking gigs in America's largest cities along with the occasion tour through more rural areas. After benefiting from the apprentice and master loyalties of stock theater in the middle of the century, most actors now had to swim in more industrialized waters, where loyalties ran shallow and exploitation ran deep. Anyone looking for evidence of the fleeting brutalities of the combination system should look no further than the practices of road producers in financial trouble, who ruthlessly and routinely left actors stranded in out-of-the-way towns without train fare home.[56]

Not a moment too soon, in the opinion of many actors, the Actors' Equity union became a force to push back against such practices. Though this union was formed in 1913, most theater historians agree that it was not until after the successful strike of 1919 that it wielded serious power within the industry. Some readers may consider performers to be outside of the scope of this study, focused as it is on craft work, but their inclusion is both appropriate and important. By analyzing the formation of the actors' union as a key step in the development of an external market for skilled performers, replete with specialists of every conceivable stripe and skill, this chapter will push the definition of theater craft as far as it can go.

It is no accident that the actors of this era spoke of their work as a "craft," just as so many continue to do today. Before industrialization, back in the days of Ada Rehan and Augustin Daly, actors tended to learn their trade from mentors. There was little in the form of an organized craft to speak of, since so many performers were learning from idiosyncratic mentors. Veteran players and especially actor-managers took less experienced actors under wing for mimicry and repetitious training. The system was by no means perfect, especially for those actors who devoted inordinate amounts of time to training younger competitors only to find themselves out of a job. The stock period had plenty of *All About Eve* jealousies and rivalries along these lines. There were also more than a few famous defections, when talented apprentices broke free of their Svengalis to become masters in their own right.

Much of this changed after 1900, when actors began to learn their trade in profoundly different ways more fitting of the label "craft." They began to train in classes, in schools, and through standardized techniques. Many, though not all, seized upon the innovations of Constantin Stanislavsky as early as the 1910s. By the 1930s the Americanized version of these acting trends famously took shape through the Group Theatre and the teaching of Lee Strasberg. In addition to these new acting techniques, many performers in the earlier decades of the twentieth century had to train and drill in a vast new panoply of special skills, from dialects and diction to dance. Teachers of these skills and techniques cropped up to meet a geyser of demand in New York City. They existed to a lesser degree in other cities, but nowhere were the specialists, coaches, and teachers of the theater as numerous, or as ubiquitous, as they were in Times Square. After two decades of snowballing growth, the 1922 *Business Listings* named a jaw-dropping 122 different specialists of this ilk.[57]

With all these coaches and teachers heading to and from their studios on midtown sidewalks and with advertisements adorning their windows, one wonders whether actors were assaulted by visual reminders of the skills they had yet to master as they walked to work. Passersby were certainly reminded that productive, law-abiding small businesses predominated, especially on 42nd Street. Each teacher or proprietor of this sort played a small role in sustaining the commercial theater as an integral component of New York City's economy.[58]

The rise of paid teachers and instructors was also significant as a marker of increasing specialization among performers. In most economic sectors, increased specialization among the workforce went hand in hand with industrialization. This was certainly true for actors working in the commercial theater.

Actors may have gained specialties, coaching, and the like, but nothing heralded their industrialization more than the founding, and the strengthening, of their Actors' Equity union. To protest their lack of rehearsal pay, being fired without grounds, being ditched without train fare, and heaps of other indignities, the 1913 organization staged a stirringly successful walkout in 1919. After being deprived of performers for thirty days and having lost about $37 million of income, New York City's producers finally caved in to almost all of Equity's demands. Some of the more irascible, established, or old-time producers, such as George M. Cohan and David Belasco, refused to acknowledge the union or hire its actors even after the strike was settled, but most of Broadway's mavens were game. They paid for rehearsal time, they signed contracts giving far more rights to actors, and they pushed Broadway even further into its industrialized future.[59]

Actors were not the only skilled performers to gain these types of rights and privileges as the twentieth century unfolded. Musicians were equally successful at securing fair remuneration for their work and for their time. Having done so a few years before the Equity performers, musicians had provoked old-timer Henry W. Savage, builder of the "factory for making plays," to grouse in 1912 that "the expenses of supplying music have more than doubled in the last ten years on account of the demands from the musical union. This season we have to pay to members of the orchestras on tour not only their wages, but their transportation, board, lodging, and sleeping-car fares."[60] One wonders how Savage felt in 1919 when he learned that he would have to pay these costs not only for musicians but for actors as well.

The truth of the matter, whether Savage, Cohan, or Belasco liked it or not, was that this was where the theater was headed and would continue to go through the 1920s and beyond. From stagehands and lighting designers to musicians and dancers, just about every single person working on Broadway came to be represented by a union, which set work rules and lobbied on their behalf. This system worked reasonably well until October 1929. After that point no one, not even the strongest of Broadway's unions, could shelter performers and craftspeople from the economic storm.

Chapter 3

"Sing for Your Supper"

Theater-Related Craft Work
in Radio, Film, and Television

A S THE DUST settled after the great crash of 1929, Broadway producers and proprietors struggled like most other Americans. Shrunken
personal fortunes wreaked havoc on theatrical investments, while the number of shows per year dropped to new lows.[1] The industry's leaders and
craftspeople were flexible and dynamic, having weathered previous economic downturns, but the grim 1930s were unlike anything they had seen.
Broadway insiders must have known that the straits were dire when the
well-funded Theatre Guild, a pride of the industry for many, announced
that it was finished for the season in mid-April 1931, two and a half months
early. As the *New York Times* explained, "The Guild, it now turns out, has
decided not to produce any more new plays on Broadway this season. So
have so many other people, for that matter. One of the results of this scar-
city of new productions is that three of the leading scenery building firms
are now engaged in a price war."[2]

Dwindling contracts and bidding wars were certainly frustrating, but
some theater-related businesses suffered an even worse fate; they contracted
with deadbeat producers and never got paid. McDonald Construction
endured this outcome not once but twice in 1932. After the veteran producer Abraham R. Erlanger passed away, McDonald's owners scrambled to
collect on his bankrupt estate. With an estimated one million dollars owed
to McDonald and myriad other contractors, their efforts were in vain.[3]
Only three months later, the bankruptcy of Morris Green left the same

McDonald firm with $15,756 in unpaid fees. Like the Erlanger case, this one bankruptcy left dozens of contractors in the lurch. The designer Cleon Throckmorton lost his one-thousand-dollar designer's fee from a recent Morris Green show, while fifty-five Actors' Equity chorus members were each stiffed for forty dollars in wages.[4]

At a time when wages, design fees, and payments for show construction became more difficult to collect, the sums in question also shrank. On repeated occasions through the 1930s, the League of New York Theaters and Producers, comprised of theater owners and producers, demanded wage cuts from Broadway's unions. In 1932 the league went after IATSE, asking stagehands to agree to a 33.3 percent pay cut at the signing of their new contract in September.[5] IATSE's leaders reluctantly agreed, presumably to keep as many of their members working as possible.

Other theatrical unions, such as the United Scenic Artists (USA), did not wait for producers to demand concessions and seized the initiative with a creative fix for their ever-dwindling number of work hours. In 1935 the USA imposed a strict thirty-two-hour workweek on its painters in order to distribute available work hours as evenly as possible. Union leaders also decided to allow members to delay dues payments on a case-by-case basis. Originally intended for only the least fortunate of the bunch, this leniency policy soon applied to an alarming number of brethren.

At New York University's Tamiment Library, one can read the hand-written notes sent by USA painters to their financial secretary Charles Roman in 1935 pleading for a break from dues payments. Many of these notes provide a remarkable, heartbreaking look at the plight of those who lived through the Great Depression. In February 1935 Manuel Essman wrote, "I know that I am months behind in my dues. I once more ask for your leniency. My own position has been pretty desperate."[6] Another painter, Russell C. Lemior, wrote not only of his financial woes but also of his frustration with the thirty-two-hour workweek: "I have done my utter-most to keep money aside for all of my obligations, but have totally failed. I have a big family as you know and they are all out of work . . . I have given many a days [sic] work and I do not begrudge same for they have needed it too and badly, but I do not think it works out just fairly for the stock man who never gets a days [sic] work."[7] The poignancy of these notes was not lost on USA's leadership. By 1935 Charles Roman was put in charge of a relief fund that would aid anyone earning less than ninety dollars a month.[8]

It is tempting to assume that the Depression sapped the city's theatrical production center of its early twentieth-century vibrancy. This famously depressing age, however, was not quite the interruption to show business that its grim reputation would suggest. These were certainly leaner years in theater craft and construction, but escapist fare had its appeal on the Great White Way just as it did on the silver screen. Dramas, operettas, musical comedies, and shows in the vaudeville and burlesque styles continued to play and to profit throughout the 1930s. It was not until the end of the decade that the count of new shows per year dipped below one hundred, numbering just ninety-eight in 1939. The number of theater-related businesses still active in the *Business Listings* also held unexpectedly steady through the 1930s, dropping only 11 percent between 1929 and 1940.[9] One proprietor, Edward Kook, even "grew and prospered" during the Depression, because of an innovative catalog he produced in order to sell and rent his lighting equipment nationally.[10]

So what then were the trajectories of the beleaguered, transforming industry in the 1930s and 1940s? Both the industry and its Manhattan production center were resilient and adaptable, bolstered by several interwoven trends. First, despite the ripe old age of many theatrical craft buildings at this time, fewer structures met the wrecking ball than in other districts. Try as they might, the visionaries of the Regional Plan Association could not completely paint this swath of midtown with their utopian, white-collar brushes, because too many successful and beloved theaters stood in their way. Another key trend of the Great Depression and the 1940s was the harvesting of dormant Broadway theaters for alternative uses such as live radio broadcasts and film screenings, which kept playhouses standing even if they no longer hosted plays. For obvious reasons, the playhouse owners of the 1930s had a hard time saying no to those interested in renting, regardless of the physical impact that the alternate use would have. For those lucky enough to contract with the Federal Theatre Project, the tenancy was more traditional and did not harm their properties. Most nontraditional tenants, however, did considerable damage. This trend accelerated after 1948, when television broadcasting flourished in midtown Manhattan. Broadway performers, far from being replaced by television, stood proudly in the spotlight for many of the medium's earliest broadcasts. For roughly the first four years of television history, at least, the tiny swath of Manhattan known as the theater district continued to have disproportionate national influence on popular culture, by playing host to numerous television shows.

In all cases of alternative media striking up rental agreements in Broadway playhouses or temporarily putting theater-related shops to work, the benefits of the arrangements were short-lived. Radio faded in popularity, while both feature films and television broadcasting migrated to the West Coast over time. By the end of the 1950s, the high point of alternative media in Broadway had passed, and the craft proprietors of the theater district were left to rely mostly on stage shows. Given that the number of shows per year would never return to the dizzying heights of the 1920s, this meant fewer contracts and fewer jobs than ever before. In a sense, alternative media on Broadway left theater owners and industry leaders with a temporary, false sense of stability. When radio, film production, and television largely disappeared from the Times Square district, they left it more challenged than ever before.

Resilience After the *Regional Plan*

Way back in 1925, before the Regional Plan Association had been formed, the "old gray lady" of Times Square, otherwise known as the *New York Times*, published a revealing article about the relocation of a lumberyard from West 38th Street near Broadway to the far west side between 10th and 11th Avenues. As the *Times* told it, this storied old lumber business had finally succumbed to its inevitable displacement from the city center. Opened there in 1864, the firm had survived at the same spot into the mid-1920s, despite the fact that most surrounding lots had succumbed to tall buildings long ago. When *Times* reporters noted that Wright Lumber was finally selling its land, they pointed out that the property had doubled in value in just two years and that "it was the part of practical wisdom to sell, as the plot was too valuable to devote to lumber uses."[11] The thread in the story woven by the *Times* was that Wright was a charming throwback in its original location, a surprising survivor of a bygone age.

Those who continued to use large quantities of lumber several times a month to craft stage scenery in midtown might have been surprised to read that their craft work and their suppliers were no longer "practical wisdom" by the 1920s. Yet this was how many influential New Yorkers began to think after World War I; they took it as gospel truth that blue-collar uses were simply unnatural in midtown. Nowhere were these assumptions more pronounced than in the 1929 planning manifesto titled *Regional Plan of New*

York and Its Environs. The central idea of this document, penned by the newly formed Regional Plan Association, was that businesses engaged in hammering, welding, sewing, painting, and other craft and construction activities had no place in central Manhattan. Though this notion had begun to percolate earlier, when skyscrapers first sprouted in the district, the *Regional Plan* gave it voice, visibility, and legitimacy.[12]

On the surface the *Regional Plan of New York and Its Environs* may seem an innocuous treatise, nothing more than a call for organization within the chaotic metropolis. Its authors reacted to the mixed uses of midtown as follows: "In the very heart of this 'commercial' city, on Manhattan Island south of 59th Street, the inspectors in 1922 found nearly 420,000 workers employed in factories. Such a situation outrages one's sense of order . . . one yearns to rearrange things to put things where they ought to be."[13]

If these utopian yearnings had stayed mostly on the page, then innocuous this plan would be. But they did not. Immediately following the publication of the *Regional Plan*, scads of planners, developers, and governmental leaders sprang into action, hacking into midtown's industrial fabric to make room for a postindustrial economy geared to the automobile. With each passing year after 1929, droves of office buildings and parking garages mushroomed in Manhattan, creating space for white-collar operations. City elites who championed the *Regional Plan* were especially successful on the eastern fringes of midtown, near Grand Central Station. Within this area their success in crafting a towering white-collar district was rapid, unbridled, and staggering in its totality. By the 1950s this section of the city had indeed transformed dramatically, more or less according to the well-articulated blueprint of the Regional Plan Association.[14]

Nowhere were postindustrial reclamations of cherished midtown real estate more successful or prominent than on the streets just northwest of Grand Central, at Rockefeller Center. On a wide stretch of blocks between 48th and 51st Streets, just east of 6th Avenue, the Rockefeller family harnessed the power of its beastly fortune to execute a complete overhaul of the city fabric. Twenty acres of aging but industrious buildings, filled with boutiques, dressmakers, fabric suppliers, and secondhand clothing stores for decades on end, were unceremoniously flattened to their foundations. In their stead arose a dizzying tower-in-the-plaza complex comprised of nineteen buildings, underground parking garages, state-of-the-art radio studios, and the now-legendary Radio City Music Hall. The complex did have copious new offices available for rent, but these decidedly white-collar spaces were certainly not intended to be the new home for a displaced fabric store or a secondhand clothing shop. Even if there had been allowances for tenancy by the displaced businesses, none of them could have possibly afforded the rent. Midtown's theater-related shop proprietors were resilient in an ever-changing city, but this did not mean that they were rich.

Rockefeller Center was therefore part of New York City's larger structural shift, because it left smaller shop proprietors in the lurch. This is not how the complex is usually analyzed within the city's history. This is a space that is well understood by the wider public as a bold, successful real estate gamble of the Depression and by planning historians as a step forward into the Miesian, tower-in-the-plaza future of the mid-twentieth century. But this complex was also a major catalyst for economic change, single-handedly causing structural economic shift by its very existence. Its developers destroyed untold dozens of walk-up buildings that had been available to small theater-related businesses since the turn of the century, replacing them with a planning island of relentless white-collar orientation.[15]

This is not to say that Rockefeller Center harmed the New York City economy per se, but only that it facilitated transformation. Though many thousands of dollars poured into midtown because of Rockefeller Center's construction, precious few of these sums were spent on anything even remotely related to the theater. Interestingly, the original design for the complex featured a new opera house as its centerpiece, but over the course of the 1930s this plan was replaced by one more geared to radio broadcasting. In its final incarnation, the completed Rockefeller Center did have some spaces dedicated to costuming, scenery, and lighting, but they were available only to the center's corporate broadcasting tenants. The economic life of Rockefeller Center had an insularity that matched its tower-in-the-plaza design.

Even though Rockefeller Center turned its hard, marble-and-granite-covered back on the district's smaller theater-related shops, its overall impact was not all that damaging to the Broadway industry in the long run. There may not have been room, conceptually or literally, for Broadway's scrappy supply businesses within the complex, but there were still plenty of viable, affordable options for tenancy on nearby streets. Some of Broadway's more white-collar entrepreneurs, such as the producers Robert Whitehead and Harold Prince, did take up residence at 1 Rockefeller Plaza, running their offices and collecting donations from "angels" from distinguished addresses.[16] But most craftspeople and proprietors proved resilient in the face of midtown's rapid transformations, seeking out new work spaces after their previous ones had met the wrecking ball.

Craftspeople in the right trades could secure jobs at Rockefeller Center, but this would have meant giving up their autonomy as independent proprietors. The stage rigger Peter Clark made this shift after he signed on to design and rig the legendary Radio City Music Hall in the mid-1930s.[17] He and his team of rigging experts had worked on a contract basis on Broadway through the 1920s, using a building on West 30th Street as their home base and workshop. They had shared this space with several other businesses and specialists until Clark and his employees became the exclusive riggers of the new music hall. Though this small group became beneficiaries of Rockefeller Center largesse, their former colleagues did not. Once they had secured the talents of Peter Clark Incorporated, the producers of radio broadcasting at Rockefeller Center had no need to contract with any other third-party firms. They had in-house specialists on call, operating as a self-sustaining institution rather than an employer of local contractors.

That Rockefeller Center generally excluded, ignored, and bypassed Broadway's theater-related proprietors who did not happen to be Peter Clark was not the problem. Even during the rough-and-tumble years of 1930s depression and early 1940s warfare, the Broadway industry continued to generate a decent number of contracts for its local theater craftspeople. The problem with this shining new city of the future, as embodied by Rockefeller Center, was that the theater industry got no glittering complex of its own. In all the years after 1929, when city leaders spent lavishly on office tower complexes, municipal parking garages, new stadiums, a United Nations headquarters, public housing towers, bridges, and highways of all imaginable shapes and sizes, they did not break ground on a single building devoted to theatrical development. New playhouses cropped up on occasion during the 1930s and 1940s, but no city project emerged to meet the craft and construction needs of the vitally important theater industry.

Rather than nurturing, sustaining, or investing in this crucial piece of the midtown economy, city leaders such as Fiorello LaGuardia, Robert Moses, and the Rockefeller brothers sought to replace it. The public records of their actions in slum clearance, urban renewal, and midtown redevelopment suggest that they would have eradicated even more of midtown's chaotic yet affordable mix of walk-up buildings if they had been given the chance. Meanwhile the smaller loft or walk-up buildings that did survive in midtown struggled with age, obsolescence, and decay.[18]

Though planners, real estate developers, and city leaders were tremendously successful at remaking the district surrounding Grand Central Station and bringing Rockefeller Center to fruition, they traveled a bumpier road toward the white-collar city to the west of 6th Avenue. Here it was equally true that those calling the shots had internalized the assumptions and antiindustrial biases of the *Regional Plan*. Many were equally convinced that they had a mandate to shunt blue-collar operations to the periphery, and most did not see small, blue-collar businesses as natural parts of the local economy. As on the east side, they certainly had strong support from real estate developers, who stood to profit far more from the construction of skyscrapers than the construction of theatrical shows.

Try as they might, however, leaders on the west side were unable to wipe the urban slate clean of its industrial smudges, as the east-siders had done. There were simply too many operational, profitable, popular theaters standing in the way. No massive wave of creative destruction could wash through Times Square or its surrounding blocks, in the super-block style of Rockefeller Center, because it would inevitably smack into an immovable clump of historic obstacles: Broadway's theaters. At least until the 1960s, Times Square's storied old playhouses and hotels were comparatively sacrosanct, even if their stoops, mansard roofs, or dentils were getting a little long in the tooth.

In the age of the *Regional Plan*, actual playhouses, with stages and red velvet curtains, were welcomed into the urban fold. As "outraged" as Regional Plan Association leaders may have been by the jumbled mix of shops in and around Times Square, there is no evidence that they took any issue with playhouses themselves. Much to the contrary, power brokers such as Mayor Jimmy Walker, Governor Al Smith, the builder Robert Moses, and others actively celebrated these buildings when they cropped up like mushrooms in the 1920s and when they continued to trickle into existence through the 1930s. As they christened these shiny new sites of theatrical consumption at ribbon cuttings and opening-night parties, they showed that a theater per se was not a problem—not a problem, that is, as long as the unseemly craft or construction work of the stage was kept hidden away from the watchful eyes of their planners. In the increasingly polished and consumption-oriented city center of the 1930s and 1940s, New York City's leaders called for Times Square to be more showroom than assembly line and more department store than garment factory.

This squeaky-clean vision for the theater district never stood a chance. Since at least 1900, there had always been more spaces devoted to theatrical craft, construction, administration, rehearsals, and coaching than to performances. Tucked as they were next to, behind, and even above local playhouses, these spaces played bathwater to the proverbial baby of the Broadway stage. Planners could not scrub midtown west clean of its light manufacturing without scouring Broadway into oblivion in the process. Given that theater owners found creative ways to keep their buildings viable during the Depression, through trends of repurposing and alternate media described below, and given that playhouses had a nostalgic appeal for the city's populace, few met the wrecking ball.

Even as eastern midtown was overrun with wrecking crews and new skyscrapers, western midtown's theaters stood fast, refusing to yield the urban stage. The theater district's larger supporting cast of humble, theater-related walk-ups and loft buildings were therefore shielded as well. It was within these buildings, devoted wholly or partially to craft, construction, and administration, that the national production center resided. Work spaces for designers, carpenters, seamstresses, wig makers, agents, coaches, and other specialists were certainly less visible or valued than a theater with a brightly lit marquee, but they were of momentous importance to America's commercial theater. Before alternate spaces for this work arose within regional theaters and performing arts centers around the nation, these buildings constituted the delicate, surviving roots of a still-vital Broadway industry.

Saved as they were by their larger, show-filled neighbors, these smaller buildings did suffer under the regime of the Regional Plan Association. Though rarely destroyed, they suffered the fate of marginalization. They were already somewhat obscured by the machinations of many a Broadway producer, actor, and adman, who labored tirelessly to convince audiences that what they saw was stage "magic" rather than meticulous, professional stagecraft. After 1929 the craft and labor of the stage went from hidden to virtually invisible, because the *Regional Plan* was a blueprint for the city's future in which they had no place. The *Regional Plan* codified and promoted the idea that these craft and administrative activities were a distraction from the economic logic of midtown.

Having been saved from the wrecking ball by the ongoing vitality of the playhouses they supplied, Broadway's supply buildings and craft shops continued to generate compelling works of stagecraft through the 1930s and 1940s. From the elaborate sets and costumes of the escapist play *Dinner at Eight* to the gritty, more realist sets and costumes of the musical *Porgy and Bess*, Broadway's specialized suppliers continued to excel. Each time the performers of this era kicked up their heels or recited a monologue, they became part of not just Broadway but also light manufacturing history. In the 1934 musical *Anything Goes*, for example, Ethel Merman shared the stage with sixty-two other performers, each making numerous costumes changes and all romping on an elaborate set evoking a cruise ship. These components had to be built somewhere. Throughout the 1930s and 1940s that somewhere was still midtown Manhattan.[19]

Despite the undeniable importance of these components, they were apparently too trifling to be deserving of notice by planners. It did not help that the ramshackle buildings where most costume and scenery construction took place were relatively old and unsightly. To the eye of a 1930s planner, they were too small and too old for the modern city. Save for the McGraw-Hill and Candler buildings, there was not a single tower of note if one looked west and south from the top of the Empire State Building. Any planner influenced by the sleek, modern visions of Robert Moses or Le Corbusier may have assumed two things about this particular swath of Manhattan: that the buildings were obsolete and that the area was "blighted."[20] Neither was true.

Even the most cursory examination of these seemingly unimpressive structures would have revealed their economic value. *New York Times* reporter Bosley Crowther recognized this incongruity in 1936, writing that "on the riverward side of Tenth Avenue in [*sic*] West Thirtieth Street—past the smoky forge of Owen Lavelle, horseshoer, and a sleazy row of warehouses where packing-box commerce is done—stands a dull, unlovely building from which (you'd never suspect it) emerge the first physical embodiments of what eventually become some of Broadway's most handsome productions."[21]

The "embodiments" Crowther referred to were the sets of McDonald Construction, one of the most prominent and profitable scenery firms of the age. McDonald not only owned its building at 534 West 30th Street but also built dozens of notable Broadway shows in the 1930s and 1940s, including the landmark musical *Carousel*. If it was a productive "wonderplace" on the inside, did it really matter that the firm's thirty-year-old building was "unlovely" on the outside? With McDonald and another tenant, the "makers and venders [*sic*] of stage rigging," sharing the 534 West

30th Street building and with two other scene shops on the same block, surely West 30th was a productive part of the local economy.[22]

Marginalized as they were, even the most productive of Broadway's supply, construction, and rehearsal buildings languished into the 1940s, aged and unimproved. Many were demolished to make room for parking structures. Whether dug deep below the surface as multilevel basements or erected several stories high, these types of buildings were the most common form of new construction near Times Square in the years leading up to World War II. They certainly facilitated theatrical consumption during years when more and more consumers arrived for shows via automobile, but parking garages in western midtown inevitably meant that yet another batch of small and affordable structures had disappeared.

Of all the buildings destroyed to make room for parking, none had a story quite so dramatic as that of the 48th Street Theatre. In this unusual example, an actual playhouse was destroyed, but by gravity and the ravages of time rather than by a wrecking crew. When the storied playhouse was built back in 1912, it was standard practice to install a large water tank above any new theater. After several deadly fires at the turn of the century, these heavy tanks were created to douse the playhouses at a moment's notice, saving audiences from fire, yes, but also from death by trampling.[23] When the 48th Street Theatre got its ten-thousand-gallon water tank, it was rigged up in the rafters, mounted on sturdy steel beams. For decades, as stars such as Katherine Cornell and Montgomery Clift trod the boards, the filled tank hulked above them.

Over many years the steel beams gradually corroded. Though the theater was well used as a stage house, as home to the Equity Players, and as a radio and film house in the 1940s, this corrosion somehow escaped notice. Even when it was reclaimed for "legit" theater in the 1950s and stagehands were once again climbing its trusses and manning its fly spaces, no one made any waves about the water tank. By 1955 the beams had corroded to a point that would seal the fate of the building.

Only a few months after the groundbreaking play *Tea and Sympathy* ended its run at the theater, the old beams finally gave out. On the morning of August 24, 1955, ten thousand gallons of water came crashing through the ceiling, onto the stage, and even through the windows of adjacent apartments, soaking a bewildered mother and son at their kitchen table. The damage was so extensive that the theater could not be saved. Within a few years the site was converted into a multistory parking garage.[24]

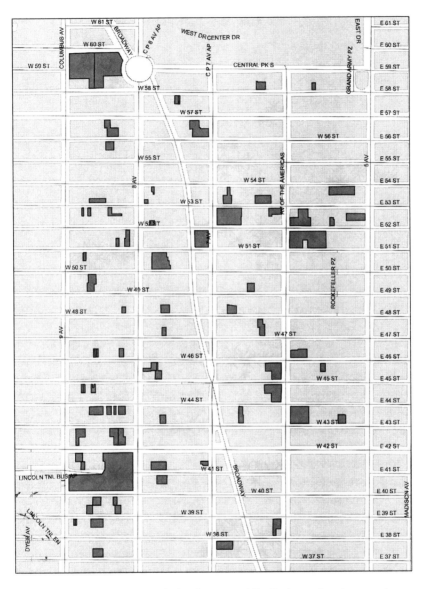

Figure 10. Map of spaces remade for the automobile. Dark gray locations are those converted into open parking lots, freestanding garages, or underground garages between 1933 and 1955. The Coliseum at West 60th Street and the Port Authority Bus Terminal are included as automobile-oriented facilities. Based on Sanborn fire insurance maps from 1933 and 1955. Generated by the author using Geographic Information Systems software.

Alternative Media on Broadway

Like the old 48th Street Theatre, the playhouses and theater-related buildings not replaced by parking facilities continued to age through the Roaring
Twenties, the dirty 1930s, and the war-torn 1940s. Precious few playhouses
benefited from makeovers, renovations, or improvements or any sort until
long after World War II. In an age when the number of stage shows per
year dwindled, those who owned theaters had to find alternative tenants.
The most famous solution to this problem was for a theater owner to slap
a white screen up on the stage, shoehorn a projector into the rear of the
house, and start showing films. More than twenty playhouse owners used
this strategy in the 1930s. A less well-known but equally important tactic
for riding out the Depression was for an owner to rent his space to one of
the many radio producers in need of broadcast space with a "live studio
audience." Long before television, it was these radio tenants who began the
colonization process on Broadway.

In the bold new age of big-budget radio, performers and theater-related
craftspeople adapted quickly to stay employed. Live radio broadcasting
from the Times Square district obviously reduced local demand for visual
components, such as backdrops, set pieces, and costumes, but it was not
the total interruption in the flow of theater-related goods that one might
suspect. Some radio shows, such as Ed Wynn's *Fire Chief* at the New
Amsterdam, continued to utilize basic backdrops and silly costumes to help
keep audiences in stitches. Broadway's expert contractors were perfectly
situated to supply these components, and supply they did throughout the
entire mid-century era.

Joining radio as another piece of the Times Square entertainment puzzle
was the film industry, which had been routinely spawning castings, rehearsals, and film shoots in Manhattan for decades. Given that most film shoots
had no need for live studio audiences or theaters, however, this alternative
media was less connected to Broadway's playhouses than radio. As employers of theater-related contractors and shops, New York City film producers
did promote the ongoing vitality of Broadway's shops when they purchased
components such as lights or costumes, but overall their role in this mix
was mostly as competitors for audiences.

When television joined the radio and film industries in the colonization
of fallow playhouses, beginning in 1948, the adaptability and resilience of
midtown's theater-related craftspeople were strikingly evident. The relationship between this new medium and Broadway was the most intimate of

all, because television broadcasters needed a whole slew of dancers, singers, costumers, wig makers, rehearsal studio proprietors, and other experts who were useless for most radio gigs and film shoots.

Once produced, the radio shows, films, and television programs of this era did compete with live stage shows for audiences, but this is not a project about the consumption of entertainment. Rather this study of the production of components will briefly shift focus to radio, film, and television because this is where many experts in Broadway stagecraft found additional work at mid-century. There was no sudden or catastrophic collapse of the theater-related trades in the 1930s and 1940s but only a slow creep of jobs away from the theater toward alternative media.

Over time the gradual harvesting of Broadway's vast theatrical infrastructure for other uses did have deleterious, unintended consequences for the district. Radio, television, and film projection tenants did not use playhouses as stage crews did. They walled off and ignored many of the spaces once used by stagehands, riggers, and lighting experts. As rental tenants, they were not expected to make repairs or improvements. They tended to depart after only brief tenure, leaving their rented theaters in disrepair.

Most important, the contracts that theater-related craftspeople and supply-shop proprietors secured for radio, television, and film work were generally less consistent and smaller in scope than those of stage shows. In this way, even though the theater district thrived as a multifaceted entertainment center through the 1950s, the seeds of its decline also took root. By the 1950s and 1960s the presence of all three alternative media in midtown Manhattan waned rapidly, for myriad reasons to be explored below. By the late 1960s the theater industry's delicate, interconnected industrial district, built up over the course of the past six decades, would rapidly unravel.

Radio and Broadway

Originally radio functioned as little more than a high-tech megaphone for live entertainment, broadcasting the sounds of New York City's popular culture to local, regional, and then national audiences. This remained true for most of the 1920s, when the Broadway industry also happened to be positively buoyant.[25] In the early days of radio, stage producers had little to complain about. They could and did use radio technology to broadcast hit songs from their musicals to massive audiences, transmitting music from new shows into living rooms far faster than vinyl or sheet music ever could.

Even after the turn of the 1930s, when radios transitioned from a luxury to a standard middle-class amenity and broadcasting became even bigger business, relations between the stage and radio industries remained more or less copacetic. Radio did pose a potential threat to live theatergoing by bringing top-notch entertainment directly into the American home, but this threat was mitigated by its vast potential as an advertising tool. Stage producers of the 1930s not only transmitted hit songs to massive audiences with broadcasts but also experimented with radio advertisements for their shows, just as did their colleagues who sold automobiles or soap.

As broadcasting grew unabated in the early 1930s, some Broadway leaders grew wary of its impact on older modes of distributing their songs. Sheet-music publishers and their composer clients were particularly concerned. According to the general counsel of the American Society of Composers, Authors, and Publishers (ASCAP) in 1932, broadcasting had taken a noticeable bite out of sheet-music profits, and radio royalties were not making up for composers' losses.[26] Though this trend was troubling for the ASCAP crowd, other Broadway power brokers focused instead on harnessing radio's awesome broadcasting power to promote new stage shows.

This went far beyond spoken or musical commercials. The Broadway cast recording, a foundation stone of the industry for most of the twentieth century, was created not only for sale on vinyl but also for radio broadcasting. When the producer Florenz Ziegfeld famously captured the voices and orchestrations of Jerome Kern's *Show Boat* in 1927, for example, he was able to distribute copies of the RKO recording for broadcast without having to pay anyone for a live performance. Preserving this show as an RKO recording had the added benefit of reliability, reassuring Ziegfeld that the *Show Boat* he disseminated would be free of unwanted coughs, vocal cracks, sharp trumpet notes, or other auditory pitfalls of live broadcasting.

Radio broadcasters played *Show Boat* frequently in 1928, making this the most successful of Broadway's early cast recordings. With the hit songs "Bill," "Ol' Man River," and "Can't Help Lovin' Dat Man" becoming national standards by the end of the decade, *Show Boat* cemented Jerome Kern's place as one of America's most popular composers. In an age when a new score by an industry leader such as Kern could fill a house on Broadway, composers used radio to keep their star burning as brightly as possible.[27]

The benefits of radio extended well beyond the confines of the five boroughs, helping touring shows to sell tickets nationwide. Though they bemoaned the damaging impact of radio on sheet-music sales in the early 1930s, ASCAP's leaders did acknowledge that after the broadcasting of popular songs, "sure-fire hits did capacity business in the larger cities." Broadway producers cashed in on widely broadcast songs by shoehorning them into touring musicals, regardless of whether they fit the shows.[28]

Another fringe benefit of live broadcasts was back in the city, where Broadway's musicians sometimes got hired. It was often true in live radio that when composers worked, so did musicians. At Hammerstein's Theatre for a onetime WEAF broadcast in 1931, producers hired a full orchestra to play George Gershwin's lush, challenging music. In the theater district of the early 1930s, these paid gigs were a godsend. Musicians clearly suffered from unemployment as most others did, in ways that radio broadcasting could not fix, but at least these events generated some paid work.

For live radio broadcasts without music, such as "radio plays," connections to the local theater-building economy were fewer. Radio plays, which debuted in the 1920s and peaked in popularity during the 1930s, featured nothing more than actors' voices, sound effects, and perhaps some musical scoring, depending on the piece. These intimate, auditory experiences broadcast from the small studios within Rockefeller Center and similar spaces required no massive orchestra, no live studio audience, and certainly no scenery, costumes, or dance troupes. They did provide paid work to actors, and perhaps they generated business for rehearsal studio proprietors or dialect coaches on occasion, but they were otherwise many steps removed from local stagecraft.[29]

Of all the intersections between Broadway and radio, the most profound was full-fledged tenancy, when a radio production occupied a dormant theater for more than just one night. The first experiment in this vein occurred in 1932, when the comedian Ed Wynn performed his wildly popular *Fire Chief* show before a "live" or amplified audience in the roof garden of the New Amsterdam Theater on 42nd Street. This space, where Florenz Ziegfeld had once hosted capacity crowds for "Midnight Frolics," had been mostly dark since 1929. When Wynn performed his radio-oriented comedy routine for an audience of 675 and producers encouraged the crowd to "behave naturally," the uproarious laughter and applause became broadcast gold. The *Fire Chief* team broadcast this show from the same space every Tuesday night for several years. For the first time in entertainment history, listeners across America could laugh along with an amplified audience as they enjoyed a comedian from many miles away.[30]

After Wynn's success, other performers followed suit, requesting that they too be freed from the soundproof glass that had divided them from their audiences in the earliest days of radio. By the end of 1933, stars such as Rudy Vallee and Al Jolson were performing for live studio audiences within dormant Broadway theaters. At least one night a week and sometimes more frequently, these broadcasts filled an otherwise darkened theater with patrons, support staff, technicians, producers, and actors. For the men who owned these spaces and the workers hired for these events, even one event per week was better than none. As the 1930s waned, radio producers continued to book vacant Broadway theaters for broadcasts with enough regularity that the live studio audience became a staple of comedy broadcasting.[31]

Radio producers were useful as midtown employers, but they could never hire as many people as Broadway's impresarios. A live broadcast such as *Fire Chief* put some sound technicians, agents, and actors to work but did precious little for stagehands, designers, or costumers. During the entire duration of its multiyear run, *Fire Chief* utilized only "a curtain bedecked with advertising material," "two large [Texaco] gasoline pumps on each side of the stage," and a few silly costumes for its star.[32] Compared to a Broadway musical, this was a pittance of production value.

By way of contrast, Irving Berlin's musical *Face the Music*, playing downstairs in the main house while Wynn was upstairs, featured a whopping seventy-two performers, each needing several costumes.[33] Even in the constrained roof garden space, stage productions as recently as 1928 had needed scenery depicting, for example, "John Black's office, the home of Judge Fish, and a yacht."[34] Each of these settings required furniture, walls, and at least one painted backdrop. Other, previous shows, especially the annual *Follies* in the main house, featured costumes so prominently that portions of the revue became veritable fashion shows.[35] In comparison to any of these stage productions, the components of Wynn's *Fire Chief* broadcasts were unimpressive.

Another obvious drawback of radio shows was their limited potential to employ the city's talent pool. Broadcast producers had absolutely no use for dancers and had to steer clear of physical comedians. Some radio producers succeeded in booking the hottest acts of vaudeville or Broadway only to realize that the pratfalls, sight gags, and facial expressions that had

made such hits onstage were virtually useless on radio. Sure, sublime physical comedy could get the live audience roaring, but home listeners would
be perplexed. There are many amusing anecdotes from the early days of
radio, when directors had to reprimand physical comedians for neglecting
home listeners.[36]

Foreshadowing the David Letterman phenomenon of the late twentieth
century, crowds of "anxious" hopefuls lined the sidewalks of the theater
district in the early 1930s waiting not for bread but for their chance to see
stars such as Ed Wynn "in action at the microphone."[37] In this way, tourism
for the purpose of attending a live broadcast began long before television,
bolstering the safety of Times Square sidewalks in the 1930s by filling them
with law-abiding visitors.

In addition to Wynn, Vallee, and Jolson, dozens of other performers
got into this act. One of the most famous was Major Bowes, host of a
weekly amateur hour from 1934 to 1946. Although his show first launched
from Radio City, it relocated to the Manhattan Theatre on 53rd Street and
Broadway in 1936, where it settled in for an impressive decade-long run.
Bowes's show was a unique chance for singers and actors to be discovered,
but it was also a weekly production requiring a full orchestra, stagehands,
and ushers. This cultural phenomenon also brought an audience of thirteen
hundred people to the northern edge of Times Square once a week. Many
Bowes attendees came from the five boroughs, but plenty of others traveled
from other cities or states to join the fun.[38]

Looming even larger than the Bowes broadcasts were the 1930s events
at the legendary Hippodrome Theatre, which could seat almost five thousand. In the gargantuan space, producers staged some of the most highly
attended radio events of the decade. Although the Hippodrome did not
broadcast with the regularity of Major Bowes, when it did it was an
immense magnet for law-abiding visitors to Times Square. Indeed when
operas broadcast from the Hippodrome in the 1930s, the space was so
crammed with people that home listeners complained of hearing coughs,
sniffles, and rustling in addition to arias and arpeggios.[39] Along with boxing
matches and political stump speeches, these types of broadcasts generated
massive audiences, probably the largest of the entire Times Square district.

Less prominent than either the Hippodrome or Major Bowes but influential en masse were the dozens of lesser-known programs broadcasting
from empty Broadway theaters in this era. From the Playhouse Theatre on
48th Street down to Maxine Elliott's on 39th, the tenancy of radio shows

within Broadway houses was a widespread, albeit short-lived, facet of the midtown economy. The Great Depression may have killed off vaudeville,[40] but the "fabulous invalid," as Moss Hart nicknamed Broadway in 1938, kept right on kicking, partly because of radio.[41]

The history of radio "on Broadway" is key to understanding why this district declined so rapidly and so completely after the 1950s. Radio tenants used far less space in rented theaters than did their stage-based forebears, leaving many areas unvisited and therefore neglected. At the New Amsterdam, for example, live theater through the 1920s had sent riggers, stagehands, actors, producers, musicians, and audience members into every imaginable space of both the main house and the roof garden. When performers opened closets in their dressing rooms, stagehands climbed into fly spaces, musicians packed orchestra pits, and ushers manned the aisles, all were given the opportunity, if not the obligation, to notice and report building problems. As these buildings were home to stage shows, few corners were not regularly monitored on a weekly or even a daily basis.

More to the point, each of these stakeholders had a vested interest, as either producer or consumer, in the niceties of the venue. When the venerated New Amsterdam was home to "the Great Ziegfeld," it is hard to imagine a scenario in which a plumbing, electrical, or structural problem went unreported for longer than a day. Legendary producers, famous for producing exquisite scenery and costumes, tended not to let roof leaks drip onto the well-coiffed heads of their guests. In the stage age, Ziegfeld had every reason either to fix problems himself or demand that building owners Klaw and Erlanger fix them immediately.

After the *Follies* left the New Amsterdam in 1927, intermittent radio tenants began to utilize the building very differently. Those who did darken this theater's door to work on radio shows such as *Fire Chief* were well aware that their events were auditory ones, and they had no reason to go rooting around in spaces not essential to their broadcasts. Audiences, having flocked to see stars at the microphones, were equally disinterested in the physical condition of the houses surrounding them. In the rare event that a radio show staffer or nosy audience member stumbled upon a building problem, it is unlikely that a producer would have paid much heed when he was judged solely by the sounds he sold.

As if the deafening silence regarding the physical condition of Broadway's playhouses were not ominous enough, radio tenants arrived on Broadway just when the district's oldest houses began to suffer serious structural problems. The story of the 48th Street Theatre, briefly occupied by radio and then destroyed by a long-forgotten water tank, illustrates the very real consequences of this ill-fated timing. The physical neglect of playhouses was not so dramatic as to have them collapsing in droves, like so many houses of cards, but it did prove damaging. This was especially true because radio tenants were only one form of nontheatrical tenancy.

Film entrepreneurs and, later, television producers proved equally keen to rent vacant Broadway houses when stage production stalled after 1929. Whether screening a film or staging a television broadcast, most of these entertainment industry professionals were as disinterested as radio producers in maintaining the spaces they rented.

Film and Broadway

Compared to radio, which had a complex, often beneficial relationship to theater, the film industry's impact on Broadway in the late 1920s was simpler; it was a threat, and a serious one at that. After the first "talking picture" debuted in 1927, some stage producers were positively apoplectic about the clear and present danger that "talkies" brought to their bottom line.[42] Adding insult to injury, when film producers harvested Broadway's dormant playhouses for moving pictures, they tended to leave behind even more physical damage than radio broadcasters did. The film industry did put some theater-related businesses to work in the 1930s and 1940s, but this cross-fertilization was limited because so many of the businesses were on the Hudson, while the bulk of the work was near the Pacific. By midcentury, when Hollywood dominated feature films, New York City continued to produce films but mostly shorter pieces such as newsreels, cartoons, and sponsored industrial films. On occasion New York City did serve as a stunning visual backdrop for feature movies, but far more shoots after 1920 took place on Burbank back lots than in Brooklyn or on Broome Street.

While most of these transitions were gradual, the meteoric rise of talking pictures and the simultaneous dropping off of stage entertainments in the early 1930s were certainly not. As was the case with radio, the profitability and dynamism of Broadway through the 1920s had overshadowed any threat posed by the vigorous film industry. For the first few decades of the twentieth century, at least, the producers, building owners, craftspeople, and performers working in these two forms of media kept things reasonably copacetic. On October 6, 1927, however, this relationship was fundamentally altered with the opening of *The Jazz Singer*. Talking pictures began to rattle and hum with all sorts of sounds previously offered only by Broadway and vaudeville.

Silent movies had already absorbed some elements of melodrama, slapstick, and physical comedy from the stage, but films after 1927 quickly sang out with all of the vocal inflections and intonations that made stage shows so fun and compelling. Films with synchronized sound easily incorporated double entendres and "blue jokes," stealing the mantle of lowbrow entertainment from vaudeville. Although New York City would always have some form of crass stage comedy, vaudeville rapidly dwindled after 1927, and Broadway transformed. Especially after the great crash of 1929, vaudeville all but disappeared from the American stage, while Broadway developed into a more rarefied medium of relatively highbrow entertainment. Though this process unfolded slowly over many years, it is key to understanding why Broadway produced a shrinking number of shows per year after the 1920s. Film had begun to speak to the masses as a more well-rounded form of popular entertainment, leaving Broadway producers with fewer tricks that could not be replicated on the silver screen.[43]

While the one-two punch of the talking picture and the stock market crash of 1929 neatly dispatched vaudeville,[44] the fabulous invalid of Broadway kept on, albeit with new constrictions. In the new economic landscape of the 1930s, Broadway producers had to compete with films offering stars of equal caliber, songs of equal popularity, and even dance sequences that rivaled those of the live stage. With the innovative cinema work of Busby Berkeley appearing on the silver screen in the 1930s and with Hollywood stars speaking and singing on-screen, Broadway's producers struggled to fill their houses. Some even struggled to keep their houses, as many a fallow Broadway playhouse was snatched up and converted into a fertile site of film screening.

Film projection houses in Times Square or on 42nd Street were hardly a novelty in 1929. The Strand and the Rialto had opened as major projection houses in Times Square as early as the 1910s. What made the early 1930s so different was the way that film projectionists harvested Broadway's existing playhouses. Beginning in 1930 these conversions progressed at a fast clip, with one theater after another transitioning from eight live shows a week to five or six film screenings a day. All told, by the end of the decade over twenty Broadway theaters had been converted, and few would host live theater again, at least for many decades. This was especially true on 42nd Street between 7th and 8th Avenues, a symbolic stretch of the district that had been immortalized in song but was also a crucial logistical center teeming with theater-related shops, rehearsal studios, and the offices of producers and agents. By 1937 every single one of the historic theaters on 42nd Street had been gobbled up for film projection.[45]

As was the case with radio tenancy, this trend left many a Broadway playhouse in a sad state of disrepair. When the storied New Amsterdam finally succumbed to film in January 1937, the incentive for facility upkeep dropped even lower than it had been during the days of Ed Wynn's *Fire Chief* broadcasts. Simon H. Fabian had purchased the building specifically for projection and had only a few areas of concern.[46] The lobby and box office needed to be reasonably clean, the seating needed to be decent, and the projection room needed to function. Fly spaces, dressing rooms, an orchestra pit, storage rooms, and the roof garden became neglected, closed-off spaces. Deterioration set in quickly, and the building began a famous slide into disrepair.

Had film projection, a common alternative use for theaters, kept Broadway's stagehands, electricians, and component craftspeople working more or less the way that stage shows had, its arrival in the Times Square district would have been business as usual. This was not the case. When playhouses converted from stage shows to film projection, available jobs in the buildings plummeted. A stage show, even a play with only two actors, required a stage crew of at least ten, if not twenty, and the entire panoply of box office workers, ticket takers, ushers, and concessionists needed to handle an audience. For a musical, producers had to add a full orchestra and various corps of dancers and singers to this mix. For film projection in the same building, one needed only a box office staff, ticket-takers, projectionists, and perhaps a teenager or two selling popcorn. There was a small silver lining of stability to projection-related jobs, because movie houses did not go dark when their latest attractions closed, as theater houses did. But the impact of this stability on the local job market was negligible. All told, few theater-related craftspeople gained much employment from the projection of films, other than the musicians occasionally hired to play along with silent films in the 1910s and 1920s.

It was in film production, rather than projection, that theater-related craftspeople were most likely to find employment. Sadly, this too was became a diminishing prospect as the 1930s and 1940s unfolded. In the

1910s especially, film production in the five boroughs and its environs had
been in bloom. From midtown Manhattan to Fort Lee, New Jersey, several
major movie-making operations set up shop, most famously in 1919, when
Paramount Pictures redeveloped a studio site in Astoria, Queens. Thomas
Edison's company made films first in West Orange, New Jersey, and then
in the Bronx until 1918. *Business Listings* for 1922 reveals independent
shops for both "film cutting" and "film storage" in the heart of Times
Square. Eaves Costume, a leader in the industry, had supplied hundreds of
costumes and other supplies to D. W. Griffith in the 1910s while also supplying raiment to Paramount and Cosmopolitan Studios. Even through the
1920s, when feature film production had famously shifted to Hollywood,
studios such as Paramount and First National were still producing feature
films in New York City, tallying up a combined total of forty such films in
1926.[47]

Film production, had it survived with more breadth and depth in the
New York region, may have proved an effective survival strategy for costumers, scenery builders, and other specialists who saw their prospects for
theater work shrink at mid-century. It did not. Although some types of film
production continued to flourish in New York City, feature film shoots
dwindled. Between World Wars I and II, New York shoots tended to be
newsreels, short films, cartoons, or industrials rather than features. One
particular challenge to feature-film production in the region had been the
dearth of the expensive sound equipment needed for talking pictures. While
these machines were readily available throughout Hollywood by the 1930s,
they were rarely considered worthwhile investments for most New York
studios.[48]

Theater-related shop owners and expert craftspeople interested in working on feature films had only a few choices as this type of shoot gravitated
toward the Pacific. They could head west and never look back, as did
Charles LeMaire, a costumer who had designed for Brooks Costume and
Florenz Ziegfeld in New York but never returned after 1943, when he signed
with Twentieth Century Fox in Los Angeles. They could maintain New York
shops for theatrical work and fly out to California to design for film, as
Irene Sharaff, the Tony-winning costumer of *West Side Story*, did through
the 1950s and 1960s. At mid-century it was common for leading talents in
both scenic and costume design to split their time between New York and
California. As an alternative, those who worked in execution rather than

design, such as the employees of Dazian's Theatricals, could weather this shifting geography by opening branch supply offices. By 1941 Dazian's stationery showcased its surviving New York office, a branch office at 731 South Hope Street in Los Angeles, and two other storefronts in Philadelphia and Boston. Finally shop owners and craftspeople could push their unions, especially United Scenic Artists, to create broader jurisdictions that included feature film work in California.[49]

This is precisely what United Scenic Artists business representative Rudy Karnholt tried in 1948, after a couple decades of diminished film production in New York City. He spearheaded an effort to recruit Hollywood designers to his union, hoping to strengthen numbers, gain political clout, and take USA's jurisdiction to both coasts. The campaign failed. Out in Los Angeles the film industry had its own unions and its own problems. When L.A.'s scenic designers had been on strike in 1947, New York's scenic artists and craftspeople had been powerless to help them. In the decades following Karnholt's campaign, even more jobs in design and construction would leave New York City for Hollywood. With businesses firmly rooted in Manhattan, mid-century proprietors watched as their work opportunities dwindled.[50]

None of these strategies succeeded in pulling the lion's share of the available work in film production back across the country. Meanwhile none of the playhouses colonized for film screenings during the crisis years of the early 1930s returned back to the Broadway fold as the decade progressed. The closest they got to stage productions was burlesque, a form of entertainment particularly ill-suited to increasing the amount of fabric being worked into costumes within midtown.

The most famous of these theaters, the New Amsterdam, never suffered the indignity of hosting the twirling pasties of burlesque, but it did remain out of commission as a theatrical space at least until 1937. In this year a group of enterprising producers found a way to bring the roof garden back online by renting it out for Broadway rehearsals. Despite the uncontested dominance of film screening on the block and the continued screening of films downstairs, these producers succeeded in reactivating the upstairs site as a productive space. This small beachhead of theatrical space on 42nd Street was not only a symbolic victory but also an incubator for Arthur Miller's iconic play *Death of a Salesman*, which rehearsed in the decaying but functional roof garden space in late 1948.[51]

Figure 11. Emil Friedlander of Dazian's, Inc., presenting costumes, ca. 1945–52.
Courtesy of the Billy Rose Theatre Division, The New York Public Library
for the Performing Arts, Astor, Lenox, and Tilden Foundations.

The Federal Theatre Project

While the larger economy and the costs of producing live shows tilted much of Times Square toward film after 1929, one weighty federal program did tip the district back toward theater, albeit briefly. It was called the Federal Theatre Project (FTP), and this component of the Works Progress Administration (WPA) was centered, not surprisingly, in New York. The administration of the project was a small boon to the local economy, filling rental spaces at 110 West 48th Street and 1991 Broadway with bursts of professional, theater-related activity, and it is true that more FTP productions took place within the five boroughs than anywhere else.[52] As a generator of local craft and construction work, however, the Federal Theatre Project was not quite the engine one would suspect. Despite its strong concentration in a city filled with more costumers, scenery builders, and component suppliers than any other, the project secured most of its components in-house, through experts on its payroll, and was therefore relatively disconnected from Broadway's third-party shops.

The intensive concentration of the project within Gotham reveals much about the continued, New York–centric lopsidedness of commercial theater during the 1930s. In a sense the Federal Theatre Project, operating just a decade before regional theaters revolutionized the geography of the American stage, was the last chapter in a long history of uncontested New York City dominance.

Though WPA employees crafted most of the project's components themselves, the Federal Theatre Project did rely on Manhattan's theatrical infrastructure for rehearsal space. This was one aspect of production that FTP specialists simply could not provide themselves. They may have had a staggering total of "more than 12,700 workers" on their payroll, "a majority of whom worked behind-the-scenes," but generally speaking, painters and seamstresses did not tend to own playhouses. Without a commercial producer at the helm who might own a theater and offer it for rehearsals, FTP productions had to branch out. One rehearsal studio proprietor, David Ringle of 1607 Broadway, was a repeat beneficiary of FTP largesse in this regard. His studios appear in FTP administrative schedules as a rehearsal location frequently, especially in the summer and fall of 1936.[53]

Another method that the administrators of the FTP used to rehearse their shows was to secure rental space in a playhouse earlier than was usually the case, long before opening night. The Adelphi, Maxine Elliott, and

Lafayette theaters all benefited from this form of early tenancy throughout the 1930s, when the FTP would move its productions in for a long stretch of development and rehearsals.

Other methods of FTP production had no such silver lining for the owners of Broadway's local building or business owners. When the traveling players of the FTP's Caravan Theatre show loaded up their five traveling trucks for performances in farther flung locations throughout the five boroughs, their mission was certainly not to reinvigorate midtown's theatrical economy. They had a mandate to bring theater to the multitudes as affordably as possible and therefore eschewed the finely crafted trappings of the typical Broadway extravaganza.[54]

It is important to note that even the most minimalist of FTP productions provided employment for at least some of the theater industry's skilled workforce. Those lucky enough to make the FTP payroll as painters, actors, or choreographers during the 1930s must have been grateful for the opportunity, but they must also have known that this federally backed project was not going to be laying its golden eggs into perpetuity. Despite several years of positive productivity, the project ultimately lacked the longevity to buck the larger trends of this era. It burned briefly and brightly in New York City and beyond but ultimately left the Broadway industry as adrift as it had been before.

As the Depression was finally mitigated and then ended by World War II and the Federal Theatre Project closed for good, many a playhouse was still out of the Broadway loop, having been converted for radio or the movies. This left Broadway producers with fewer options for rehearsals and performances, which gradually raised the costs of renting playhouses. With the stock of theaters diminished, the costs of rehearsal space up, and the Federal Theatre Project only a memory, Broadway producers faced an uncertain future in the early 1940s. This uncertainty was only exacerbated by the advent of television broadcasting in 1947.

Television and Broadway

As much as the radio and film industries did to enervate Broadway, the most significant challenge to live theatergoing in the mid-twentieth century was television. Unlike film, television was not an immediate and obvious threat to Broadway, and the two industries were surprisingly copacetic throughout the 1940s. When the television industry matured and left New York City, however, it left Broadway's industrial district weaker than ever before.

Early television was all about New York City. Its technology was developed there, its shows were filmed there, and even its plots, including those of *The Honeymooners* and *I Love Lucy*, were set there. Many early television shows from 1947 to 1952 were telecast from old Broadway, vaudeville, and radio theaters between 41st and 59th Streets. By the late 1950s, however, the television industry had outgrown this home base, and scores of television shows and production companies were relocating to southern California. Many designers, craftspeople, and performers followed them. This trend dealt a triple blow to theater professionals who stayed in New York City. Their first challenge was losing some of their most talented colleagues and collaborators. Second, anyone who stayed had to contend with a stock of underutilized work spaces, weakened unions, and insolvent businesses. Even more deleterious than either of these challenges was the advent of a mature, diversified television industry, one that could compete much more effectively against Broadway for audiences.

As exciting as television was for those watching at home, it was even more exciting for those performers lucky enough to be involved in some of the first telecasts. Bob Hope, one such performer, was featured in a highly experimental, thirty-minute broadcast from the Paramount Building in Times Square in 1947.[55] After having performed for vaudeville audiences at the Palace and *Follies* audiences at the New Amsterdam, Hope was suddenly thrust before a multicity audience through the new technology. Stage stars such as Hope dominated the medium in its first year. For a special four-hour broadcast from the Palace Theater, for example, the ABC network relied on Broadway stalwarts Beatrice Lillie and Ray Bolger, along with a few other performers. Bolger is best known as the scarecrow from *The Wizard of Oz*, but at that point in his career he was doing just as much work on Broadway as in Hollywood. Radio stars succeeded in migrating as well. In 1948 radio performer Milton Berle made the switch to television, broadcasting his *Texaco Star Theater* variety show from Rockefeller Center.[56]

The historian James Baughman has explained that the overlap between Broadway and television involved far more than casting, suggesting that "early T.V.'s heavy reliance on Broadway combined with live telecasting to give the newest medium a heavy theatrical flavor."[57] In other words, these performers were not just Broadway stars who happened to appear on television; rather they were featured *as* Broadway stars. Many sang their signature songs from the stage or revived comedic characters and skits that had proved popular before live audiences. This is an important distinction to make regarding early television, because this early era of Broadway on television is lesser known than famous, scripted shows. At this stage television functioned briefly as more of a broadcast technology than a distinct form of entertainment.

The example of John Raitt performing on *The Ed Sullivan Show* in 1954 is an excellent case in point. At the time of the broadcast, Raitt was at the peak of his Broadway popularity, having starred in *Carousel* in 1945 and having just opened two months earlier as the lead in the hit musical *Pajama Game*. On the August 22 broadcast of *Ed Sullivan*, episode forty-nine of season seven, Raitt sang songs from both shows. He performed the song "Hey There" out of its *Pajama Game* context, in a fanciful medieval stage setting, and then sang "Soliloquy" from *Carousel* on a saloon set. Despite unconventional scenery, the performances do not seem to have deviated much from what had appeared on Broadway.

Other early television broadcasts utilized larger portions of hit shows, such as extended scenes or "production numbers." Countless broadcasts of *Ed Sullivan*, the *Colgate Comedy Hour*, and the *Milton Berle Show* in the 1950s and 1960s featured elaborate production numbers pulled directly from the stage. Nearly the entire cast of *Pal Joey*, for example, took the stage of Hammerstein's Theatre to perform a series of musical numbers on *Ed Sullivan* in 1952. With them arrived scenery pieces, costumes, and backdrops from the Broadhurst Theatre imported just for this *Ed Sullivan* broadcast.[58]

Stars and production numbers tapped directly into the marketing potential of this new medium, turning New York City's dominance of early television into an asset for producers. For the shop operators, landlords, and business proprietors of the Broadway industrial district, however, the most significant tie between the two industries was not people or songs but buildings.

Following a precedent set by radio and film, many of television's earliest broadcasts occurred in old playhouses. Several of these theaters had been radio venues in the 1930s and 1940s before yielding to television. There were many reasons why television took root in Gotham during its infancy, but one stands out above all the others: AT&T's coaxial cables stretched only from New York City to Boston, Philadelphia, and Washington, D.C., and early television relied wholly on these cables for transmission.[59] Television innovators therefore looked for broadcast space somewhere along this urban axis but within close proximity to performers, costumers, lighting experts, and musicians.

This search led them straight to Broadway. In 1948 the DuMont Television Network revived the Craig Theatre on 54th Street, which had largely failed as a stage house, to broadcast several short-lived shows. The network also rented the Ambassador Theatre from the Shubert Organization between 1950 and 1956. Joining DuMont in this practice were the aforementioned *Milton Berle Show* at Center Theatre (Rockefeller Center), Ed Sullivan's *Toast of the Town* at Maxine Elliott's Theatre (39th Street and Broadway), and Sid Caesar's *Your Show of Shows* at the Majestic Theatre on Columbus Circle. Adding to the mix, CBS broadcast many short-lived programs from the old Mansfield Theatre on West 47th Street between 1950 and 1960. Even though coaxial cables soon reached to dozens of other cities, television producers continued to utilize vacant Broadway theaters. By the end of the 1960s, television broadcasters had also taken over the Biltmore, the Ziegfeld, and Al Jolson's 59th Street theaters.[60]

At first this trend benefited both industries. For television producers, this location enabled them to tap Broadway's existing talent pool, personnel networks, and infrastructure. At least during television's infancy, they did not have to cultivate and build up these vital components on their own. For Broadway theater owners, these rentals helped to fill awkward or unprofitable playhouses that might otherwise have struggled for bookings. Not all Broadway houses were created equal in the competitive theater environment of the 1950s and 1960s. Some had been constructed with fewer than one thousand seats, while others had cramped dressing rooms, insufficient backstage and fly spaces for scenery, or deteriorating physical plants. Any one of these characteristics could make a theater unattractive, especially as weekly profit margins grew tighter by the year. It was precisely this type of underutilized theater that owners tended to rent to television producers. When the managers of Maxine Elliott's Theatre booked *The Ed Sullivan Show* as a tenant in 1948, they secured steady rental income for a forty-year-old building that had stood dark for several Broadway seasons.

After *The Ed Sullivan Show* left in 1950, however, developers quickly demolished the aging and unimproved theater. This development spoke volumes about the challenges faced by even those theater owners lucky enough to secure television tenants. Some houses, such as Maxine Elliott's, were hamstrung by their original designs. Built for its eponymous namesake at the peak of her popularity, the 1908 Maxine Elliott's may have been "one of the most lavishly designed playhouses of its time," with copious dressing rooms and backstage space, but this left room for only 934 seats. This crippling detail limited weekly revenues during the playhouse's entire history. Even for sold-out hits, the 934-seat house could not compete as a money-maker with its 1,200-seat neighbors.[61]

This is one of the reasons why, despite having showcased notable plays such as Lillian Hellman's *The Children's Hour* (1934), and despite having been the intended location of Mark Blitzstein's historic *The Cradle Will Rock*, the often dark little theater succumbed to radio broadcasting in 1941. When Sullivan's *Toast of the Town* opened in the old, intimate house in 1948, the honeymoon between the live studio audience and the performers may have been a fine one, but the broadcast became such a hit that it outgrew its original home. By 1950 CBS had remodeled the much larger, far more lavish Hammerstein's Theatre on 53rd Street specifically for *The Ed Sullivan Show*, leaving the Maxine Elliott's bereft of both a tenant and structural improvements.

Not even its brief burst of television fame could save the storied old house. Nearly fifty years old and outmatched by neighboring venues, the old playhouse met the wrecking ball after being purchased by the Shubert Organization and then quickly resold to a developer. When developers destroyed the beautiful, aging theater to make room for an office tower in 1959, landmarking laws were few and far between.[62] At 39th Street and 6th Avenue, the theater stood directly in the path of a booming midtown office corridor, and its fate was sealed.

The historical march toward demolition was strikingly similar for several other theaters. First, a radio broadcast or film screening crew moved in during the 1930s, generating fewer jobs but bringing a modicum of life to a dormant house. After World War II theater producers did reacquire some of these theaters, but just as many stood dark or were harvested as television broadcast spaces. Like their radio forebears, those who acquired or rented old playhouses for television broadcasting tended to delay or completely ignore issues of refurbishment, renovation, and maintenance. After the DuMont Network vacated the Ambassador Theatre, for example, J. J. Shubert complained woefully about what they left behind, writing, "[T]hese people who take the theaters for the purpose of television . . .

destroy the theater."[63] When most television programs departed for the greener pastures of Hollywood, the spaces they vacated were in deplorable condition. It was precisely these theaters, poorly maintained for years, that were most in danger of being razed.

The Majestic Theatre at Columbus Circle and Al Jolson's 59th Street Theatre both fit this pattern. Each was a venue for live shows before transitioning to radio or television, and both were wiped from the map by the 1960s. In the case of the Majestic Theatre, where the stage versions of *The Wizard of Oz* and *Babes in Toyland* had debuted at the turn of the century, the force behind demolition was an individual quite familiar to scholars of urban history: Robert Moses.

In the 1950s, after the departure of Sid Caesar's *Your Show of Shows*, the Majestic was even older than Maxine Elliott's. It had been built in 1903 at a remove from the central concentration of Broadway houses and had always struggled as a result. It also happened to stand in the path of one of Robert Moses's pet projects, the Coliseum. As in many other Moses projects, wrecking crews got to work before local leaders understood what was happening. They had razed the stately playhouse in 1954 even though it was still functional and was conveniently situated close to costume shops on both 61st and 62nd Streets.[64]

The new facility that arose on this site had no space for television broadcasting, let alone theater-related craft or businesses. At the Columbus Circle Coliseum, scenic design or display specialists could have easily contributed to the many conventions that occupied the facility after 1954. Instead of creating work spaces, however, Moses designed a massive parking garage. While the Majestic Theatre had brought a charming pedestrian entrance and graceful architecture to Columbus Circle and accommodated a mix of live theater, cinema, and television broadcasting for decades, the new Coliseum was comparatively monolithic, static, and unaesthetic. It served only one purpose, conventions, and with its large garage, it favored the automobile over the pedestrian.

Despite the small role that television broadcasting played in the demolition of several Broadway houses, not all was lost as the new medium went mainstream after 1950. Because early television was tightly concentrated near Times Square, it sometimes meant jobs for Broadway's skilled craftspeople. Soon after television began to flourish in 1948, Broadway's United Scenic Artists union succeeded in negotiating a contract with NBC, ABC, CBS, and DuMont, securing a 15 percent hourly raise for their members

working in television.[65] As a growing cadre of television producers began
to hire from USA's ranks for the creation of backdrops, scenery, costumes,
and other components, the union succeeded in maintaining its membership
base through diversification.

The 15 percent raise was certainly welcome, but this did not necessarily
mean that craft specialists had it easy in the age of television. In the same
year that they secured this raise, USA members also had to pay higher dues
to help defray the rental costs of their union office. No longer able to afford
its rental space on 42nd Street, USA moved to 234 West 56th Street, where
the union no longer had adequate space for its membership meetings. Acting secretary George Sullivan explained these developments to the membership in 1948: "[M]embers may expect a raise in dues . . . a rise in union
expenses makes this necessary. It is impossible to rent space like was done
at 42nd Street. The present rate is higher and yet parent body must hire
extra meeting hall, because present location is not large enough."[66] Through
the 1950s and 1960s membership meetings took place in local hotel ballrooms, including those of the Edison, Claridge, and Manhattan Hotels.[67]

As they gathered in these ballrooms, the designers, painters, and carpenters of United Scenic Artists hashed out their working conditions in the
rapidly expanding television industry. Minutes from these meetings are
filled with discussions of television work in the 1950s, when some costume
and scene shops aggressively pursued contracts. In a 1951 interview, a
spokesperson for Brooks Costume, a major Broadway costumer, explained
that roughly 40 percent of that company's income came now from television. In the same article, the rival Eaves Costume company "reliably
reported" that a full 50 percent of its income came from the new medium.
Even if these spokespeople were exaggerating the extent to which their firms
had secured television contracts, it is undeniable that theater-related businesses, in general, did a significant amount of television work in the 1950s.
One USA member, the scenic proprietor Peter Rotundo, got positively
entrepreneurial about his television work by 1952, advertising special "T.V.
packages" to producers complete with scenery, camera crews, and lighting
technicians. Another, veteran scenery builder George M. Vail, got into television work late in his career despite having spent an entire career building
only for the stage. As a partner in Chester Rakeman studios, Vail helped to
build scenery for CBS television between 1949 and 1952.[68]

This work was far more than just taking something from a Broadway
show and rigging it up for *The Ed Sullivan Show* or *Your Show of Shows*.

When John Raitt sang "Soliloquy" and "Hey There" on the aforementioned *Ed Sullivan Show* broadcast in 1954, he did so in front of several elaborate scenery pieces and a painted backdrop. These were not imported from any existing Broadway show but rather were built and painted by USA members specifically for the broadcast. USA had a signed contract with CBS for this type of work and worked diligently to enforce it.[69]

Ultimately the mutually beneficial, tightly compacted working relationships between television producers and theater-related craftspeople were relatively short-lived. Much of this had to do with the limitations of studio space in New York as compared to California, described in the 1952 *Saturday Evening Post* as follows: "New York had been, up until now, the TV capital. . . . But in New York the whole industry is crying for studio space. Old theaters, the private dining rooms of hotels, abandoned churches and car barns are used for stages. One program started last summer originates in Philadelphia because no space whatever could be found in New York."[70]

From the mid-1950s forward, the television industry stalled in New York but surged ahead in southern California. Stars, shows, technicians, and specialists relocated to the Los Angeles basin, and the shows they crafted there were developed with their own styles, independent of the Great White Way. This happened quite quickly, as if an exciting wave of television activity had washed over Times Square only to retreat just as quickly. With fewer chances to work in television through the late 1950s, theater-related business proprietors had to work even harder to cobble together their annual incomes.

The irony of this exodus for Broadway's industrial district was that many television shows left just when theater-related craftspeople were reorganizing, recombining, and relocating to better accommodate them. When Brooks Costume moved from its 6th Avenue work space, which it had occupied for over forty years, to West 61st Street in 1952, the stated reason was "to be near the television studios of the Columbus Circle district."[71] Peter Rotundo's specialty "TV packages" were featured prominently on the scenery builder's letterhead in precisely the same year. The proprietors of these businesses could not have picked a worse time to gear their operations to television.

Lured by new facilities and less cantankerous union relations, television producers voted with their feet, moving many of their shows to Los Angeles. By the mid-1960s shows created in the "city of angels" constituted a vast majority of all television programs in the United States. United Scenic

Artists, saddled with more craftspeople than work hours, struggled to maintain the hourly pay secured by the 1948 contract. By 1964 things became worse when New York's television producers indicated that they would no longer pay into USA pension and welfare funds. In response the union went on strike, prompting several New York producers to threaten to "move to California." As the strike dragged on, the producer Herbert Brodkin made good on this threat, taking both *The Defenders* and *The Nurses* to Los Angeles in May 1964. These shows and the jobs associated with them never returned.[72]

At the time of the strike, television producers and union leaders did make good-faith efforts to cooperate, especially through the Joint Council of film and television unions. Union leaders on the council agreed that television labor costs in New York City were unpredictable, and they worked to standardize wages, overtime pay, and weekly hours across several unions. Although they worked to create a labor landscape in New York that resembled Hollywood, space constraints undercut their efforts. It had long been true that New York had comparatively fewer studio spaces available for broadcasting. It was also true by 1964 that Los Angeles had the space and the economic climate to promote the construction of new studios, while New York had neither. The Joint Council publicly acknowledged that "when only one stage is available, time and money are wasted in tearing down and building sets between scenes."[73]

The inefficiencies of New York City's cramped and limited studio spaces proved insurmountable. By the 1970s television shows that filmed in New York had become the exception. Even one of the most beloved New York City shows, Johnny Carson's *Tonight Show*, finally made the move to Burbank in 1972. As Carson explained about Burbank, the "facilities are better . . . studios are better . . . it's all in one building. If we want to do a sketch, all I have to do is call . . . and I've got it tomorrow. The facilities in New York are terrible."[74] At Rockefeller Center in the 1960s, Carson's popular show had employed members of Cameramen's Local 644, Motion Picture Film Editors Local 771, the Script Supervisors union, Make Up and Hairstylists Local 708, Studio Mechanics Local 52, and Motion Picture Machine Operators' Union Local 306.[75] After 1972 neither these skilled experts nor any of Broadway's theater-related craftspeople stood a chance of working on the show if they stayed in New York.

Simultaneously television producers began to bypass Broadway's talent pool when casting performers and musical acts. In the 1950s Broadway's nominees for the Tony Awards and the performers on *Toast of the Town* were generally the same people.[76] In the 1960s, when Ed Sullivan hosted the Beatles and the Doors, television was part of a new age in popular music, which had much less to do with Broadway. Just as television jobs for New York City craftspeople become fewer, so did gigs for New York City performers decline. Broadway "production numbers" continued to appear on television variety shows in the 1960s, but not as often. Even though exciting new programs such as *Saturday Night Live* (1975) kept New York City broadcasting alive in subsequent years, their producers could not hire nearly as many craftspeople as had worked for Ed Sullivan, Sid Caesar, and Milton Berle.

Despite decades of use by alternative media such as television, Broadway's aging infrastructure went from utilized to neglected to downright downtrodden as the century progressed. The performance and construction spaces of the industry, built for commercial theater and then colonized by radio, film, and television, were in bad shape by 1950 and in even worse shape by 1960. As theaters came crashing down to make room for office towers and alternative media failed to employ with any sort of longevity past the year 1960, it was not surprising that the business of those firms still employed on Broadway shrank. More ominously, many of these businesses simply disappeared altogether.

Chapter 4

"Oh, What a Beautiful Mornin'"

Show Construction at Mid-Century

WHILE MANY THEATER-RELATED business proprietors and craftspeople heard the siren song of radio, film, and television production from the 1930s to the 1960s, others stayed the course, supplying and building only for Broadway. As the explosive growth of the 1920s gave way to the inertia of the 1930s and the restricted supplies of the 1940s, the working conditions for these individuals inevitably changed. What is most fascinating about the middle decades of the twentieth century is how seemingly positive developments became Trojan horses of unexpected, injurious consequences. This was especially true of the iconic 1943 show *Oklahoma!*

There was, of course, much to celebrate in the crafting of this show, one of the most famous of its time. The impressive density of the shops and suppliers that built *Oklahoma!* demonstrates how deeply Broadway remained rooted in Times Square in the 1940s and 1950s. Even though the winds of change blew more fiercely each year, detailed analyses of *Oklahoma!*'s craft and construction reveal that most of the industry's stagecraft remained stubbornly fixed in place. Collectively the work of fabric suppliers, costumers, scenery builders, and other theater-related experts during these decades was a clear demonstration that America's theatrical production center was alive and well, still operating efficiently and locally on the same streets it had occupied for decades.

When the show debuted in 1943, however, it stayed open for five years at a time when most shows were lucky to run for one. Originally constructed by shops and suppliers within a ten-block radius of Times Square, this Rodgers and Hammerstein musical took over the St. James Theatre on 44th Street and did not yield the stage until 1948. While it is true that theater-related shops got to build for several railroad touring companies of *Oklahoma!*, all departing from New York City, it is also true that a more traditional four- or six-month run would have meant more new shows over these five years, and therefore more construction work. When *Oklahoma!* set a new precedent for a long-running hit, its producers unwittingly contributed to the larger, overall decline in new shows per year. This iconic show and its national touring companies also contributed, indirectly, to a powerful decentralization trend in show building that propelled shops and work spaces out of their former Times Square locales.

Show Development at Mid-Century

As was true for so many industries, World War II jolted Broadway out of its economic malaise, flooding midtown sidewalks with soldiers on leave and filling theaters with patrons. It took some doing, however, to get raw materials for the theater in the early 1940s, when the United States was saddled with strict rationing. The economy was indeed rebounding, but this would not mean brighter days for Broadway's craftspeople until they could access materials. To get lumber for scenery, industry leaders had to plead their case with the National War Labor Board.

The scene shop proprietor George Vail's urgent letter to this board in 1942 reveals the difficulty such leaders had in convincing others of their economic importance. In the correspondence Vail argued that his shop, while not traditionally industrial, was part of a vital economic sector employing perhaps one hundred thousand people.[1] Sadly, Vail's initial requests for lumber were denied in 1942, and it was not until 1943 and 1944 that Broadway regained some of the vigor of the 1920s. It would certainly not be the last time that governmental leaders failed to see the economic value of Broadway's craftspeople.

As ignored and misunderstood as they may have been, shop crews such as Vail's found a way to muddle through, hammering out components as best they could. When a group of leading craftspeople, including Vail, signed contracts to construct *Oklahoma!*, little did they know how different this show would prove to be. The musical was a seamless amalgamation of song, dance, and drama, with spoken scenes that transitioned smoothly into songs, and songs that advanced the plot. Even the dances, especially the famous dream ballet, did their part to advance the plot. This seamlessness helps explain why the theater historian Mary C. Henderson names *Oklahoma!* as "a theatrical event that changed the course of the American musical" and why Ethan Mordden stated that "the very title of the show has become a summoning term meaning 'the work that changed the form.'"[2]

The artistry of Broadway was constantly in flux, but the fusion achieved in *Oklahoma!* was a major, unprecedented step forward. Previous musicals had pulled songs and playwriting closer together, but none had, in the words of the theater critic Brooks Atkinson, "raised the artistic level of the Broadway musical stage to the point where it had to be taken seriously as literature." Flowering through the collaborations of composer Richard Rodgers, lyricist Oscar Hammerstein II, director Rouben Mamoulien, and choreographer Agnes de Mille, the show was so groundbreaking that it is frequently cited as the birth of the modern musical. After it opened on March 31, 1943, it not only ran for a whopping five years but also spawned a best-selling cast album, three national tours, and a feature film.[3]

On another, more basic level, however, *Oklahoma!* was just another compilation of wood, fabric, skilled labor, and other stage components to be forged in the crucible of Broadway's production center. The skilled workers who transformed these materials into a salable product were members of the same unions that their forebears had belonged to in the 1920s and 1930s, and they rehearsed and crafted in some of the same spaces. In this way *Oklahoma!* was not just the brainchild of Rodgers, Hammerstein, Mamoulien, and de Mille but was also birthed through the elaborate networks of Broadway's interconnected, tightly concentrated industrial district. Analyzing the show along these lines reveals how craftspeople sustained and were sustained by a vital, local, theater-building economy. Without the depth and breadth of Broadway's industrial district, *Oklahoma!* may have been a great idea on paper but never the smash hit that played the St. James Theatre for five years.

Upon inception *Oklahoma!* was little more than a high-risk investment opportunity for a few dozen well-heeled New Yorkers. The show originated when Theresa Helburn of the *Theatre Guild*, one of the industry's most respected production groups, suggested a musicalization of the play *Green Grow the Lilacs* to composer Richard Rodgers. While Rodgers explored a songwriting partnership with lyricist Oscar Hammerstein II in the spring of 1942, Ms. Helburn solicited investments for the fledgling show. The first-time partnership between Rodgers and Hammerstein has become the stuff of theater legend, but without the efforts of Ms. Helburn and the guild, their score may never have made it out of the lounge room of the 44th Street Lamb's Club, where they honed their material at the piano in 1942.[4]

The guild's role during this incubation period was to arrange "backers' auditions." These events were chances for the show's creators, and sometimes trusted singers, to perform new material for potential investors, either in a borrowed living room, a rehearsal studio, or a music room. In the case of Oklahoma!, backers' auditions took place at the Steinway Piano building at 57th Street and 6th Avenue. This location, a personal favorite of Richard Rodgers, made it possible for the music to be played simultaneously on two pianos, for a richer sound. The actors Joan Roberts and Alfred Drake, already tapped to play the romantic leads, sang from the score to potential backers on numerous occasions throughout the summer and fall of 1942. By early 1943 the guild had raised enough of the eighty-thousand-dollar budget to begin rehearsals and component construction.[5]

Each of the eighty-seven shows opening in the 1942–43 season went through a similar process, but it is difficult to know how their capitalizations compared to Oklahoma!'s because producers often held their financial cards close or purposefully dissembled about their finances. As points of comparison, the 1943 musical A Connecticut Yankee cost fifty thousand dollars, Death of a Salesman cost one hundred thousand dollars in 1949, and the play Stalag 17 cost thirty thousand dollars in 1951.[6]

Using these budgets as reference points, it is reasonable to say that the average show of the era cost roughly sixty thousand dollars. If the eighty-seven shows of Oklahoma!'s season had each capitalized sixty thousand, the total theatrical investments for the year would have totaled more than five million dollars. In an age when the contractors, artists, and businesses employed by these investments were overwhelmingly located in a one place, this sum was a major boon to the Times Square economy.

Though the sums invested in new Broadway shows had tremendous economic value and would even count by this author's measure as research and development funds, Broadway's chroniclers rarely describe them this way. Instead they emphasize how Broadway's funds came from "angels." The angel character was ever present in 1940s theater journalism, appearing in circulars such as Playbill, the New York Times, and the New York Post. Journalists portrayed Broadway investors as either high-stakes gamblers or

Figure 12. Cover image of Leo Shull's mimeographed publication *Angels: The People Who Finance the Broadway Theatre.* Photo by the author, 2009.

generous philanthropists, who usually lived in New York City's best neighborhoods and suburbs. In caricatures, such as those of Al Hirschfeld, angels wore expensive suits or furs and brandished cigars. In print characterizations, journalists emphasized the risk that these investors took, and they often suggested that angels knew little about the theater.[7]

There is some truth to the angel stereotype. Many investors did do nothing more than write checks, and many lost great sums of money. Meyer S. Davis, for example, invested in four 1943 shows, two of which were flops while the others turned only modest profits. Undeterred, Davis and his wife continued to invest throughout the 1940s and 1950s, so often that they were featured as angels by the *New York Post* in 1958. In a society column focused on the Davises and their investments, the *Post* made it clear that while they were avid theatergoers, neither had industry experience.[8] Not all investors, however, were quite so removed.

Rodgers and Hammerstein, for example, began to invest in their shows after *Oklahoma!*'s shocking success. Other industry investors are less well known. No theater historian has chronicled how in the 1950s the composer Jule Styne, the actress Mary Martin, and the actress Rosalind Russell invested many thousands of dollars in their own shows and those of their colleagues. Even Fanny Brice, a star of vaudeville and the *Ziegfeld Follies*, became an investor in the 1960s.[9]

Why do the personal investments of famous theater artists matter? The answer is that they were part of a crucial feedback loop, through which industry profits were used for the development of new shows. Such reinvestment in new product development is taken for granted in industries such as automobile manufacturing but has received short shrift on Broadway, where those writing about investments have focused on famously fickle, silk-stocking angels. The truth of the matter is that there were plenty of well-informed, well-connected insiders writing checks as well. Even some of the most successful theater-related businesses, such as Brooks Costume and Imperial Scenic, became angels by the 1950s, usually for shows they were also contracted to build.[10]

Other major players in the Broadway investment game at mid-century were film and recording studios such as Loew's Incorporated and Capitol Records. Loew's put up significant funds for a 1954 musical called *The Boyfriend*, while Capitol fronted $220,000 for a 1960 musical, *The Unsinkable Molly Brown*. With the hope of generating profitable film adaptations or cast recordings, these media corporations began investing on Broadway long before the 1970s, when they are best known for doing so.

From Mary Martin to *Molly Brown*, there would be little public record of these insider investments without a fascinating mid-century publication, *Angels: The People Who Finance the Broadway Theatre*. It was published by a controversial Times Square habitué, Leo Shull, described in his *Variety*

obituary as a "red-faced, bottomlessly angry but often funny man." A theater enthusiast and native New Yorker, Shull began publishing mimeo-
graphs with news of the stage from the basement of the 44th Street
Walgreens in 1941, reportedly hiring the aspiring actors Lauren Bacall and
Kirk Douglas to hawk his printouts in Times Square. Although he had
many publications, his most singular achievement was *Angels*. This mimeographed circular, published every few years, listed all the names, addresses,
and investments of recent Broadway angels that Shull could get his hands
on. With each new edition, Shull would send teams of out-of-work actors
onto local sidewalks and into Sardi's restaurant to sell *Angels* to aspiring
producers. The oldest surviving edition dates back to 1946, with subsequent
editions available from 1955, 1958, 1963, 1979, and 1982.[11]

Shull's strategy was as ruthless as it was simple. He did nothing more
than compile publicly available information on investors who had used the
vehicle of a limited partnership in New York State. This was a means of
organizing investors that grew popular in Broadway in the early twentieth
century, as the industry modernized and costs escalated.[12] The limited partnership's popularity stemmed from boundaries of profit and liability. Lead
producers were general partner(s), with more liability and more profit,
while smaller investors were limited partners, with almost no liability and
a smaller share of the profits. Investors were required to file with the state,
which made their payments and home addresses matters of public record
in the years that Shull was publishing. He could therefore dig up this information and publish it without breaking any laws. Mid-century producers
did occasionally publish their own investors' names as a way of saying
thank you, but they did so without listing dollar amounts, in what appears
tantamount to a gentlemen's agreement.

Shull's *Angels* therefore angered many, as revealed in the condemnations
he received in the *New York Times* and *Variety*, but he was careful not to
violate the law. When a production was organized without a limited partnership, Shull had no legal access to investment data and did not seem to pursue
it. The Theatre Guild, for example, did not need limited-partnership investors
because if its national subscribers, and *Oklahoma!* is notably missing from
Shull's first edition. Other productions had their own reasons for not forming
limited partnerships or for not filing with the state. Of the eighty-seven shows
in the 1942–43 season, Shull scored financial data for only twenty.[13]

Even though these twenty shows were just a quarter of the whole season,
they still reveal telltale patterns of capitalization. First and foremost, most

of the investors lived in Manhattan. Although some hailed from places as far-flung as Beverly Hills and Ohio, a full 70 percent resided in New York's smallest borough. Another 15 percent had addresses in Westchester County, other New York counties, or unlisted locations, while the final 15 percent lived in other states. The preponderance of Manhattanites is not surprising, but the out-of-state checks do present an interesting contrast to the fund-raising environment created by the regional theater movement a decade later. While regional theaters and performing arts centers may have intercepted funds such as these by the 1950s and 1960s, evidence from the 1940s suggests that it was entirely possible to collect investments from Californians, Texans, and many others.

As the investors for *Oklahoma!* and other 1940s shows mailed their checks to producers, they were key players in Broadway's "development work." Jane Jacobs wrote passionately about this type of work and its importance to cities in *The Economy of Cities*, a follow-up to her famous book, *The Death and Life of Great American Cities*. Suggesting that dynamic city economies made possible the development of new ideas and products, Jacobs explained that "development work is a messy, time- and energy-consuming business of trial, error and failure . . . but the exorbitant amounts of energy and time and the high rates of failure . . . do not mean the development work is being done ineptly. The inefficiency is built into the aim itself; it is inescapable." She went on to compare city economies to research laboratories. If a lab were to fund four scientists, she reasoned, and have only one research breakthrough, no one would question the money spent on the other three. It would be understood as the cost of research, and one in four would be recognized as a high rate of success.[14]

Despite the striking relevance of Jacobs's theories to Broadway's angels and its hits and flops, no one, not even Jacobs, has framed commercial theater along these lines. When investments are carefully considered, commercial theater at mid-century sharpens into view as a theatrical laboratory, writ large upon the industrial district. Yet those who have written about Broadway's finances in the past, be they critic, journalist, economist, or historian, have dismissed theatrical investments as a form of frivolous entertainment for the wealthy. Studies of Broadway's finances, such as Thomas Gale Moore's 1968 book, have focused overwhelmingly on theatrical consumption, as measured through ticket sales, prices, and Times Square tourism. Moore wrote convincingly of the benefits of Broadway tourism, publishing data on theatergoer spending. His data suggested an

average of seventy cents spent on midtown dinners for every dollar spent
on tickets. Similar studies in 1975 and 1993 struck the same note, emphasizing tickets and tourism and imploring city leaders to help promote existing shows. Nowhere in these discussions did development work take center
stage.[15]

Newspaper coverage of the commercial stage was equally devoid of this
analysis. When productions "hit" as *Oklahoma!* did, generating 2,000 percent returns[16] and promoting visits to Times Square for years on end, the
theater press was quick to laud the Great White Way as an engine of city
tourism. When shows flopped, however, returning no profit and closing
after just a few performances, they were lambasted and even ridiculed as a
disastrous waste. The myopic focus of scholars and journalists alike on
consumption stems from the inherent difficulty of seeing value in Broadway's flop shows.

For those who write about the stage, few things are as enticing as the
big-budget Broadway flop. Failed shows have elicited so much morbid fas-
cination that there is an entire book on the subject.[17] More public and more
spectacular than just about anything possible in a laboratory, flop shows
inspire discussions of what went wrong, rather than the educational utility
of failed experiments. In most discussions of flop shows, it is assumed that
the funds raised for the show have, in essence, disappeared overnight.

But what of the sums paid to contractors, especially those secured prior
to a show's trial by fire on opening night? By the 1910s United Scenic
Artists had negotiated a tripartite fee schedule with Broadway producers.
The first third of a designer's or scene shop's fees was paid up front, when
contracts were signed. The second third was due upon delivery of scenery,
backdrops, surreys, or baskets. These first two payments enabled shop owners to pay the weekly wages of their rank-and-file employees. The third,
sometimes elusive payment was due after opening night. Knowing that the
third installment depended on the show's success, savvy shop owners
endeavored to have the first two pay for raw materials and wages. When
shows flopped, this usually meant that a shop proprietor had lost an opportunity to profit, not that USA's designers, painters, and journeymen went
unpaid. For smaller suppliers, such as those working with ribbons, shoes,
or wigs, it was common to be paid in full prior to opening night.[18]

Measured in wages or components produced, a flop and a hit generated
roughly the same amount of craft and construction work. It was only the
elusive third payment, often constituting the shop proprietor's profits, that

was put at risk by a failed show. If the dire predictions about *Oklahoma!* had come true and the musical with "no gags, no gals, no chance"[19] had floundered, contractors such as Capezio, LaRay Boot Shop, and I. Weiss & Sons would have already been paid, and the designers and major suppliers would have had at least two-thirds of what was expected. Before the reviews hit, much of the show's eighty thousand dollars had already been spent on wages and tangible products.

There were exceptions to these rules, of course. When Charles Geoly, proprietor of Eaves Costume, decided to rent costumes to a new and untested producer, Phil Baker, for the 1941 musical *All in Fun*, little did he know that Baker's experience would prove to be anything but fun. The show teetered on the brink of insolvency during its Boston tryout, and Baker never paid Geoly for twenty-three thousand dollars' worth of costumes. Despite sending his son Andrew up to Boston to raise a ruckus at the stage door with a sheriff and an attorney in tow, Geoly was never able to collect on this unpaid costume bill.[20]

These interruptions in the normal business cycles of Broadway have always made headlines, but evidence suggests that it was far more common for these bills to be paid than unpaid, especially as the chaos of the early Depression subsided. Given how many of these bills and wages were fully paid, those investing in Broadway during the 1940s, 1950s, and beyond were therefore doing development work, whether they knew it or not. At an estimated ratio of one hit to three flops per year, angels, theater artists, and business investors wrote the checks that put blue-collar Broadway to work.[21]

Once a show had its budget intact, the next important developmental step, for both *Oklahoma!* and the larger industry, was to hire a creative team and a cast. Even as dozens of craftspeople, skilled laborers, and designers started work in January 1943, the only newsworthy aspect of *Oklahoma!* was the hiring of Rouben Mamoulien to direct, Agnes de Mille to choreograph, and Betty Garde and Celeste Holm as leading actresses. The comings and goings of creative leads and actors had long captured the public imagination more than the hammering or sewing of craftspeople, and the *Times* could hardly expect to sell newspapers with headlines such as "Painters Paint Backdrop" in its "News of the Stage" segment.[22]

Next, the Theatre Guild then had to flesh out a chorus of singers and an entirely separate chorus of dancers through auditions. In the last two weeks of January, de Mille held dance auditions at the Guild Theatre, conveniently owned by the producers and vacant, while the rest of the team auditioned singer-actors at the St. James Theatre. Both sets of auditions were scheduled for weekday afternoons, just a short walk from the transportation hub of Times Square.[23]

Oklahoma!'s auditions, held with little advance notice, suggest a mid-century industry replete with local talent. Although performers moved in and out of the theater district as they pleased and there was no fixed roster of actors as in stock or repertory, the 1943 district was home to a deep talent pool. Residence hotels and apartment houses, some catering to performers, helped to make this possible, as did a network of part-time jobs for thespians. The overall impact of performers living, working, and socializing in and around Times Square was to create a wonderful efficiency in casting. Some performers were so close to auditions that they could simply walk down the block. Such was the experience of Celeste Holm, *Oklahoma!*'s original Ado Annie. She walked to her audition from a job waiting tables at the Stagedoor Canteen on West 44th Street, just a few hundred feet from the St. James.[24] Even though Ms. Holm's experience was unusual, it is safe to say that those casting *Oklahoma!* had at their disposal a highly accessible, talented pool of performers.

By February 1, 1943, as carpenters, designers, and painters worked toward a synthesis in scenic design and as more than a dozen full-time employees at Brooks sewed costumes,[25] *Oklahoma!*'s cast could begin rehearsals at the unoccupied Guild Theatre, where de Mille had auditioned her dancers. The fact that *Oklahoma!* could have both auditions *and* rehearsals within a Broadway house is notable. This was a crucial advantage of producing on Broadway at mid-century. More often than not, the houses of the 1940s and 1950s had theater-related tenants both day and night. When the *Oklahoma!* creative team started auditions at the St. James, the comedy *Without Love* was also playing there, eight times a week. The *Oklahoma!* crew simply wrapped up their sessions in time for the star Katharine Hepburn to tread the boards in the evenings. During the rehearsal process, when *Oklahoma!*'s performers needed more space than was available amid the *Without Love* scenery, they practiced songs, lyrics, and scenes in basement-level rooms. In March, Hepburn's comedy closed, and the farmers, cowmen, and other characters of the musical claimed the main stage for technical and dress rehearsals. The cozy arrangement between the productions was fairly common, but in this case it was particularly easy because the Theatre Guild produced both shows.[26]

The double booking of one production in performance and another in development was an unsung, highly productive practice for many a playhouse owner in the mid-twentieth century. They either collected fees for a daytime rental or offered the space in the hope of securing a profitable main-stage tenant. In the case of *Oklahoma!*, the early commitment made by the St. James's owners to the burgeoning musical paid off in spades.

For producers who could not secure a double-booked theater, there were plenty of affordable studios able to handle rehearsals in this era, even for dance-heavy shows requiring more space. The 1940 Manhattan *Yellow Pages* list roughly ten midtown spaces that would have worked for dance, acting, or music rehearsals, including the Jane Gray, Haven Rehearsal, Kyser Kay, Midtown Music, Nola, and Dave Ringle studios. In 1950 there were fourteen spaces listed between 39th and 57th Streets near Times Square and Broadway's suppliers. Open for business in the day and often into the early evening, these spaces had a daytime function that complemented and supported the district's evening economy. Just about the time when rehearsal studios were locking up for the night, a different wave of performers and theatergoers headed into the theater district for shows that were already up and running.

Scenery and Lighting

No matter how well Joan Roberts, Alfred Drake, and the rest of the cast honed their performances at the St. James, they had no show unless the guild succeeded in acquiring the right sets, costumes, shoes, wigs, properties, lights, draperies, and other specialty components. From the most mundane boot to the famous "surrey with the fringe on top," all needed professional construction with the right balance of style and durability, and to be ready in time for the first out-of-town "tryout" performance.[27]

Even though *Oklahoma!*'s set pieces and backdrops were relatively straightforward,[28] the guild still needed two contractors for the work. In early 1943 the scenic designer Lemuel Ayers solicited bids from various shops, settling on Vail Construction for scenery and the Robert Bergman studio for painting. In a proverbial chicken-and-egg relationship, the contractors absolutely had to work together. Some of Vail's lumber and plywood pieces were to be covered by Bergman's stretched, painted canvases, while others had to stand, harmoniously, in front of painted backdrops.

Over a period of four to five weeks, Vail did work on West 47th Street near 10th Avenue, while Bergman's painters worked a short walk away, on 39th Street near Broadway. For meetings to coordinate their work, Bergman also had an office on West 42nd Street.

Also during this crucial stagecraft process, producers had the chance to weigh in. Guild leader Lawrence Langner had a look in mind for the scenery, and to this end he asked designer Ayers to refer to a particular style of rustic painting. Throughout the first few months of 1943, this type of collaboration unfolded at the St. James Theatre, at the Theatre Guild's office on West 53rd Street, and over the phone. The entire creative team shared sketches, works in progress, and conversations to ensure that the show's components would coalesce properly.[29]

It is difficult to know exactly how many carpenters and painters worked under Langner's and Ayers's guidance, but standard United Scenic Artists contracts of the era suggest a team of three to four scenic construction workers working for roughly four weeks and about three painters working for roughly two weeks. Although this was hardly competitive with the payroll of a contemporary Times Square powerhouse such as Paramount Pictures, it is important to note that when construction for *Oklahoma!* began, an entire array of local raw materials suppliers for canvas and lumber, strung-up lights, hung baskets, and the famous "surrey with the fringe on top" were also put to work.[30]

In terms of the design style, much of *Oklahoma!*'s scenery was a purposeful throwback to a simpler time and place, but one particular aspect stood out as a reflection of contemporary design trends. It was the dwelling for the character of Jud, designed by Ayers as a dark, claustrophobic, "expressionist den of iniquity." This was not done to achieve some sort of Belasco-style realism, nor did it have any of the elements of spectacle. It reflected the style that had come to dominate on Broadway by 1943, known as "New American Stagecraft." Theater artists working in this style related their designs to theatrical plots, but with a layer of abstraction. With origins in 1915 and several decades of development, the style had definitely gone mainstream by the 1940s.[31]

The innovators of the New American Stagecraft, especially Robert Edmund Jones in the 1910s, Norman Bel Geddes and Lee Simonson in the 1930s, and the decorated Jo Mielziner, who worked extensively from the 1930s to the 1970s, had little interest in designs that were entirely realistic or entirely fantastical. Mielziner's design for *Death of a Salesman* in 1949, for example, had realistic shapes that would be legible to audiences but also alterations to these shapes that were loaded with meaning. For the home of Willy Loman and his family, Mielziner designed a loosely interpreted A-frame house informed by the themes and tone of the play. The Loman home was cramped but tidy, and the room of sons Biff and Happy were purposefully designed in close, claustrophobic proximity to the rest of the house. Mielziner's design was certainly aesthetically appealing, but it had nothing of the spectacle or opulence that had defined an earlier generation of designers. His scenery related to what the play was *about*, and therefore transcended the simple question of where the play was *set*. Mielziner's "clever set," which provided several playing spaces within one piece of scenery, also cut costs for the producer Kermit Bloomgarten, who was saved the expense of several distinct, freestanding playing spaces.[32]

Neither literally realistic nor extravagantly spectacular, most scenic designs at mid-century occupied an artistic space that lay somewhere in between. Another excellent example is Mielziner's design for the 1950 musical *Guys and Dolls*, which had playful, gritty, and slightly cartoonish scenery to match Frank Loessor's score and the broadly drawn characters of the libretto. When designers such as Mielziner did their jobs well, they supported and even enhanced the artistic statements of a show's creators.

Given the subtleties of these mid-century designs, it is not surprising that designers and USA scene shops worked intimately. Design sketches alone were insufficient for proper construction. To build *Salesman*, the scene shop Nolan Bros. could not simply generate any old A-frame house containing rooms for dramatic scenes. They had to work extensively with Mielziner in late 1948, first from his sketches and then in person, as he, the playwright Arthur Miller, and the director Elia Kazan all spent considerable time at the Nolan shop at 533 West 24th Street. The producer Kermit Bloomgarten had devoted a quarter of the play's budget to scenic design and construction, so it makes sense that he and the rest of the production's leaders would work overtime to ensure that what was built satisfied both playwright and designer.[33]

As abstract design elements such as Jud's living quarters in *Oklahoma!* and the Loman home became standard on Broadway, questions of stage lighting became more important than ever. For the spectacle shows of earlier decades, lighting was relatively imprecise. Scenery could and did fade into the background, especially if too much brightness would reveal its flaws. Realist shows such as those of David Belasco had been up to the glare of bright lights, but turn-of-the-century technology was limited. By the 1940s stage lighting had blossomed significantly, in terms both artistic and technological.

In the age of *Oklahoma!*, stage lighting had grown to include everything from follow spots and footlights to color palettes that set the tone for a scene. Artistry and technology advanced in tandem, leading the Broadway industry to a complicated place. It was becoming difficult for one designer to handle all of the lighting, scenery, and costumes in a show. It had not always been thus. In 1924 Robert Edmund Jones had designed all of the lighting, scenery, and costumes for a production of *Hedda Gabler* on Broadway. By 1948 a production of the same play at the Cort Theater had two designers, one for scenery and one for costumes. *Death of a Salesman* in 1949 had Mielziner credited as both scenic and lighting designer, with Julia Sze credited for costumes. With each passing year, lighting technology became even more advanced and complicated, prompting a proliferation of designers credited for lighting. Although *Oklahoma!* had no separately credited lighting designer, many late 1940s shows did. Such a design credit was positively de rigueur by the 1950s.[34]

These changes involved far more than just an increase in the amount of work. What the new lighting designers did was qualitatively different from what their forebears had done. They no longer labored primarily to make scenery and actors visible. Much like their colleagues in scenic design, they began to contribute to the milieu of the pieces they were lighting. This was yet another step toward specialization in the larger industry.[35]

As options for lighting a scene proliferated, mid-century designers such as Peggy Clark had to manage a mind-boggling array of concerns with each lighting and equipment choice. Consider, for example, the tasks put before Clark in a 1951 memo from the production supervisor regarding the lighting for Harold Lang, the lead actor in the musical *Pal Joey*: "Peggy—this memo is to give you further ideas on what Bob wants in lighting—so you can plan on your equipment. . . . If the angle from the booth makes it impossible to spot Harold when he is on the trampoline and pedestal in *Chez Joey*, it will be necessary to have two spots, one on stage left and one on stage right in different colors to hit him . . . not from above but from head height." Clark was being asked to light a moving target twice, at particular angles and from particular places in the house. It is no wonder that the lighting plots and design maps of where lights would hang within theaters were massively oversized and many pages long.[36]

Table 1. Contractors Credited for *Oklahoma!* in *Playbill*

Contractor	Components Supplied	Location
Vail Construction	Scenery construction	530 W. 47th St. (at 10th Ave.)
Robert Bergman Studios	Painting	229 W. 42nd St. (office) (shop at 39th and Broadway)
Dazian's	Draperies and fabrics	142 W. 44th St.
I. Weiss	Draperies	445 W. 45th St.
Brooks Costume	Costumes	1150 6th Ave.
LaRay Boot Shop	Dance shoes	W. 46th St.
Robert Lerch Wigs	Wigs	67 W. 46th St.
Capezio	Ballet shoes	Several stores in Times Square
Jessie Zimmer	Stockings	Unknown
Lamb's Club	"Show conceived"	132 W. 44th St.

Sources: Contractor and component information is from *Oklahoma! Playbill*, NYPL-BR; location information is from Manhattan *Business Listings*, 1943, NYPL-MRR.

Costumes and Draperies

Like scenery and lighting, costumes in the age of *Oklahoma!* were beginning a profound metamorphosis. To serve the naturalist plays of Arthur Miller, Tennessee Williams, and others, costume designers were moving toward threadbare, tattered, or otherwise lived-in garments. The costumes of *Oklahoma!*, however, did nothing to fan these winds of change, because they were historic or "period" in nature. To produce them, Langner steered the designer Miles White to historic clothing catalogs "for ideas"[37] and then hired Brooks Costume, with a large facility on 6th Avenue and 45th Street, for execution. Joining Brooks as suppliers of specialty components were the LaRay Boot Shop, Lerch wigs, and Capezio, a prominent supplier of ballet shoes. The full list of businesses credited for *Oklahoma!* in *Playbill* is shown in Table 1.

The proximity of these businesses to the St. James and to each other was crucial for the creation of components with a unified appearance. The playhouse was the site where dress and technical rehearsals took place, when the entire array of components, from ribbons to backdrops to leading ladies, was combined into a salable product. When Brooks had completed the costumes, designer Miles White could see them on actors with the wigs and under the lights at dress rehearsals, all within hours of completion. If Robert Lerch wanted to better match his wigs to White's costumes or to actors' skin tones, he needed to travel only two blocks, to his stock of hair and wigs on 46th Street. Even after the show had shipped off for an out-of-town tryout, the creative team could take small components with them as they traveled back and forth by rail to New Haven. When leading lady Joan Roberts's wig was deemed insufficiently "girlish" during the New Haven tryout period, an easily accessed, specialty ribbon from Brooks Costume solved the problem.[38] Small changes such as these were easy in an age when vendors were close to the theater district and to both of Manhattan's major train stations.

By being so well situated in midtown, contractors were also poised to make repairs or supply replacements. The contributions of Capezio and LaRay Boot Shop, for example, were put to the test by Agnes de Mille's grueling dance rehearsals. Should the heel of a woman's character shoe or a male's boot snap, the unlucky performer or an assistant to the production team would need to walk only a block or two to get it fixed or replaced. Wigs did not break per se, but they certainly could be damaged or lost in the chaos of dress rehearsals. Even costumes, usually repaired with ease during rehearsals by in-house IATSE wardrobe mistresses, could be rushed over to Brooks for major surgery as needed.

For *Oklahoma!*'s period costumes, the Brooks shop was ideal because it worked with both custom orders and a stock of rentals. James E. Stroock's firm was at the top of its game in the 1940s but certainly not the only game in town. Its top competitor was Eaves, a full-service costumer occupying seven floors at 151 West 46th Street. Advertising its rental collection as "the largest stock on hand in the East," Eaves was clearly a major midtown operation. The shop had a "research department" and claimed "50,000 costumes in stock," "wigs to rent and made to order," and "arms and armor," while also offering "designs and sketches . . . made by Eaves artists." Not to be outdone, rival house Brooks claimed in its own advertisements "the largest collection of the world's finest costumes. . . . the kind Broadway stars wear."[39]

Ultimately whether one collection was finer or larger was immaterial. What mattered for *Oklahoma!* and for all other shows at mid-century was that there were fifty-two costume shops or individual contractors available for hire in New York City, and a full thirty-six of them, as listed in the Manhattan telephone directory, were squarely within the theater district.

They ranged from about fifteen fully unionized shops[40] to a mix of small costume stores and one-person specialists. More affordable, individual costumers were ideal for producers who needed maximum flexibility, while costumers offering only rentals also served an important purpose. They provided producers with an eminently practical option for simple costumes, especially of a popular period. Through the browsing, renting, cleaning, delivery, and return of hundreds of costumes every month, these rental firms anchored their locations with a healthy dose of reputable, daytime business activity.

One such firm was Charles Chrisdie Costumes, founded down on the Bowery by Charles Sr. back in 1873. In 1940 the Chrisdie company moved its stately array of period costumes up to 41 West 47th Street, occupying all five floors of a walk-up building. Although the shop quickly relocated to 148–50 West 52nd Street, its 1942 relocation was not for a lack of business. The two floors that Chrisdie secured on 52nd Street were twice as wide, suggesting a successful if not growing firm. Offering convenient browsing among the "thousands" of period pieces at a site close to most mid-century rehearsals, Chrisdie was also staffed to alter the garments that the company had already rented out. When the widow of Charles Jr., Mrs. Alice Evans Chrisdie, retired in the early 1960s, she sold off the rental collection to various buyers, and the firm ceased to exist.[41]

For those producers who needed one-of-a-kind garments, stemming from inventive sketches, Chrisdie's rentals were not enough. Such costumes needed to be made from scratch, at a greater cost but with greater specificity. Made-to-order costumes were far more labor-intensive, even generating work for temporary hires at a major shop such as Brooks or Eaves. At the Brooks shop, there was enough work at mid-century to employ fifteen to twenty full-time seamstresses, cutters, beaders, and other employees.[42] The other shops engaged in made-to-order costuming, including those of Helene Pons, Veronica Blythe, and Barbara Karinska, were smaller but still large enough to work on Broadway. Although the number and size of these shops in the 1940s and 1950s suggest a vigorous trade, there was also a major development in the artistry of Broadway that threatened their bottom line. Named by contemporary critics as "naturalism," this trend in playwriting and design had the potential to undercut the livelihoods of dozens of made-to-order specialists.

The key to naturalism's impact on Broadway was the ready-made clothing store, a rarity at the turn of the century that had become all but ubiquitous by the 1940s. When playwrights such as Clifford Odets, William Inge,

Arthur Miller, Eugene O'Neill, and Tennessee Williams began to push the boundaries of Broadway with their naturalist writing, they created characters of the recent past or the present day. Nearly every character to appear onstage was meant to do so wearing unremarkable, contemporary clothing, the kind found at ready-made or secondhand stores. In the stage directions for *The Glass Menagerie* in 1945, for example, Tennessee Williams stated that Amanda Wingfield should wear "one of those cheap or imitation velvety-looking cloth coats with imitation fur collar."[43] This was hardly the kind of custom-made gown that would get the sewing machines of Brooks or Eaves humming. Savvy producers of these new shows quickly realized how easily they could meet their costuming needs through other means.

In this production environment, made-to-order costume shops had to fight to stay relevant. Costume designers and craftspeople had quickly recognized that plays or musicals calling for everyday clothing would be a threat to their livelihoods. In 1941 more than three hundred designers in United Scenic Artists voted to pass the following: "resolved that . . . A Contract for all costume designs or finding of costumes for period or modern plays . . . must be registered in the office of the local union for every production."[44] In other words, while made-to-order craftspeople could never stop producers from renting or buying costumes, the union could at least require that all Broadway shows hire designers.

Despite their efforts, members of USA continued to find themselves at loggerheads with Broadway producers over ready-made clothing. In August 1950 a *New York Times* headline read "Costumers Local Threatens Stage," because USA had threatened to strike if producers continued to circumvent their jurisdiction. Producers had been displaying everything from Brooks Brothers suits to thrift-store garments on Broadway without hiring either the costume workers of the International Ladies' Garment Workers' Union or the designers of USA. Union representatives explained to the *Times* that "their livelihood depends exclusively upon this work." The producer Mike Todd offered a counterpoint, highlighting "the impracticability of ordering a 'custom-made worn-out suit.'" The producer John Golden chimed in as well, saying, "[I]t's all right with me, if they can make them (the garments) cheaper than anyone else." Todd, one of the most vociferous producers during the controversy, went so far as to say that United Scenic Artists demands violated the Taft-Hartley Act.[45]

Producers and costume workers had a long history of feuding, but this mid-century flare-up was especially rancorous because spectacle shows, reliant on eye-popping, made-to-order costumes, had lost so much ground on Broadway since the 1930s. David Belasco had offered "photographic realism" several decades earlier, but most of his contemporaries had opted for the shiny fabrics of spectacle shows. Even through the lean years of the Great Depression, made-to-order shops were busy because of the appeal of escapist shows. By the 1940s, however, a dominant new mode of realistic expression on Broadway had rendered costume craftspeople less essential. In Eugene O'Neill's 1946 classic, *The Iceman Cometh*, the denizens of a dive bar wallow in self-doubt and tattered clothing. In *Death of a Salesman*, Arthur Miller specifically called for the mother character to have runs and holes in her stockings. Most of Tennessee Williams's plays called for clothing that was simple, realistic, or even drab. Even on the musical stage, the costumes for shows such as *Porgy and Bess, On the Town,* and *Carousel* were relatively realistic and understated. They were certainly a far cry from the glittering garments of an escapist comedy such as *Anything Goes.*

As these artistic changes grew entrenched on Broadway, the ease with which producers could meet costuming needs at thrift stores, department stores, or even their own closets had precipitated a major confrontation. In the heated public debates of August 1950, United Scenic Artists came down hard on what its members perceived as scofflaw producers, resolving that "all garments to be used on the stage" must be "manufactured by members of our union" and that "no buying of any ready-made garments will be allowed."[46] While the USA's hard line did rein in the use of ready-made garments in the short term, they were not eliminated altogether.

Despite the occasional tussle between unions and producers, most of the costuming work at mid-century went smoothly. This was especially true because the city of New York and its hinterlands were rich with garment-making talent and because Times Square remained a safe destination for daytime workers of all stripes. The story of Emma Z. Swan, a Brooks costume seamstress in the 1940s, 1950s, and 1960s, is an excellent case in point. According to a tribute letter from a friend, sent to the Museum of the City of New York in 2001 to honor Swan's work, she was a "tall," "elegant," skilled, and high-ranking Brooks employee who commanded a team of seamstresses five days a week, after commuting via train and ferry from Roselle, New Jersey. Although the letter does not detail Emma's path from the West 39th Street ferry terminal to Brooks Costume, this was a common commute through a district not yet known for crime problems. The author of the letter even mentions that Swan "often returned late at night when a production got close to opening night," additional evidence that Times Square was reasonably safe for Broadway craft workers day and night.⁴⁷

The conditions on the blocks surrounding Brooks mattered far more than commutes. Over the course of a costuming workday, it was common for trusted employees to walk to nearby shops in search of fabric. In the case of Emma Swan, the tribute letter states that she worked with designers to help "them choose what fabrics . . . would look great and move well on stage." Everyone at a costume shop knew full well that garments had to look right under the lights while also being suited for choreography. To fill this tall order, seamstresses and costume workers such as Swan often shopped at specialized fabric stores such as Gladstone's, Maharam, and Dazian's.

Specialty fabrics were crucial for a smooth show-building process. The costuming issues of the 1957 musical *West Side Story* are an excellent case in point. The designer Irene Sharaff had crafted "blue jeans" using "a special fabric . . . dipped and dyed and beaten," because actual blue jeans would have both constricted the dancers and killed the look. Sharaff made her decisions in consultation with Brooks Costume and the choreographers Jerome Robbins and Peter Gennaro, who were running dance rehearsals close by at Chester Hale Studios on West 56th. Without this collaboration Brooks ran the risk of supplying garments incompatible with the show's aggressively balletic choreography. The producer Harold Prince learned this the hard way when he proposed cutting costs with regular Levi's and was met with quick opposition from his entire production team. Had a costume order of Levi's or a similarly incompatible fabric moved ahead without close, in-person consultation with choreographers, this may have cost thousands of unnecessary dollars.⁴⁸

In the age of *Oklahoma!* and *West Side Story*, general fabric suppliers were a dime a dozen in midtown, poised to supply beautiful, flowing fabrics that would dance and sing in the light. Only Gladstone's, Maharam, and Dazian's, however, specialized in fabrics enabling performers to literally dance and sing under hot lights eight times a week. Located between 6th and 7th Avenues in the West 40s, these shops were within walking distance of each other, overlapping in their supply and therefore serving as a collective resource for made-to-order costumers. They were extremely close to the costume houses that needed help, in one case on the same block. Of the three, Dazian's was the oldest, dating back to 1842, while Louis Maharam and Louis Gladstone had opened their shops more recently, in the 1930s.⁴⁹

In the spring of 1943 costume designer Miles White and Brooks owner James Stroock, tasked with finishing *Oklahoma!*'s costumes, had every reason to darken the doors of all three specialty shops in search of the perfect fabrics. In the case of Dazian's, this great-grandfather of the stage fabrics business was also the contractor for *Oklahoma!*'s draperies. Also known as soft goods, these large, hanging panels of fabric were a crucial part of show construction at mid-century. After scenery was built, backdrops were painted, lights were hung, and costumes were sewn, all of these components had to be framed so that the audience would see only what was intended. Given that the built-in curtains of Broadway houses were rarely up to this challenge, firms such as Dazian's regularly supplied draperies.

For each new show, shops such as Dazian's had to measure, design, and cut draperies. Even if an existing show simply moved to another theater, new draperies were almost always needed since stage and proscenium sizes varied widely. In the case of *Oklahoma!*, Helburn and Langner had hired both Dazian's and another leader of the trade, I. Weiss & Sons. From their shop on West 45th Street near 11th Avenue, the proprietors of I. Weiss joined Dazian's in the work of framing the entrances and exits of the actors, the appearance of the scenery, and the sight lines of the audience. Both companies had many Broadway credits to their names by 1943, and their skilled workers knew how to hang just the right fabric panels in the wings and from the proscenium of the St. James Theatre.

In addition to scenery, lights, costumes, and draperies, most mid-century shows needed at least a few wigs, and many required specialty dance shoes. To meet these needs, Langner and Helburn called on the talents of Robert Lerch for wigs, the LaRay shop and Capezio for shoes, and a fellow named Jessie Zimmer for stockings. Even these small-time suppliers had to be proximate to rehearsals in order to do their work properly. Even something as small as a wig could be controversial, especially if an actor found it cumbersome or unappealing. Such was the case at the opening of a play in 1942, when the *New York Times* reported that producers replaced the "ostentatious replica" worn by actor Guy Sorel with one "more becoming" after much complaining. Fellow actor Russell Collins, presumably the scene partner of Sorel, commented that he was "happier without the encumbrance."[50] These small, amusing incidents demonstrate that even wig makers needed to be ready to replace or adjust components, for reasons as varied as damage, vanity, theft, or even absent-mindedness.

There were no such wig controversies the following year when *Oklahoma!* opened on March 31, 1943. At the eleventh hour, the production team had needed to pay scenic designer Lemuel Ayers for one additional painted drop, but other than that the components had congealed well during out-of-town tryouts in New Haven and Boston. As the show's creators and performers prepared for their opening night party at Sardi's restaurant, the work of contractors and union craftspeople was already finished. Most would have been working on other projects. During *Oklahoma!*'s long run, these shops may have picked up small bits of replacement or repair work, but their days as the show's incubators had passed. As a story of theater assembled within the industrial district of midtown, that of *Oklahoma!* does not begin but rather ends on opening night, March 31, 1943.[51]

Of all the contractors who worked on this historic musical, two in particular would have taken special notice of the show's unprecedented long run. These were the drapery suppliers, employees of I. Weiss & Sons and Dazian's. Unlike costumers or scenery builders, these specialists and their colleagues in the trade at Lee Lash Studios, Charles Kenney, Universal Scenic & Drapery, and J. C. Hansen had few other options. They had built their businesses in an age when shows turned over rapidly. For a draperies shop, a show's "closing notice," dreaded by performers and musicians, must have been welcome news. It indicated that more work was soon to come. When Broadway shows began to shift toward longer runs after 1943, these specialists had fewer chances per year to ply their trade.[52]

Of all the drapers, Dazian's was best positioned to weather this storm. The shop had both draped and costumed productions up and down Broadway through the latter half of the nineteenth century. In 1902 the shop had followed the theater uptown to the newly christened Times Square, opening in a new building at 142 West 44th Street. For most of the twentieth century, the firm's midtown location was perfectly situated between active theaters and the garment district.

Dazian's was also distinguished for its multinodal approach to theater supply in the age of *Oklahoma!* By 1941 the firm not only had branch offices in traditional theater towns such as Chicago, Boston, and Philadelphia but had also branched out to Los Angeles.[53] This was due to Dazian's success in supplying specialty fabrics to major movie studios such as M.G.M., in both Los Angeles and New York. A 1943 magazine feature on the New York shop chronicles the milieu that Miles White might have entered when he stopped by to choose *Oklahoma!*'s fabrics: "Dazian's main store is a colorful mad-house. In one corner you may find a doting mother selecting spangles with which to garnish her daughter's dancing school costume while upstairs Metro-Goldwyn-Mayer may be discussing specifications for 5,000 costumes or 50,000 make-up sponges."[54]

With a rich history in New York and a broad base of work in other cities, Dazian's survived into the post–World War II era, although not at its 44th Street location. At some point between 1963 and 1966, the firm left the theater district for a space at 40 East 29th Street.[55] This relocation was representative of larger, decentralizing trends in the 1950s and 1960s, which pulled dozens of shops such as Dazian's out of Times Square with compelling centrifugal force.

Decentralization in Show Construction

As the case study of *Oklahoma!* demonstrates, the shops supplying and building for Broadway in the 1940s were as tight as a Richard Rodgers harmony. More than just physically proximate, they shared a skilled labor pool and routinely collaborated. As a result they collectively activated "external economies" of scale, typical for businesses in industrial districts. They benefited from "cheap, rapid transfer of material" and "frequent face-to-face communication to deal with the problems that inevitably arise when new products are made," in a fashion similar to other geographically specific sectors of New York City's economy, such as brewing in Brooklyn or diamonds on 47th Street. They received raw materials from the same suppliers, shared larger construction jobs, and recruited from the same pool of skilled workers. As a product of midtown's industrial district, *Oklahoma!* was as local as it got.[56]

This tightly concentrated craft work was not of obvious, towering economic value to midtown Manhattan. Fewer than ten contractors were actually hired, and the Theatre Guild's $80,000 budget paled in comparison to the $737 million budget of the entire city in 1945.[57] The walk-up buildings utilized by the guild and its contractors were literally dwarfed by those of large manufacturers or white-collar firms. Unlike its midtown neighbors, the guild was also a temporary employer, providing only five to six weeks of work for the employees of Brooks, Robert Bergman, Capezio, LaRay Boots, Vail Construction, and other small-time suppliers. All told, as a craft and construction project, *Oklahoma!* employed only about seventy-five people.

This was just one of eighty-eight productions in the 1942–43 season, however. The built components and craft work of these shows do impress in the aggregate. The costumes for these many shows included the glamorous gowns worn by Gertrude Lawrence in *Lady in the Dark*, the tattered raiment of the Lester family in a revival of *Tobacco Road*, and the stately yet worn dresses of Anton Chekhov's *Three Sisters*. Scenery specialists painted endless rows of army tents, in careful perspective, on backdrops for Irving Berlin's *This Is the Army*. They also used wood, canvas, and paint to conjure the boardwalks of Atlantic City and an editor's office at a fashion magazine. Lighting designers, riggers, and electricians used trusses, colored gels, and carefully angled spotlights to evoke the brooding despair of Richard III, the sparkling opulence of the *Ziegfeld Follies*, and the straightforward realism of a Washington, D.C., living room.[58]

Granted, some of these eighty-eight shows had little to no production value, and it was true that one-person vehicles or farcical revues needed fewer components than full-scale musicals or plays. But more often than not, the shows of this ten-month season employed several designers, several businesses, and dozens of unionized workers, each for weeks at a time.

Although the history of this show-building economy is seemingly slight, its theater-related businesses were so tightly concentrated, so thoroughly unionized, and so busy in the age of *Oklahoma!* that they made an indisputable, positive, and productive impact on the midtown economy. The United Scenic Artists union could boast of 315 members in 1941, and in scenery alone they had fourteen union shops by 1945, each with many permanent, salaried employees.[59] The swollen ranks of these workers had much to do with Broadway's dominance of the national theater market and touring companies, but they also stemmed from the vigorous number of new shows opening each year in Times Square. Between 1947 and 1968 an average of sixty-three new shows opened per year in New York City, each built by the same concentrated network of craft specialists who had constructed *Oklahoma!*[60]

Although the original stage version of *Oklahoma!* was clearly part of this classic, centralized tradition, its unprecedented eight-year tour, ending in the late 1940s, along with its three simultaneous tours of the 1950s all contributed to larger trends of show-building decentralization. Rather than pulling theater craftspeople and artists together for collaboration, the expanded phenomenon known as *Oklahoma!* began to disperse theater craft from midtown. The first and most obvious way in which the show had unintended, deleterious consequences was by claiming the stage at the St. James and not giving it up for five years. The long run of this show and others that followed suit left Broadway's theater-related shops with fewer new shows to build. If more work became available outside of New York City, as it did during the 1950s and 1960s, theater craftspeople, shop proprietors, and other experts might seek the greener pastures in regional theaters. As Chapter 5 will chronicle, many of them did.

Oklahoma!'s national tours promoted decentralization when they switched from railroad to bus and truck transport. The first, very famous national tour had traversed the nation via railroad. As this touring company began to pull into railroad stations with heaps of crafted components in tow in 1943, and eventually played every state in the nation by 1951, it was not all that different from its predecessors. Its traveling components were crafted in Manhattan by the same contractors who built the main-stage production, and the rail-based tour was yet another notch in Broadway's belt of national dominance. The theater historian Robert Simonson explains railroad tours as follows: "Before WWII, Broadway shows reached cities outside New York by one method: train. Sets would be loaded into railway cars, then ride the tracks to Philadelphia, Boston, or some other major East Coast hub, and there be unloaded and transported to the stage. In the case of Detroit, a spur led directly to a loading dock at a theater." By the 1950s, however, the touring productions of *Oklahoma!* and other hit shows were built and distributed much differently.[61]

On wheels rather than rails, the "bus and truck" tour producers of the 1950s did not gather components in a central location, near a railroad station. Instead they collected finished components from locations outside of New York City and were actually required to do so by law. In 1948, when the Interstate Commerce Commission (ICC) ruled that Clark Transfer could truck scenery across state lines, the ruling forbade Clark from hauling scenery within fifty miles of Gotham. When the new bus-and-truck tour model was experimentally used for the plays *Death of a Salesman* and *Mister Roberts* in 1949, their producers were bound by law to build and launch far from Manhattan. Although these rules were intended to protect Broadway from imported, non-union-built scenery, they also promoted decentralization in show building by increasing the market for scenery constructed outside of New York. The bus-and-truck haulers of the 1950s were not the first firms to move scenery on wheels and roads. A company named Globe Theatrical Transfer, for example, had relocated scenery locally within New

York City in the 1920s. The crucial difference by the 1950s, however, was that these new theatrical transfer companies could work with a burgeoning number of regional theaters and performing arts centers.[62]

When the Theatre Guild built *Oklahoma!*'s touring shows in the 1950s, they sought to replicate the crafted components of the original, but in a manner more friendly to the new age of bus-and-truck dispersal. This sent them to firms such as Kaj Velden Scenic in Fort Lee, New Jersey, which had a history on West 54th and 52nd Streets in Manhattan but had relocated to Fort Lee in 1948. By hopping across the Hudson, proprietors David Steinberg and Kaj Velden had upgraded from roughly twenty thousand to seventy-five thousand square feet, which they found in the former home of a defunct movie studio. In a region rapidly being remade for the automobile, where touring scenery and backdrops would be transported by truck anyway, Kaj Velden's new space "for building and storing stage sets" was ideal. Unfortunately the relocation proved ill-fated when a 1952 fire destroyed over a million dollars worth of stored scenery, including touring scenery for *Oklahoma!*[63]

That the move to New Jersey resulted in disaster for Kaj Velden Scenic and the Theatre Guild is purely coincidental. But this coincidence was symbolic nonetheless, as the products of a vibrant mid-century industrial district, having been moved out of their natural "habitat," tragically went up in flames. Far more significant than this small, symbolic scenery fire was the conflagration of FIRE (finance, insurance, and real estate) skyscraper development that spread through midtown in the decades after *Oklahoma!* Office towers, along with the highways and parking garages built to support them, would soon be shoehorned into western midtown, pushing theater-related craft out of the district with alarming speed.

This transformative era from the 1950s to the 1980s was not the first time that theater-related contractors had flourished outside of Manhattan. The *Julius Cahn–Gus Hill* directory of theater- and film-related suppliers reveals that Lee Lash Studios was painting backdrops in Mount Vernon, New York, as early as 1922 and that in the same year the Eldredge Company did its theatrical printing on Flatbush Avenue in Brooklyn. Although the firm does not appear to have worked much on Broadway, there was also J. R. Clancy theatrical distribution company in Syracuse, New York, with representatives in twenty-one different cities nationwide.[64]

The next generation of theater-related contractors to open outside the city's limits, in the decades after World War II, were not supplements to a thriving theatrical infrastructure, as Lee Lash, Eldredge, and J. R. Clancy had been. They were either refugees from midtown or replacements for a collapsing network of theater-related businesses within the city. Business listings from New York City mapped with Geographic Information Systems software demonstrate this geographic shift in no uncertain terms. Through the 1920s non-Manhattan business listings for theatrical trades were few and far between. The maps from 1929 (see Figures 13 and 14) show an intense concentration in the city center.

By the 1950s shops of this type had also sprung up in Brooklyn and New Jersey. The stockpiling of these shops in the city center continued unabated, but an additional layer of distant contractors was also emerging. These first waves of decentralization, in which shops spread to Brooklyn and Fort Lee, were not inherently destructive. They unfolded during a time of overall expansion in Broadway's construction trades. Indeed the 1960 *Business Listings* had more entries in costuming, theatrical equipment, and scenery than had appeared in 1950. It was not until the 1970s and 1980s that the decentering trend began to have unexpected, deleterious consequences within midtown.

The map of theater-related businesses from 1980 starkly portrays the hollowing out of Broadway's industrial district. The open circles in Figure 17 represent theater-related businesses no longer listed by the time the 1980 *Yellow Pages* appeared. These defunct firms clearly outnumber those still in operation.

The change in the number of theater-related businesses was as striking as their dispersal from the city center. After peaking in the 1920s at 142, these shops dwindled slightly in the 1930s and early 1940s. The count then held steady through the 1950s at more than 100 and expanded impressively during the 1960s, reaching a new peak of 220 by 1970. Measured through the Manhattan *Yellow Pages*, Broadway construction was still a growth industry through the 1960s. The problem for the industrial district, however, was that little of this growth occurred in the midtown core, as evidenced by the maps above. Even more ominously, the total number of theater-related shops in Manhattan plummeted to only 47 by 1980.[65] Instead of reviving in Manhattan, theater-related craft work arose in entirely new locations: regional theaters and performing arts centers.

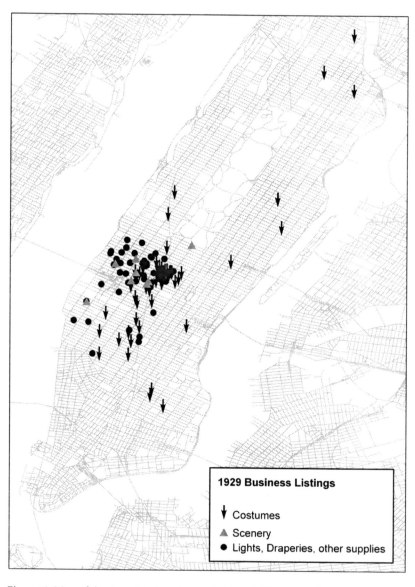

Figure 13. Map of theater-related businesses in 1929 in New York City. Based on *1929 Business Listings*, New York Public Library, Microform Reading Room. Generated by the author with Geographic Information Systems software.

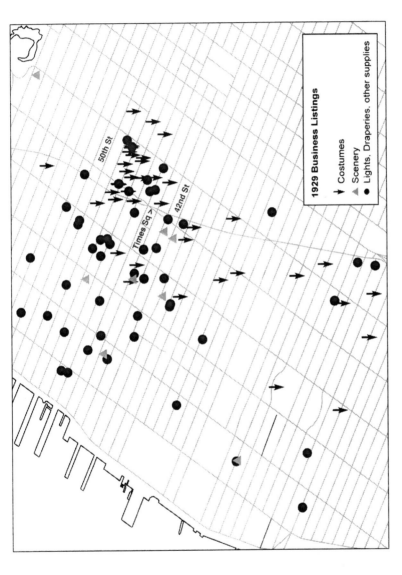

Figure 14. Detailed view of 1929 in midtown Manhattan. Readers should note the preponderance of costume and supply businesses in and around Times Square, along with the tendency of scene-shop proprietors to operate on the far west side, west of 7th Avenue. Based on 1929 *Business Listings*, New York Public Library, Microform Reading Room. Generated by the author with Geographic Information Systems software.

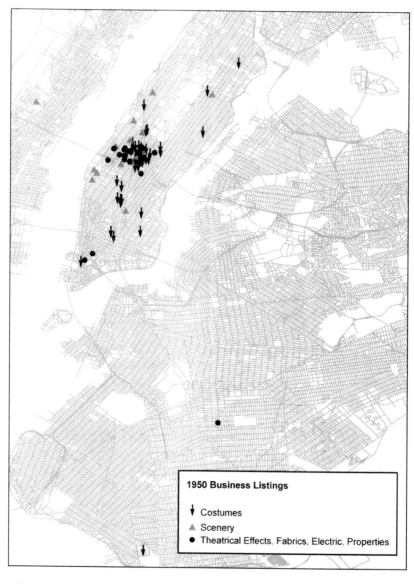

Figure 15. Regional view of theater-related businesses in 1950. Readers should note the decentralization of shops to Brooklyn and New Jersey, along with the persistence of costume/supply shops in Times Square and scene shops on the far west side. Based on 1950 *Business Listings*, New York Public Library, Microform Reading Room. Generated by the author with Geographic Information Systems software.

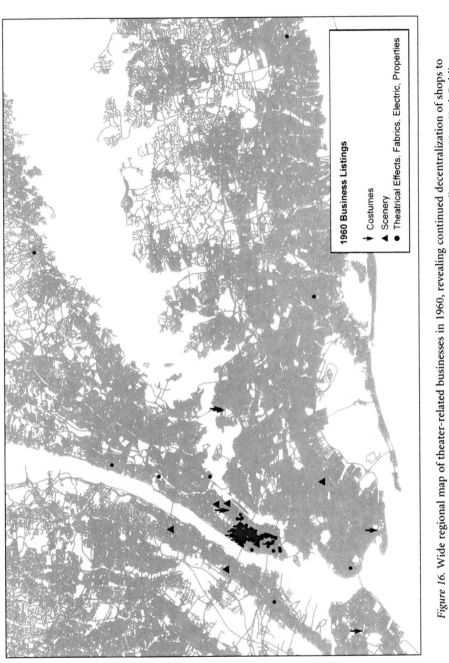

Figure 16. Wide regional map of theater-related businesses in 1960, revealing continued decentralization of shops to Long Island, Staten Island, New Jersey, the Bronx, and Connecticut. Based on 1960 *Yellow Pages*, New York Public Library, Microform Reading Room. Generated by the author with Geographic Information Systems software.

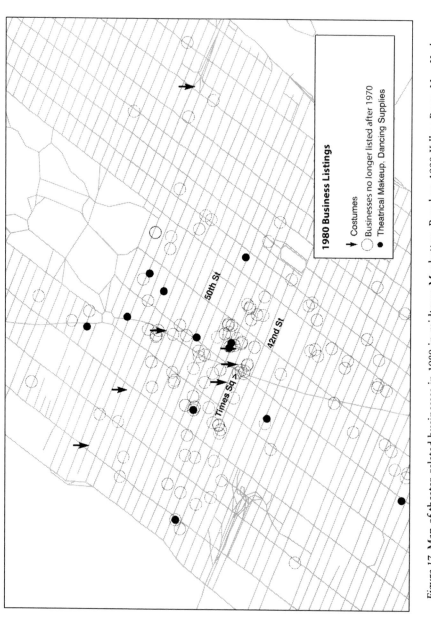

Figure 17. Map of theater-related businesses in 1980 in midtown Manhattan. Based on 1980 *Yellow Pages*, New York Public Library, Microform Reading Room. Generated by the author with Geographic Information Systems software.

Chapter 5

"Sunrise, Sunset"

The Decline of Broadway Craft and
the Rise of Regional Theaters

ONE CAN HARDLY blame her. When she got the offer in 1963, Barbara Karinska was a seventy-seven-year-old veteran of the costume trade. No spring chicken, she had already gone through most of the highs and lows of her profession. The chance to have a more steady, predictable existence must have sounded appealing to one who had experienced almost all that an independent costume shop proprietor could. This "regal" craftswoman had won an Academy Award for her work on the 1948 film *Joan of Arc*. She had collaborated with one of Broadway's greatest composers, Leonard Bernstein, creating costumes for the critically acclaimed musical *Candide* in 1957. For years she had costumed the distinguished New York City Ballet, and in 1962 she had been tapped for one of America's most prestigious design awards. Besides having been there and done that, Karinska had other reasons to say yes in 1963. The neighboring shops on her block of West 44th Street were significantly less refined than they had been when she opened in 1938, just as the "spacious" but "dilapidated" loft she rented at 112 West 44th Street had seen better days. So when her friends at the glittering new Lincoln Center, as high profile as it was well funded, invited her to close her shop and relocate to a state-of-the-art work space only about fifteen blocks uptown, she said yes.[1]

Karinska's journey to her new shop at 20 West 57th Street was not as transformative as Irving Berlin's from the lower east side to Times Square, but the skilled seamstress still underwent a remarkable transformation

Figure 18. Barbara Karinska in her workshop, ca. 1960–64. Courtesy of the Billy Rose Theatre Division, The New York Public Library for the Performing Arts, Astor, Lenox, and Tilden Foundations.

when she hitched her wagon to starry Lincoln Center. By heading for greener pastures uptown, Karinska ceased to be a third-party contractor. This Ukrainian-born craftswoman closed the doors on her 44th Street shop in 1963, taking her entire crew of roughly fifteen to thirty skilled costumers out of the contractor game. After having functioned in this capacity for twenty-five years, the shop's skilled workers were gobbled up by a mammoth institution, and they disappeared from midtown's small business landscape.[2]

In her new space, Barbara Karinska and her expert team engaged in the same craft work but according to new rules. They had been recruited because of the long-standing artistic partnership between Karinska and

New York City Ballet choreographer George Balanchine, who desired an in-house costumer at Lincoln Center. As tenants of the new institution, Balanchine and Karinska would keep some of the artistic license they had enjoyed in prior decades but would also have to answer to Lincoln Center's board of directors.

In the beginning Balanchine had helped Karinska to get started as an independent contractor on 44th Street back in 1938. At the new shop on 57th, Karinska and her costuming crew answered to Lincoln Center and the New York City Ballet year-round, rather than only when under contract. While there were no famous flaps, fights, or flare-ups that made the papers, there is no denying that the power dynamic changed. Karinska and her craft workers relied on the annual roster of shows at the ballet as they had done before, but they were now on an institution's payroll. She may have had posture "as regal as if two pages were carrying her train," and who knows, maybe she really was to costumes what William Shakespeare was to literature, as George Balanchine quite boldly and famously claimed.[3] But she still had the board to answer to when the new arrangement was launched in 1964. Even the most regal of bearings and the most towering of reputations were no match for the power of old money.

There was far more at stake here, of course, than the autonomy of one Madame Barbara Karinska. Her migration to an institution was part of a larger trend, one that vastly transformed the American stage. The trend in question was slow in unfolding but momentous in its sweep. It represented nothing less than a spatial redistribution of theatrical craft work within the United States. It is this redistribution that inspired the following sentiments, the first penned by the journalist John Gunther in 1947 and the second by Arthur Laurents for the 1959 musical *Gypsy:*

New York is the publishing center of the nation; it is the art, theater, musical, ballet, operatic center; it is the opinion center; it is the radio center; it is the style center. . . . New York sets the tone and pace of the entire nation.[4]

Miss Cratchitt: "New York is the center of everything—" Rose: "New York is the center of New York." (*Gypsy*)

Gunther could write so smugly of New York's centrality in 1947 because so many American arts events indeed took place there. By the time Laurents playfully questioned New York's centrality in 1959, however, vaudeville was dead, Broadway was transforming, and a tectonic shift in theater geography had already begun.

Historians of the regional stage, performing arts centers, and the fine arts outside of New York have dutifully documented the redistribution of shows and performances, utilizing narratives of decentralization and even antimonopoly activism, but none has framed this dispersal in terms of craft.[5] Even those who have written of the exodus of blue-collar jobs from New York City, under the rubric of deindustrialization, have neglected to address theater-related craft work. This is probably because the economists and urbanists who write of deindustrialization seek bigger fish, and their impressive studies of manufacturing-job loss would benefit little from featuring the closure of a shop as small as Karinska's.[6] Yet these closed shops mattered a great deal in the history of midtown, just as the newly built shops of the regional stage opened up unprecedented terrain for national stagecraft.

The spatial reorientation of theatrical craft workers and craft shops played out over several decades. After 1965 or so, many dozens of shops began disappearing from New York City. A handful were absorbed by nearby institutions, but most disappeared altogether. In their place new shops for crafting costumes, scenery, and the like mushroomed in cities such as Seattle, San Francisco, Los Angeles, Dallas, Houston, and Minneapolis during the 1960s and 1970s. By the 1980s the post–World War II redistribution of American theater craft was stark.

For workers, these changes often meant a migration from contractor work to institutional employment. As the Karinska case demonstrates, such relocations could change the power dynamics of theater craft while also raising sticky issues of artistic license and autonomy. The scads of scrappy craft workers who had dominated Times Square at mid-century may have suffered the indignities of deadbeat producers or landlords hiking up rent, but when push came to shove they were rarely under the thumbs of any people but their head designers or shop proprietors. Assuming that jobs were more or less available to those with the right skills, as they were through the 1940s and 1950s, any worker who did not mesh with her or his shop foreman could try another boss a few blocks away.

In the brave new institutional landscape of the 1960s and beyond, however, theatrical craft workers spread out nationally and tended to get jobs with institutions, more likely to be the only game in town. The overall number of jobs dwindled, and evidence suggests that those working for institutions such as the Seattle Repertory Theatre and the Dallas Theatre Center had considerably less artistic autonomy than their third-party, Broadway predecessors had. Although contract work for Broadway continued, the number of shops was diminished, and the sun had set for most independent businesses. Meanwhile through regional theaters, performing arts centers, and the Off-Broadway movement, a new era dawned for institutional craft shops dispersed liberally around the nation.

New Lighting and New Spaces

Much like Madame Karinska, Edward Kook said yes. He was invited to Lincoln Center not to make costumes but to light them. In the early 1960s Kook was one of the most respected names in stage lighting and the proprietor of Century Lighting, Inc. This "growling, self-made, deal-hustling, Runyonesque character" began his theatrical career as an accountant for Display Stage Lighting, and he most likely started without knowing a follow spot from a footlight.[7] In a turn of events worthy of *The Producers* by Mel Brooks, however, this mere accountant tinkered with the lights enough to become a master of the trade. By 1929 he had founded Century Lighting with partner Joseph Levy, and through lighting innovations they stayed afloat in Manhattan during the lean years of the Depression.

The first of Kook's novelties was his catalog of lights and trusses, featuring products for sale and rental nationwide. By offering to ship his specialty goods anywhere, Kook broadened his costumer base beyond Broadway, addressing the growing demand for professional lighting outside of New York City. The second of Kook's innovations was a light that could cast various intensities and colors from a single bulb. He stumbled upon this discovery in 1931 because he continued to futz with lighting technology in his laboratory at 351 West 52nd Street and because he had help from fellow enthusiast Maude Adams, known primarily as a stage actress. Adams and Kook did not invent the first lighting system that could dim, brighten, or change color in an instant, but they certainly modernized it. Prior to 1931 stagehands and electricians stood behind Broadway's lights with a mix of shades, screens, and colored gels, manually sliding them in front of bulbs to achieve the desired effects. The new Century Lighting bulb did this work on its own. As long as it burned hot enough within its metal casing, electricians could adjust its brightness or color with the turn of a knob. When Kook's skilled crew began using them in Broadway playhouses after 1931, little did they know that their work was a first step toward the automated, electronic lighting systems of the 1960s.[8]

Through the 1930s and 1940s Kook's Century Lighting joined Kliegl Brothers Stage Lighting as one of the most frequently hired of Broadway's theater-related businesses. Under Kook's leadership, Century lit many of Broadway's top plays, such as *The Glass Menagerie* in 1945 and *Death of a Salesman* in 1949, all the while operating on the far west side, in close proximity to the other industry specialists. Given that Kook reportedly "spent as much time backstage in the theaters of Broadway as he did in the shop of Century Lighting," he became quite the expert.[9] The firm did relocate once before Kook sold it in 1963, but the second work space at 521 West 43rd Street was still squarely within Broadway's industrial district. Given the company's success and its central location, it may seem surprising that Kook would abandon the excitement of independent contractor work for an institutional existence at Lincoln Center.

As he explained in interviews at the time, Kook made this switch because of his frustration with the ad hoc chaos of Broadway, where innovation in lighting was, for all practical purposes, logistically impossible. In this way Kook left commercial Broadway with a clearer sense of purpose than Karinska and her garment team did. Explaining his decision to the *New York Times* in 1963, Kook derided Broadway lighting as "antiquated" and "laborious." Swimming with the tide of history, Kook had become fascinated with the prospect of permanently installed, electronic lighting systems.[10]

Unfortunately the historic, proscenium-based playhouses between 52nd and 41st Streets were poor candidates for Kook's excellent idea. They had neither the space nor the wiring for what Kook had in mind. Down to the last playhouse, these buildings were designed around static, rectangular boxes framing the stages and dividing them from the audiences; these were known as prosceniums. It was from the prosceniums that the classic red velvet curtains hung, and it was around the prosceniums that lighting crews climbed, squeezed, and scrambled to install lighting prior to the 1960s. Dangling in the fly spaces above the stages or in the wings and teetering on ladders above the plush velvet orchestra seats, Broadway's specialized crews affixed lights to balconies, ceilings, boxes, and prosceniums wherever they could. What made this cumbersome process more of an art than a science was that no Broadway house had the dimensions of any other. Even if Kook had found a theater owner willing to invest in his bold new idea, he would have been hard-pressed to wedge it into the cramped space. Within any existing playhouse Kook's lighting system would have been, at best, a round peg that did not quite fit in its squared-off proscenium.

The only lighting system that worked within Broadway's idiosyncratic playhouses was inefficient, expensive, time-consuming, and a source of frustration to Kook. The work that his firm did in 1958 to light the play *Look Homeward, Angel* perfectly illustrates why the proprietor found the status quo so irksome. Just a few years before he agreed to join Lincoln Center, Kook worked at the Ethel Barrymore Theatre on a contract job with his crew of seventeen unionized electricians. Their task was to install two hundred heavy, metal-encased lights, and to do this they worked almost around the clock for two full days. They climbed forty-foot ladders to the ceiling, proscenium, and balcony to pull off this feat, staying until 5:15 A.M. on their final day of work. With overtime pay, each man earned more than fifty dollars on this last day, nothing to sneeze at in 1958. When the play closed in April 1959, a team of equal size had to spend just as much time taking the rented lights down. Such was the Sisyphus-like, ad hoc lighting system of Broadway.[11]

If the lighting for a relatively popular, long-running play seemed inefficient to Kook, imagine his irritation with a flop show that closed after only one performance. In such cases paid lighting crews would unfurl their ladders to disassemble the very same network of lights they had hung just a few days earlier. Though unionized electricians may have privately celebrated flops because of the extra work they generated, proprietors such as Kook lamented the way that their firms were saddling each and every Broadway production with such colossal costs. When the accountant-turned-lighting-expert made his 1963 decision to sell Century Lighting and become the lighting guru for Lincoln Center, he realized that this was the end of an era, but it was a curtain he did not regret bringing down.

What Kook was saying yes to a few blocks uptown was the opportunity to give birth to a state-of-the-art, one-hundred-thousand-dollar "electronic lighting control system" within the brand new Vivian Beaumont Theatre. Unlike the many dozens of lighting installations he and his crew had done on Broadway, this would be a permanent feature of the Beaumont's groundbreaking theater-in-the-round layout. Theater-in-the-round shows broke free of the antiquated prosceniums, thrusting the stages forward and surrounding the players with audience seating on three or sometimes even four sides. When built with lighting in mind, such facilities saved space for elaborate, flexible lighting systems. Installed just one time, these systems were dynamic enough to light almost every conceivable play or musical within the spaces.

By investing in Kook's experimental and ultimately successful system, the managers of the Vivian Beaumont saved themselves the trouble of hiring installation teams for new shows. They also saved big in terms of weekly operating costs. By the turn of the 1960s, Broadway's producers had resigned themselves to paying unionized wages to an average of four electricians each week a show was open. In other words, each time the lights went up on a Broadway show, roughly four electricians were paid to make that happen. At the Beaumont, however, Kook's electronic system needed only one electrician sitting dutifully at the switchboard entering automated lighting cues.[12]

Not surprisingly, the cutting-edge system was quickly imitated in dozens of newly built regional theaters and performing arts centers nationwide. Kook's expertise was so valued that he and his collaborator in lighting design, the great Jo Mielziner, were flown to colleges and civic centers for "all-expense-paid" consultations. At places such as the Denver Center for the Performing Arts and Wake Forest University, Kook and Mielziner showed designers precisely how they could bypass the antiquated, labor-intensive lighting methods of earlier decades. This national influence is what made Kook so interesting and so important. When the lights went up for the Beaumont's opening night on October 21, 1965, it was truly the dawn of a new era in U.S. stage lighting. Although Kook's system brought accolades to Lincoln Center, it mattered most as a model for built-in, electronic lighting systems across the country.[13]

Although much celebrated, electronic lighting systems did have a downside for practitioners of older methods. In 1965 dozens of electricians continued to earn their living by renting, hanging, and operating stage lights on Broadway and on national tours. When automated systems cropped up in regional theaters and performing arts centers throughout the 1960s and 1970s, each installed system quashed a series of potential gigs for electricians. Like the caretakers of the proverbial goose and her golden eggs, those who installed such systems got to feast lavishly on a onetime contract only to find that their trade no longer laid out quite as many full-time jobs.

Weekly rental fees for lighting firms also dried up because of these permanently installed systems. In the ad hoc age, lighting firms earned considerable income through equipment rental fees. Broadway producers paid handsomely for every light, truss, and tangled bundle of cables their shows needed to shine. Once all of this equipment was built in, these weekly fees simply disappeared. In a fascinating turn of events, demonstrating that others besides Kook wanted to cut through the Gordian knot of Broadway lighting, the maverick producer Harold Prince purchased his own electronic dimmer board for eighty thousand dollars in the late 1970s so that he could stop paying these fees.[14] Unusually flush after a string of box-office smashes such as *Fiddler on the Roof* and *Cabaret*, Prince was the only producer on the Great White Way to be so lucky. Everyone else was stuck with the Gordian knot.

It was more typical for institutions rather than individuals to invest in these systems. Invest they did. Only a decade after Kook's system was unveiled, the builders of the regional stage had proved their determination not to bleed money on rental equipment, as those cuckolds back on Broadway were doing, and had installed permanent lighting systems at the Dorothy Chandler Pavilion in Los Angeles, the Seattle Repertory, the Tyrone Guthrie Theatre in Minneapolis, the Alley Stage in Houston, the Dallas Theatre Center, the Arena Stage in Washington, D.C., and several others.

Lighting was just the tip of the iceberg, of course. Deep below their high-tech ceilings, most regional theaters eventually contained vast, state-of-the-art workrooms for costumes, scenery, and stage props. Though this regional craft infrastructure took longer to materialize, it ultimately did even more than lighting to disperse theater craft more evenly throughout the nation.

The Regional Theater Challenge

"On the streets off Times Square are about thirty theatres, most built in the first quarter of the twentieth century, with conventional proscenium stage and an average capacity of about twelve hundred. And that, for half of the twentieth century, was the American theatre."[15] This pithy summation of the theater may have rung true in 1947, but it would not remain so for long. Professional theaters blossomed outside of Gotham, and new craft jobs quickly materialized. Though Barbara Karinska and Edward Kook did not leave New York City, many of their contemporaries did. This momentous diaspora in theater craft did not happen overnight. In their earliest incarnations, most regional theaters were humble, makeshift operations. In the language of Joseph Ziegler's excellent history of the regional stage, most were "acorns" before becoming fully grown oaks.[16]

The mid-century theater artists who sought to circumvent Broadway's monopoly through regional theater were not the first to try this. Beginning in the 1910s, there had been a "little theater" movement, but it was true to its name in both craft work and production values. With productions that were invariably low budget and locally oriented, scenery was rudimentary and costumes were bare-bones. Though a handful of little theaters thrived in impressive, newly built physical plants, most of the several hundred operating in the 1910s and 1920s were nothing more than tenants in preexisting buildings. The real legacy of the movement may have been the playwright Eugene O'Neill, who honed his craft at the Provincetown Playhouse in Massachusetts before becoming legendary in New York. Other than this crowning moment, the short-lived movement did not make much of a mark. Despite the earnest efforts of many who yearned for a truly national theater, most little theaters went gentle into that good night during the Depression.

After World War II the regional theater movement began with a similar makeshift humility but quickly matured into something greater. Margo Jones, who opened a regional theater in Dallas in 1947, started within a vacant building on a state fairgrounds. Skeptics may point out that a rabble of motley thespians doing plays in a defunct fairgrounds building in Texas was hardly a revolution, but Jones insisted that this was what she and her fellow travelers in other cities would create. Boldly announcing in her book *Theatre-in-the-Round* that she wished "to live in an age when there is great theatre everywhere," this "vivid woman" and "dynamo" became a "high priestess of the movement," according to the chroniclers of the regional stage. As Gerald Berkowitz tells it, Jones "energized everyone and everything she came in contact with," and there is good reason to believe that her work and her book emboldened those who followed in her footsteps. Despite a promising start and a grant from the Rockefeller Foundation, Jones's Theatre '47 project died with her when she passed unexpectedly in 1955.[17]

Another visionary female leader of the regional stage, Nina Vance, founded the Alley Theatre in Houston just months after Theatre '47 opened in Dallas. Originally offering austere plays in a dilapidated dance studio, Vance lost her lease in 1949 and then landed in a "grimy" old fan factory building in downtown Houston. She and her team rolled up their sleeves to convert the boxlike space into a workable theater-in-the-round. In their humble digs, this group had neither the desire nor the budget for professional scenery or costumes. Like so many other regional theaters, however, the Alley got these professional components when Vance and her team moved into a multi-million-dollar facility in the 1960s. With grants from the Ford Foundation of $2.1 million in 1962 and $1.4 million in 1964, a land gift from a local trust, a strong subscriber base, and a citywide capital campaign, the Alley outgrew its infancy. Between 1966 and 1968 the civic center in downtown Houston was abuzz with construction, not only to build the Alley's two performance halls but also to carve out the subterranean rehearsal and construction spaces beneath them.[18]

These underground spaces mattered most for the geography of American stagecraft. The Alley's scene shop, costume shop, property room, and rehearsal studios enabled the institution to stand alone, as self-sufficient as possible. Houston boasted many fine businesses in 1968, but major houses for scenery or costume construction were not among them. It was possible for the Alley to rely on distant component suppliers, but high prices and shipping costs made this impractical. It was far wiser for the Alley's leaders to invest in facilities for their own homespun stage components.

A similar maturation and relocation occurred about 240 miles to the north, in Dallas. The city's first regional theater may have passed with Margo Jones in 1955, but the enthusiasm she had stirred up in Dallas lived on. Less than five years after losing Theatre '47, donors joined forces with the Ford Foundation to create the even more elaborate Dallas Theatre Center, designed by none other than the celebrated architect Frank Lloyd Wright. Wright's design was a bit constricting in terms of craft space, but the original Dallas Theatre Center (DTC) was still able to provide work spaces for three costumers, three scenery builders, seven properties specialists, and one electrician when it opened in 1965.[19]

Unlike those whose fortunes rose and fell through the contracted chaos of Broadway, these craftspeople lived a steady, salaried existence. In 1965 the original DTC facility boasted a technical and administrative staff of forty, a repertory of thirty actors, and an annual budget of $265,000.[20] Even with this many professionals on its payroll, the DTC was hardly in a position to challenge big, bad Broadway. Professional producers in New York were still churning out plenty of Pulitzer Prize–winning plays and block-buster musicals. In addition few regional theaters in the mid-1960s could claim as many paid professionals as DTC. Gradually, however, the full-time positions in regional theaters across the nation began to add up to something profound.

While Jones, Vance, and others innovated in Texas, kindred spirits did the same in Washington, D.C., Seattle, and Minneapolis. Eventually professional theaters also materialized in Buffalo, Boston, Chicago, Cleveland, Atlanta, Denver, and Los Angeles. In several cases, especially in Minneapolis, these groups formed mutually beneficial partnerships with local colleges or universities. Of the many regional theaters to be founded in this era, the Arena Stage in D.C. was especially fascinating because it flourished under the tutelage of yet another forward-thinking female leader, Zelda Fichandler. This feisty leader of D.C. theater recruited like-minded enthusiasts to create shows in an abandoned movie theater in 1950. Though it had been addled with adult films in the recent past, the building got a new use from Fichandler and her fifteen donors.[21] When the Arena Stage made its splash in the repurposed space and gained a strong following, Fichandler courted enough foundational support and local patronage to build a "multi-million dollar" facility in the early 1960s.[22]

This was not a multipurpose performing arts center that the Arena would share but rather an individual, generously outfitted regional theater, built from the ground up expressly for that purpose. This distinction is important. When cities used tax revenues to build performing arts centers, they usually expected regional theater companies to share space with other tenants and often booked Broadway touring companies to help their centers stay in the black. Even the most successful of regional theater companies, such as the Seattle Repertory, had to navigate these realities. The Arena's leaders were lucky to be part of an institution that was relatively independent and pure in breed, able to feature homegrown talent and playwrights from D.C. with regularity.

Whether they embraced or eschewed Broadway tours, there is no denying that non–New York City performance halls tipped the scales of U.S. cultural geography forcefully in the 1960s. According to a Twentieth Century Fund study from 1970, a whopping 173 arts centers and theaters were finished between 1962 and 1969, while 179 were "on the drawing boards or in construction." Even more significant than the geographic spread of these facilities was the expenditure lavished upon them by private, corporate, and governmental entities. Twentieth Century Fund economists estimated that in 1964 alone, U.S. expenditure just on performing arts buildings fell somewhere between fifty million and seventy-five million dollars. Without even taking the annual operating budgets into consideration, it is clear that the sheer cost of these facilities set them far apart from the summer stock, amateur, or little theater buildings preceding them.[23]

Despite its bumper crop of playing spaces and craft workrooms, the regional movement still needed cultural gravitas in order to thrive, especially when one considers that these shows were reviewed by tastemakers jetting in from New York City. In Minneapolis gravitas arrived dramatically in the early 1960s when the director Tyrone Guthrie, the actors Jessica Tandy and Hume Cronyn, and several other key players relocated there from Broadway. After announcing his intention to found a resident theater somewhere outside of New York, Guthrie and other theater professionals from the Big Apple took a tour of candidate cities in 1959, ultimately choosing the midwestern metropolis. One of the reasons they cited for this choice was the University of Minnesota's willingness to create mutually beneficial programs and internships in acting, directing, design, playwriting, and management.

Over the next three years, Minneapolis constructed a $2.25 million theater worthy of the esteemed director, after whom it would be named. Though Guthrie's name carried considerable weight, the real coup was probably when he signed Jessica Tandy and Hume Cronyn for the inaugural season in 1963. These married actors were not quite the Alfred Lunt and Lynn Fontanne of the 1960s, but they both had Tony nominations, and Tandy had just appeared in Alfred Hitchcock's film *The Birds*. Known to many Americans only as the diminutive biddy of *Driving Miss Daisy*, Tandy had once stood tall among American stage actresses, especially after her much-lauded turn as Blanche DuBois in the original *Streetcar Named Desire*. According to a leading history on the subject, the relocation of Guthrie along with these respected actors "further legitimized the movement and gave it national weight."[24]

Most histories of the Guthrie theater mark its inception with the completion of the performance hall in 1963. While this was essential, the true engines of this institution were the craft spaces and skilled workers hidden beneath the stage. Praised as "a small city of craft shops buzzing along 24 hours a day during peak season" and as a "veritable handicraft factory," these spaces and the experts therein enabled the institution to spring fully formed from the head of Tyrone Guthrie. Although its original lights were not as advanced as those of the Vivian Beaumont, they were permanently installed and certainly economical.[25]

Most regional theaters had begun performances in makeshift, ramshackle locations. In Milwaukee, for fifteen years prior to 1963, regional innovators had struggled with obstacles: "[N]othing was convenient, including the other buildings we were forced to expand into to house the scene and costume shops and the rehearsal hall . . . the lack of a cross-over for the actors caused a parade of costumed characters, sometimes carrying umbrellas . . . through the side alley." In perhaps the most extreme case, poor Nina Vance in Houston had cobbled her productions together around a sycamore tree reaching from her makeshift playing space through the roof, occasionally letting in the rain.[26]

Guthrie and his crew were lucky enough to skip this inchoate phase altogether, landing in Minneapolis fully formed and with a $1 million operating budget that was undoubtedly the envy of many a regional artistic director.[27] The Dallas Theatre Center, by way of comparison, had kicked off with an annual budget of only $265,000. In big-budget Minneapolis for the opening production of *Hamlet*, Guthrie was able to hire the scenic designer Tanya Moiseiwitsch and two experts originally from London, the costumer Ray Diffen and the draper Annette Garceau.

Guthrie knew Diffen from his work on Broadway, where he had executed costumes for *Camelot* (1960), *Jennie* (1963), and *Mr. President* (1963). Although Diffen did not leave Broadway behind completely after 1963, returning to work on *Tartuffe* (1965), *1776* (1969), *I Do! I Do!* (1973), and *Pippin* (1975), it appears that he spent at least half his time in Minneapolis. Moiseiwitsch and Garceau, however, seem to have moved to Minneapolis to stay. Long before the *Mary Tyler Moore Show* put the city more squarely on America's cultural map, this merry band of theater makers did its part. Both the theater and the opening production of *Hamlet* got rave reviews in the *New York Times*. The costumes and scenery got perhaps the best notices of them all. The future of this theater did not depend solely on *New York Times* reviews, but the rave certainly did not hurt.[28]

The Seattle Repertory was almost as quick to become dependent on Broadway connections and New York City cachet when it took shape in 1963. Though originally opened under the direction of the local theater artist Andre Gregory, "the Rep" got more attention when its board unceremoniously fired Gregory and replaced him with New Yorker Stuart Vaughan after just a few shows. The fact that this new director had trained with the theatrical luminaries Joseph Papp and George C. Scott in New York was enough for Seattle's newspapers to proclaim "NY Theatre Comes to Seattle" and "New Yorker Will Head Repertory Theater Here." Evidence suggests that the kowtowing to all things New York extended to the dynamic between Vaughan and his actors as well. A 1960s Rep performer described Vaughan as "one of the most eruditely arrogant men I'd ever met. He exuded an air of superiority, and every word he uttered was in a sense of finality."[29]

Like Minneapolis, the Emerald City did not have much history of professional theater—not much, that is, until the 1962 World's Fair. When the fair closed, two newly constructed performance halls stood vacant at the Seattle Center, in the shadow of the iconic Space Needle. Many of the same individuals who had organized the fair came up with the idea of the Seattle Rep, including Seattle Center manager Ewen Dingwall, the philanthropist Bagley Wright, and his wife Virginia Bloedel, the heiress of a vast timber fortune. Within a year they had not only launched the Repertory theater but had also staged a small coup to put their "New Yorker" at the helm.

In 1963 when the smaller of the two theaters became the Seattle Rep, there was no space within the entire Seattle Center for any theatrical craft or construction. Though Vaughan sought to create a "union house with high standards for scenery and costumes" when he arrived, he had his work cut out for him. With a bare-bones production staff of only twelve, Vaughan first relied on costumes and scenery crafted in affordable rental spaces in the Ballard neighborhood, five miles away.[30]

With Bloedel's timber fortune replenishing its coffers, the Seattle Rep did not have to slog through its infancy stage for long. After fifteen successful years under Vaughan and subsequent artistic directors, the Rep was able to more than double its production payroll to include thirty-three backstage employees by the late 1970s. Among these were three full-time seamstresses, three salaried scenery workers, and several other valuable, full-time craftsperson positions. By the early 1980s the Rep had so many donors and so much municipal support that these craftspeople were able to move into "set and costume construction facilities that would be the envy of any local group." As had the Guthrie in Minneapolis, the Rep's new Bagley Wright Theater had arisen atop a copious network of high-tech craft workrooms.[31]

By 1983 not only had the ranks of the salaried craftspeople at the new and improved Rep swollen, but also a wave of seamless integration in its construction and rehearsal processes had been unleashed. For the first time in its history scenery, costumes, props, wigs, and performers could gel under one roof during rehearsals. From a ragtag start-up operation in a decommissioned World's Fair building, the Rep became a fully realized, institutional center for theatrical production, even exporting shows to audiences in smaller cities throughout Washington State and Oregon. Looking back on the success of this regional troupe in 1979, the *Wall Street Journal* wrote of "A City That Staged a Fair and Got Culture," explaining that "[b]efore the fair Seattle was just another stop for the 'bus 'n' truck' road shows mopping up revenue in the provinces after a strong Broadway run."[32] By the mid-1980s the city's mature, multifaceted performing arts center was producing duplicated scenery from its own hits so that its troupe could tour cities such as Spokane.

This transition, from makeshift infancy to performing-arts-center adulthood, occurred in many cities besides Seattle and would transform the geography of theater craft as it unfolded nationally. As early as 1966 *Variety* was already reporting that more professional actors worked in regional companies than on Broadway and in its road companies combined.[33] This decentralizing trend inspired the Actors' Equity union to negotiate a new contract for its members, so that they could perform in the League of Regional Theatres if they wished. Though symbolic, performance jobs were far more mobile than craft workrooms or salaried positions in theater craft, and they ultimately did not matter as much as craft decentralization.

Additional examples from the 1960s tell an equally compelling story of theater craft dispersal. The Dorothy Chandler Pavilion had brought professional shops for costumes and scenery to downtown Los Angeles as early as 1964, while Atlanta pulled off an impressive facility of its own in 1967, complete with a 775-seat playhouse; two rehearsal studios; on-site shops for scenery, costume, and properties; and seventeen salaried actors in residence. Though the Theatre Atlanta troupe had to share an arts complex with the Southern Ballet of Atlanta and the Atlanta Symphony Chamber series, this was still impressive. By 1969 Milwaukee's civic leaders too had gotten into the performing arts center game, constructing the Todd Wehr Theatre for the Milwaukee Repertory. Even amidst the economic chaos of the 1970s, American performing arts centers kept on coming, for example in Washington, D.C., Denver, and Boston.[34]

Any of these facilities built after 1975 generally came with craft work-rooms and salaried craft positions built into the enterprise. When Portland, Oregon, got its center at the turn of the 1980s, for example, it included a space and budget for thirty-two salaried craftspeople with job titles such as scenic artist, shop foreman, carpenter, cutter/draper, costumer, wigs/hair, properties master, properties artisan, electrician, and stage grip.[35] Even in sprawling, suburban Orange County, California, civic leaders felt compelled to keep up with the Margo Joneses by opening a performing arts center with a scene shop, rehearsal rooms, and other support facilities in 1986. Orange County's center was unusual for having been built entirely with private funds, but other than that it matched the larger pattern.

Transfers and Tours

Back in the honeymoon phase of the regional movement, before most of these performing arts centers had broken ground, artistic directors spoke of liberating actors, designers, and audiences from the crass, commercial clutches of Broadway. In an interview for "Backstage in the Beer City," Milwaukee's artistic director celebrated his troupe's raison d'être in 1968: "Audiences must have at least one theatre in which they can go to see the great works of the past . . . unless cities like Milwaukee do this, the only other alternative is the jungle of Broadway—the 'show biz'—which has nothing to do with the art of the theatre, but is a way of making money."[36] This artistic director along with Zelda Fichandler, Stuart Vaughan, and many others aspired to more than just an alternative theater; they sought a superior theater.

This is why so many of them began cut off from Broadway, building shows without so much as a stitch or swatch imported from New York's historic craft businesses. The fledgling experiments of Margo Jones in Dallas, the hardscrabble plays performed under a sycamore in Houston, and even the fully fledged, celebrated *Hamlet* in Minneapolis—all were built locally. If a New York scenic carpenter or costume cutter was lucky enough to score a salaried job at a regional facility, he or she could certainly relocate. Most of the time, however, regional jobs had almost nothing to do with those who stayed put in New York.

When hit shows began to be transferred from regional theaters to Broadway, this dynamic quickly changed. *The Great White Hope*, a hit play of the Arena Stage's 1967 season, was the first notable piece to turn Broadway's show-originating hegemony on its head. In this particular case the creativity of the hinterlands circled back to employ New Yorkers. The leading player James Earl Jones so electrified audiences at the Arena Stage that New York producer Herman Levin optioned the property for a Broadway run in 1968. When the transfer production arrived for an October opening at the Alvin Theater, New York's unionized scenic carpenters, costume craftspeople, and lighting riggers secured two months of work, crafting new components to appear onstage within their jurisdiction. Even the drapery firm Dazian's got work from the gig, hanging drops and curtains behind the Alvin's proscenium in ways not needed for the Arena's original theater-in-the-round staging.

When *The Great White Hope* proved to be as much of a knockout on Broadway as it had been inside the beltway, other producers followed Levin's lead. A different but equally enthusiastic group of New York producers pounced on the Arena Stage's next hit in 1973, quickly transferring the musical *Raisin* to the 46th Street Theatre on Broadway. In doing so they put several local craft firms to work, just as Levin had. Other producers transferred plays from Houston and New Haven's resident theaters within the same decade. The dynamic between Broadway and the regionals was transformed as "a long line of plays and musicals" flowed into rather than out of New York.[37]

Something akin to an identity crisis arose for regional leaders when Broadway producers began to option their hit shows. The payments for these hits could relieve the budget stresses of regional companies, but they also threatened to undercut their experimental, non-Broadway missions. Once artistic directors began to choose plays or musicals based on their suitability for a Broadway transfer, they risked straying from their core mission. Even if a regional artistic director insisted that her or his new hit show was first and foremost a work of art, a Broadway producer could snatch it up, package it, and market it in a way that was more overtly commercial.

Another source of identity crisis for the regional stage was the Broadway national tour, which was alive and kicking during the 1960s and 1970s through musicals such as *Hello, Dolly, Mame,* and *Applause.* When the producers of these road shows scoped out venues nationally, newly constructed and comfortable performing arts centers jumped to the top of their lists. Why would the managers or artistic directors of performing arts centers book such tours if the whole purpose of their facilities was to liberate theatergoers from Broadway dreck? In theory, those making such decisions, especially artistic directors, were expected to steer clear of tours, providing their audiences with classical plays or aggressively experimental new shows. In practice, the tour managers came knocking and many performing arts centers answered in the affirmative due to bottom-line concerns.

Although the mandate for many regional theaters was to reinvigorate classics and produce bold new plays, it is not clear whether audiences were buying it by the end of the 1960s. In many cities theatergoers dutifully sat through several seasons of Shaw, Moliere, Shakespeare, and an original play or two but then began to fidget in their seats, hoping for something more. Andre Gregory, whose experimental choices as the first artistic director of the Seattle Rep had gotten him sacked, called out these institutions for their blandness in a notorious quote from the 1965 *Tulane Drama Review*. When Gregory suggested that he was "scared that the regional theatre, by the time it is mature, will have bored the shit out of millions of people all over the country," he spoke for many regional theatergoers who yearned for scripts that were less embalmed.[38] Broadway churned out an entire crop of new plays and musicals every year, so why not book the occasional tour to spice things up?

For one thing, when the managers of performing arts centers booked Broadway tours, fewer performance days remained available to their resident companies. These hard decisions left many artistic directors with two options. They could swallow their pride and share their hallowed halls with the national tour of, say, *Mame* or they could rage against the machine and risk being told by their boards of directors not to let the door hit them on the way out. This was a fate suffered by several artistic directors, from Stuart Vaughan in Seattle to Edward Magnum in Milwaukee.[39]

Another potential source of tension for regional theaters was the subscription system, in which audiences paid for an entire season's worth of shows at once. When this system worked, audiences enjoyed exciting, radical new plays or handsome, exquisitely performed classics at reasonable prices. Much of the work presented on regional stages was in fact impressive and successful, and it is important to honor this fact. The subscription system became a problem, however, when shows failed.

On Broadway if a show was truly abominable, producers at least had the decency to put it out of its misery. Subscriptions audiences for regional theaters were not so lucky. For all shows, even the god-awful ones, there were hundreds of subscribers who had already paid to see them. They could either waste their money and stay home or they could attend, knowing full well that the leads had zero chemistry, that the play made no sense, or that the production design was hideous. Perhaps all three nightmares came true in one show. In this way the masochism of the "show must go on" maxim, usually reserved for leads with laryngitis or dancers with muscle strains, could apply as well to audiences who endured performances that by most estimations should not, in fact, have gone on at all. Most shows that misfired under the subscription model were also financially painful, because they had to finish their run at a substantial weekly loss in front of a thin audience just to give a fair shake to subscribers who wanted to see it.

Despite all of these dilemmas, both existential and financial, most regional theater troupes found their sea legs in the 1960s. Neither transfer productions nor national tours took them too far off course, and the truth of the matter was that performing arts centers presented more locally built productions than touring shows, at least prior to 1990. Given their success in stealing talented performers, directors, choreographers, and designers away from New York, regional leaders probably inspired more fear among Broadway's producers than they realized. Once regional theaters gained union recognition and professional status, as most did during the mid-1960s, they employed actors, musicians, and craftspeople on similar terms as New York producers did. While none would ever out-Broadway Broadway, these organizations did pay Equity's weekly minimums for actors as well as the hourly rates required by the American Federation of Musicians. They lured countless theater artists, craftspeople, musicians, and performers out of New York City during the 1960s and 1970s, and their legacy in the grand sweep of American theater history is something to be celebrated, especially in terms of craft work.

Theater Craft Outside of New York City

Before the rise of regional theaters, theater-related businesses stuck close to New York because this was their natural, economic habitat. After theater craft was more evenly distributed, into a multitude of civic centers and theatrical basement workrooms, specialized supply shops for theatrical products also began to spread nationally. One publication more than any other captures the changing geography of the market for specialty theater goods and supplies. It was known simply as *Simon's Directory*. First published in 1955, *Simon's* was a straightforward, national yellow pages for theatrical producing. The brainchild of New Yorker Bernard Simon, the volume listed names, addresses, and telephone numbers for every theater supplier or craftsperson he could identify, from nearly every state in the union. If you were touring through Iowa and your scatterbrained stage manager misplaced crucial props, *Simon's* had you covered. If you were gearing up to open a regional show in North Carolina, suffered a short, and needed replacement lighting equipment, Bernard Simon had your back.

Updated editions appeared in 1963, 1966, 1970, and 1975, suggesting a pattern of explosive growth in theater expertise and businesses across the United States.[40] Certainly some of these companies existed prior to *Simon's* inaugural issue, and not all of these firms were launched after World War II. But the limited history of regional theaters prior to 1945 and the fact that Simon saw fit to release several updated editions indicate that non–New York theater was indeed a growth industry. As new companies sprouted or at least announced themselves for the first time in places as far-flung as Portland and Miami, they gave regional producers more options.

In this new economic landscape, the issue for Broadway's craftspeople and companies was not that such shops existed, but rather that so few of them were unionized. This had not been a problem in earlier decades, when the target market for scenery, costumes, or crafted lighting trusses was midtown Manhattan. Businesses in Boston, New Haven, or even North Carolina could have crafted as many nonunion components as they wished without posing a threat. When the components arrived at a Broadway house, IATSE's stagehands or wardrobe mistresses, who had firm control over playhouses, could simply trash them.[41]

By the 1960s, however, components could appear on professional stages nationally, and Broadway's unions had difficulty maintaining their jurisdictions. United Scenic Artists records demonstrate that union members were well aware of this changing geography and took steps to address the issue. A USA business manager wrote to the membership as follows in 1970, referring to the metropolitan region of New York City: "[T]here exists a grave danger of finding ourselves losing this work to other Unions and confining ourselves to a jurisdiction within the Metropolitan area. Our failure would cause us to lose vast opportunities for jobs." The membership heeded this advice in 1970, voting to extend jurisdiction down to Florida so members would work in film, television commercials, and even Disneyworld. To capture additional work in film design, this East Coast union also branched out to upstate New York, Maine, and Connecticut.[42]

As the union cast its net wider, there were still jobs and contracts to be had back in New York City, but these were fewer in number and harder to get than in previous decades. The regional theater revolution was partly responsible for this. Also contributing to this crisis was the wave of non-union theatrical activity that washed over Manhattan beginning in the 1950s, known as "Off Broadway."

Off Broadway

On a cool and cloudy evening in April 1952, the "erudite," bow-tie-wearing critic Brooks Atkinson visited Greenwich Village's Circle in the Square Theatre for its production of Tennessee Williams's *Summer and Smoke*. Stating in his *New York Times* review that "nothing has happened in the theater for quite a long time as admirable as this production," Atkinson sparked unprecedented ticket sales at the humble theater. Only a few years after Atkinson jolted the downtown theater scene with the legitimacy and publicity of his review, several similar groups succeeded downtown. Since then the journey of Atkinson down to the Circle in the Square has become so legendary that more than one history of Off Broadway begins with his review.[43]

No single critic or group, of course, was entirely responsible for this trend. While the Circle in the Square was certainly a major player in the rise of Off Broadway, plenty of other groups labored to create a more vital New York theater in the 1950s. There were even some, such as the Washington Square Players and the Group Theatre, that had blazed trails many years earlier. These groups had already ironed out an "Off-Broadway" contract with Actors' Equity in 1949, giving performers the freedom to work in tiny, experimental theaters downtown so long as they received a "token salary" in shows that earned little to no money.[44] What made *Summer and Smoke* so different was that this little play actually did turn a profit, and a handsome one at that.

The means by which *Summer and Smoke* made it so far into the black were quite simple. The production was stripped down to the barest of components, reducing both the construction budget and weekly operating costs.

Circle in the Square's leaders, Jose Quintero and Theodore Mann, had spent their time and shoestring budget on acting rather than fancy costumes and on careful direction rather than scenery. They were neither inclined nor expected to hire an expert such as Edward Kook or to pay weekly rental fees for elaborate trusses. Instead the lead actress Geraldine Page took to the boards under the glare of basic lights wearing a simple costume and walking an "almost bare" stage. Audiences were prepared for this, and Mann and Quintero pitched the show's raw minimalism as part of its appeal. Even though they were offering a bare-bones production at bargain-basement prices, they still had rent to pay. After the Atkinson review, they therefore ditched the tattered bread baskets they had once passed among audiences and built a proper box office instead. They collected cash from a queue of New York City theatergoers extending down their block and enjoyed packed houses for the duration of their run.[45]

After the financial success of the Circle in the Square and other groups such as the Phoenix Theatre, Off Broadway moved ever so slightly in the direction of commercial theater. Though downtown shows were still a far cry from those in midtown, the leadership of Actors' Equity decided in 1970 that Off Broadway had moved far enough into the commercial realm to justify a new contract. As it had done for its members working on regional stages, this performers' union fought doggedly for higher pay, finally reaching a deal with Off-Broadway producers in 1974.[46]

Though Equity succeeded in adapting its jurisdiction to the changing terrain of the 1960s and 1970s, other unions such as USA and IATSE had no such luck. The reason for this was quite simple. From the days of *Summer and Smoke* to the days of the 1968 hit *Dames at Sea*, Off-Broadway producers consistently built their shows with found objects, thrift-store clothing, and makeshift scenery. USA and IATSE leaders were unable to establish professional jurisdiction over Off Broadway's scene shops, costume houses, and lighting firms because these did not exist.[47]

As Off Broadway matured and profited, some theater artists resented, resisted, and renounced its modest commercialism. These artists, most notably Julian Beck, Judith Molina, and Ellen Stuart, sought to remove themselves even further from all things commercial, bringing forth yet another category of New York theater: Off-Off Broadway. In order to avoid dealing with Broadway's unions altogether, Off-Off Broadway producers took the same tack their predecessors had taken in the 1950s, agreeing to limit the number of seats in their playing spaces. After negotiations, theater artists such as Beck, Molina, and Stuart agreed to cap the seats at their experimental affairs at exactly ninety-nine.[48] As long as they kept audiences this small, they were free to serve up bizarre, fascinating theater without any worries about craft unions. Often sponsored by foundations and municipal organizations, these artists were emancipated from the bind of ticket sales and weekly operating costs, and they could let their freak flags fly through a wave of exciting, invigorating shows in the 1960s and 1970s.

In the new spaces of Greenwich Village and a swath of West 42nd Street dubbed "Theater Row," all sorts of Off- and Off-Off Broadway groups generated artistically challenging and critically acclaimed pieces after 1952. They were not in the habit, however, of hiring Broadway's unionized costumers, carpenters, or stage riggers, at least during this early period of the 1960s and 1970s. Plays that might have generated months of craft work on Broadway were instead stripped down to their most vital components and performed elsewhere. As the non-Broadway theater scene thrived and blossomed, theater-related buildings, companies, and unions in midtown struggled with age and obsolescence, both real and perceived. To make matters worse, Broadway's craft unions were wracked with corruption scandals in the early 1960s, just when the burgeoning Off-Broadway trend began to cut seriously into their business.[49] Despite all this turmoil, unionized jobs in theater craft were still available in Manhattan during the 1960s, but a sizable chunk of them cropped up in an unlikely location. They appeared twenty blocks to the north of Times Square, in New York City's very own performing arts center.

Lincoln Center

When New York City got its own version of a performing arts center in the late 1950s, the new facility generated a bumper crop of construction and design work. Many Broadway craftspeople, such as Karinska and Kook, got the opportunity to work at the immense performing arts facility. The builders of Lincoln Center, however, did not intend to contract with an array of independent businesses for each new show, in the ad hoc style of Broadway. Instead they wanted a self-sufficient, full-service center for the development, construction, and performance of shows. Like most other American performing arts centers, Lincoln Center had a wide array of skilled workers on its payroll and an impressive diversity of craft and construction spaces.

Each of the center's tenants, including the Metropolitan Opera, the New York City Ballet, the City Opera, the New York Philharmonic, and the Juilliard School, therefore had the opportunity to build, rehearse, and develop their shows in-house. If a particular opera, ballet, symphony, or play called for something beyond the means of Lincoln Center, managers could certainly hire third-party contractors, but most of the construction work took place directly beneath, behind, or above the new, marble performance halls.

In this way Lincoln Center was meant not to supplement midtown's performing arts infrastructure but to supplant it. Those who had made the center possible, including Robert Moses, the Rockefeller brothers, and Mayor Robert F. Wagner, had envisioned the facility as an escape from the city rather than a part of it. Much like Rockefeller Center two decades prior, Lincoln Center was built at a remove from the hustle and bustle of the Manhattan grid. After beginning as a Lincoln Square urban renewal project meant to clear the "blighted" residences between West 62nd and 70th Streets, the super-block development matured into a state-of-the-art cultural complex with commitments from high-profile tenants by the turn of the 1960s.

Those responsible for Lincoln Center may have celebrated the creation of a "bright and safe oasis," but the isolated monumentality of the center had unintended consequences.[50] First and foremost, hundreds of poor, working-class, mainly African American and Puerto Rican families were displaced, and earnest efforts by Lincoln Center's leaders to rehouse them affordably fell short. Second, the pedestrians, workers, and residents not displaced were now faced with a blank, windowless, marble wall on all sides of the center, save one. Most significantly in regard to theater-related businesses, the managers of this mammoth institution kept its craft and construction spaces separated from the larger economy of midtown.

It is in this third aspect, as an isolated center of craft work, that Lincoln Center most mattered to Broadway. One could argue that in certain show-building trades, such as scenery and costumes, Lincoln Center did not eliminate jobs but created them. Someone had to craft the massive scenery of the Metropolitan Opera, the painted backdrops of the City Opera, and the highly specific, dance-friendly costumes of the New York City Ballet. Craftspeople such as Karinska and her team of assistants did get these unionized jobs. As a high-profile institution, Lincoln Center had been a union work space from its inception, and it did provide thousands of work opportunities to the stagehands of IATSE, the designers of USA, the performers of

Actors' Equity, and the musicians of American Federation of Musicians Local 802. For its first decade or so, Lincoln Center did share the west side of Manhattan with scores of fully functioning Broadway construction businesses, and countless craftspeople did indeed benefit from its largesse.

In the long run, however, Lincoln Center had a subtle and destructive impact on the Broadway show-building economy. This impact took longer to manifest and was less obvious than the positive impact of new jobs, but it was damaging and real. First, the massive, state-of-the-art work spaces were not available for use by freelance producers. They were literally and figuratively cut off from the larger show-building economy for reasons institutional, financial, and even architectural. At Avery Fisher Hall, for example, the New York Philharmonic paid just a third of the going rental fee for storage and administrative space, and yet no Broadway producer got a similar deal anywhere within Lincoln Center.[51] Much to the contrary, the center's management gave priority to its premiere tenants, even bumping freelance rental groups when the Philharmonic, Metropolitan, NYC Ballet, or NYC Opera needed to tinker with their schedules.[52] The hucksters, mavericks, and risk-takers of Broadway were not invited into this marble palace for the arts. Even if they got permission to use the center's massive painting or scenery rooms, it was unlikely that they could afford them.

Of all the expert producers of the Great White Way, only Robert Whitehead was brought into the fold. He and the director Elia Kazan were hired to create shows for Edward Kook's beautifully lit Vivian Beaumont Theatre starting in 1964. Even though they had the most elaborate stage and scenic construction spaces in town, they suffered through two critically unsuccessful seasons before being unceremoniously fired by Lincoln Center's board of directors in 1966. In the same year, the composer Richard Rodgers had a similar experience. He was invited to produce a series of musical revivals at the New York State Theater. With the full backing of the board, he produced only the most popular of Broadway's mid-century musicals in the gorgeous new facility, leaning heavily on the repertoire of shows he had written himself. Despite their obvious mainstream appeal, none of these familiar shows generated enough buzz to sell out the cavernous theater. Rodgers's program ran a deficit for four years before being canceled altogether in 1970.[53] Under the strict control of the board, plays and musicals at Lincoln Center were awkward creatures within the competitive theatrical landscape of New York City. Here was a behemoth arts institution with probably the most posh craft workrooms ever to have existed on the island of Manhattan, and yet these rooms were available to only a small subset of theater artists.

Twenty blocks to the south, Broadway producers went about their business as usual while Lincoln Center's managers struggled to fit plays and musicals into their repertoire. It would not be business as usual for long, however, because the gargantuan backdrops and scenery pieces of 66th Street and Broadway did much to change audiences' expectations. Middle- and upper-class theatergoers, having feasted their eyes on the scenery of the Metropolitan Opera, began to expect, demand, and consume similar spectacles on Broadway. Within this landscape, scene shops and backdrop painters suffered enormous pressure to adapt. Many left their historic work spaces on the far west side for facilities four times larger in the outer boroughs, in Westchester County, or in states such as New Jersey and Connecticut. Imperial Scenic Studios, the builder of *Oklahoma!*'s touring scenery, had nearly quadrupled its square footage way back in 1948 by moving from Manhattan's West 50s to the Jersey side of the George Washington Bridge. Several other scene shops, notably the Feller Scenic firm in the Bronx, followed suit in the 1960s. By 1980 not a single Broadway scene shop remained on the far west side, where all of them had been only forty years earlier. Lincoln Center's jaw-dropping production values, while not entirely responsible for this geographic shift, were certainly a contributing factor.

Broadway costumers had less to worry about, at least initially. Scenery could be made to roll, fly, flip, spin, tower, or rise onstage through mechanized and electronic devices, but there was only so much one could do with fabric and a dress form. The Met may have presented audiences with finer costumes and more expensive fabrics, but Broadway costumers in the 1960s continued to enjoy plentiful contracts and decent work spaces. Still, many endeavored to increase their stock of costumes or the size of their work spaces at precisely the time that Lincoln Center came to fruition.

Historic Brooks Costume did this in 1962 when it boosted its inventory to three hundred thousand rental pieces by merging with another powerhouse firm, Van Horn.[54] Although Van Horn had been based in Philadelphia, it also had run a New York facility, complete with clerks and seamstresses, which was folded into the Brooks operation at 16 West 61st Street.[55] Skilled costumers not working at this firm had other opportunities, of course, but fewer with each consolidation or shop closure. By the 1970s Manhattan costuming was dominated by a handful of larger shops, including Lincoln Center. To compete in the post–Lincoln Center economy, aspiring costumers were better off seeking work in existing shops than they were starting their own companies.

By the 1970s the massive stages, copious dressing rooms, and well-appointed workrooms of the Lincoln Center were consistently serving up costume designers and craftspeople more space than they would ever have on Broadway. Lincoln Center did not have an unlimited budget, but the costumes on 66th Street were consistently lavish. To compete and keep up, costumers such as Brooks and Van Horn sought out bigger facilities and continued to consolidate. By 1981 the Brooks–Van Horn firm had joined with historic Eaves Costume, and the consolidated megafirm left midtown altogether to set up shop in Long Island City. Much like their scenery-building counterparts, costume houses left the Broadway industrial district rapidly in the 1980s. As they left, buildings such as Karinska's "dilapidated" 44th Street loft stood empty, and the district's interwoven theater economy unraveled, one business at a time.

The gravitational pull of Lincoln Center caused similar problems in the midtown music economy. As an employer and a work space, Lincoln Center by all accounts was lovely. The institution had a vast music library, all the latest technology in photocopy reproduction, an administrative staff to work on rights and royalties, and a well-maintained stock of instruments and accessories. In addition each of Lincoln Center's halls came complete with comfortable spaces for rehearsal and performance. Down on Broadway, rehearsal rooms and orchestra pits were comparatively cramped. As old and crowded as these playing spaces may have been, however, their locations and functions were advantageous to many types of musicians.

At Carnegie Hall the musicians of the New York Philharmonic had worked near dozens of stores that sold violin strings, saxophone reeds, and sheet music. They were also located within a block of the Steinway building and its marvelous music rooms. At the old Metropolitan Opera on 39th Street, the musicians of the first half of the twentieth century had been surrounded by myriad job opportunities at dozens of Broadway and vaudeville theaters. Both up at Carnegie Hall and down at the old Metropolitan, all musicians who traveled to midtown for jobs found themselves surrounded by a vast musical support network. On 48th Street's "music row," between 6th and 7th Avenues, instrumental supply stores, music arrangers, music publishers, performance spaces, and rehearsal rooms completely dominated the block from the turn of the century to the 1960s. Up on 52nd Street jazz clubs predominated, serving up countless opportunities for musicians to perform, experiment, and enjoy the talents of their peers. Because the network of supply stores, studios, and clubs was so broad and so deep, midtown could sustain the income and the careers of hundreds of musicians per year. Midtown also provided a nurturing environment for a variety of musical styles at mid-century, from traditional symphonic harmonies to jazz improvisations and Broadway standards.

The music economy of mid-century New York City was intricately woven into the fabric of Times Square, especially at its northern edge. When major players departed for Lincoln Center, they took with them the supply and space requirements of their organizations. A New York Philharmonic oboe player was certainly capable of traveling the twenty blocks down to Manny's on West 48th Street to pick up a spare reed, but why would he or she do so when Avery Fisher Hall had a stock of reeds and a staff of assistants on hand? Jane Jacobs, one of the most influential urban thinkers of this post–World War II era, recognized early on that Lincoln Center posed a threat to the delicate midtown economy. She wrote about the Philharmonic, the New York City Ballet, and the Metropolitan Opera as "cultural chessmen" in 1966, explaining that these groups promoted the growth of small stores, cafés, and supply businesses nearby. As Jacobs saw it, these cultural chessmen left behind a vacuum when they were extracted from the fabric of the city and isolated within an institution.[56]

From the opening of Lincoln Center to the mid-1980s, the prophetic ideas of Jacobs would prove all too true. Building after building in the West 40s and West 50s lost music, craft, and theater-related shops, and the motley assortment of tenants taking their places had entirely different ideas of what midtown audiences wanted. They were the smut peddlers, murderers, "dancers," "masseuses," drug pushers, prostitutes, pimps, and madams of the new Times Square, and they boldly rewrote the history of the space in ways that no 1920s costume cutter or 1930s scenic carpenter could have imagined.

Chapter 6

"Every Day a Little Death"

Times Square After the Collapse of
a Theatrical Production Center

ON TUESDAY, APRIL 11, 1980, as cold, blustery winds swept through midtown Manhattan, dozens of stagehands raised curtains around 8:08 P.M. to begin a slew of Broadway shows. This delayed start time, well-known to theater insiders, gave a small cushion to latecomers who hustled from subways or rushed from cabs to take their plush velvet seats at long-running hits such as *Evita*, at the Broadway Theatre on 53rd Street, or *Bent*, starring Richard Gere on 42nd Street. Those with a taste for revivals may have been headed to *West Side Story* at the cavernous Minskoff Theatre on 46th or *Oklahoma!* at the historic Palace Theatre across Times Square. Any New Yorker, suburbanite, or tourist who preferred plays could have seen Mary Tyler Moore in *Whose Life Is It Anyway?* on West 45th Street or Mia Farrow and Anthony Perkins in *Romantic Comedy* on West 47th.[1]

When the curtains came down on these and other shows around 10:00 or 10:30 P.M., many of these theatergoers would have competed for cabs in order to leave the unpredictable streets of Times Square as quickly as possible. When they saw news reports the next day, those who hurried home would have been glad they did. That very Tuesday night on the same blocks where well-heeled audiences had queued up just hours before to see their favorite film and television stars on Broadway, midtown police made several grisly discoveries. In the trash cans of West 47th and West 48th Streets, they stumbled upon the dismembered corpse of one James Eng, who had been, until recently, the sixty-two-year-old proprietor of a Chinatown garment factory.

A few days later, as snow and sleet pelted the city, detectives announced that they had arrested a suspect for the ghastly murder, an upstanding gentleman named Roy Hogan, who earned his living as a performer in "sex shows." As if this were not tawdry enough, one of the New York Police Department's material witnesses in the case was a nineteen-year-old topless dancer named Mary Ortega. Beat reporters for the *New York Times* learned that Ortega was "a close friend" of Hogan and had been seeing Eng "socially for several months," suggesting some sort of love triangle gone horribly awry. As the case moved forward, Hogan faced second-degree murder charges for the beating, murder, and dismemberment of James Eng.[2]

That same week, in mid-April 1980, as the New York theater district suffered this murderous indignity, the Seattle Repertory was presenting "Broadway's *Pal Joey*" to its audiences at the Seattle Center. Thanks to a recent Mellon Grant of one hundred thousand dollars and generous private donations, both the facility and the show's production values were first rate. Parking was copious, there was a monorail to zip theatergoers to and from downtown, and the most recent headlines about the Seattle Center were mercifully devoid of dismembered corpses. It is not known if news of the James Eng murder reached the average Seattle theatergoer in 1980, but either from reading other *New York Times* articles or from seeing films such as *Midnight Cowboy* or *Taxi Driver*, people must have known that Times Square had gotten rough.[3]

As both the image and reality of crime in Times Square conspired to steer tourists away, dozens of regional theaters and performing arts centers, in Seattle and beyond, offered convenient, professional alternatives to Broadway. Why bother traveling from Seattle to New York to see the 1980 revival of Richard Rodgers's *Oklahoma!*, for example, when a fully professional production of this same composer's *Pal Joey* was available in one's own backyard? Even more to the point, why follow through with plans to visit New York City and see Mia Farrow and Anthony Perkins in a play on 47th Street after learning of a gruesome discovery on that very street?

Headlines about body parts in local garbage cans were certainly shocking enough to unnerve potential tourists in Seattle, and they may have rattled even the most steeled New Yorkers. The horrific incident was certainly problematic for anyone looking to help Broadway hold on to its audiences, but it was also highly significant because of the location of the arrest. The building where the NYPD finally cornered Roy Hogan, 135 West 45th Street, just so happened to be the former work space of the Stage Fabrics Corporation. This supplier of specialty fabrics was one of the many theater-related businesses operating in the Times Square district during the mid-twentieth century, according to both the 1960 Yellow Pages and the 1966 *Simon's Directory*. Like so many others, however, its trail goes cold by 1970. Ten years later its emptied-out work space had become a haven for a criminal on the lam, perfectly illustrating the strong correlation between the collapse of theater-related craft and the rise of Times Square–centered crime.

On the city block where Hogan was nabbed by the NYPD, West 45th Street between 6th Avenue and Broadway, there were plenty of other buildings that slid from craft to crime over the course of the 1970s and 1980s. By first digging into the early history of this block in great detail and then analyzing the larger trends of the whole Times Square district, this chapter will demonstrate that the correlation between waning craft and rising crime is a compelling explanation for profound urban transformation. Second, this chapter will track the well-intentioned but ultimately unsuccessful efforts made by New York City leaders to curb these changes, when none of them realized that the decline of Times Square was connected to a decades-long, national trend of dispersal in theater craft away from its home city.

Theater Craft on the 100 Block of West 45th

When it was first built up during the nineteenth century, the 100 block of West 45th Street sat just to the east of a crooked midtown intersection known back then as Longacre Square. Home to an undistinguished mix of stables and low-rent lodging houses, the block also harbored three active brothels, according to a 1901 investigation.[4] The horses and harlots of this humble swath of midtown would quickly yield, however, to the many middle-class hotels, theaters, and theater-related shops that flourished in conjunction with the founding and development of Times Square.

The transformation of this block started back in 1895, several years before the *New York Times* famously relocated its headquarters to 42nd

Street and symbolically stamped its name on the area. When Oscar Hammerstein opened his massive Olympia Theatre on the southeast corner of 45th Street and Broadway in November 1895, he broke free from the industry's former center of gravity at Herald Square. He also spent lavishly on his northern outpost for theater, jolting the intersection with a grand, gargantuan structure made up of no fewer than four playhouses and an elaborate roof garden to boot.

Hammerstein's Olympia gave the 100 block of West 45th a healthy dose of middle-class respectability and even a bit of upper-crust cachet. As opening-night guests he was able to land senators, congressmen, and a prominent lawyer named Elihu Root, soon to be President William McKinley's secretary of war. He may have undercut his efforts to christen his theater with prestige just a tad by selling ten thousand tickets to a six-thousand-seat venue, which caused a small riot by those not admitted, or by inviting his guests into a building slathered in wet paint, which caused many to leave with a more lasting impression of the theater than they had expected. However, overall he succeeded in establishing a highly respected venue at the intersection.[5]

Hammerstein's over-the-top spending on architecture, Louis XIV–style decor, and amenities may have earned him prestige, but they could not guarantee a profit. Only three years after opening his grand theatrical palace, he stumbled into bankruptcy and was forced to sell. Hammerstein gave up the Olympia in 1898, but its use as a theater most certainly did not end. From its dramatic debut in November 1895 to its final season as a playhouse in 1920, this theater attracted a steady stream of craftspeople, agents, performers, and finished stage components to its doors. This was long before hit shows had multiyear runs on Broadway, meaning that the Olympia was consistently flooded with new batches of people and supplies arriving to and for the construction of new shows roughly every two or three months. For its twenty-five-year run, this stage door would have been the destination for scads of craft workers,[6] collectively anchoring this swath of the city with theater-related activity.

Farther down the block, as the city's first subway neared completion at the turn of the century, other venues catering to the middle and upper classes quickly cropped up. In 1900 the Hotel St. James opened its rooms at 111 West 45th, while the Hotel Belmont set up shop just across the street three years later. The Hudson Theater arrived on West 45th in 1902, with audience entrance doors on 44th and the bulk of the theater sitting on the

south side of the block. Only one year after this, the producer Daniel Frohman finished his New Lyceum at 149 West 45th; it featured elaborate
columns in front and a seven-story tower for theatrical craft and administration in the rear.[7] By 1904, in addition to its own sites for middle-and
upper-class consumption, this slice of West 45th Street benefited from the
esteemed Hotel Astor, which had opened just across Times Square.

Dwarfing the New Lyceum, the St. James Hotel, and even Hammerstein's old Olympia, the Astor was a seven-million-dollar behemoth, complete with five hundred rooms and a palatial roof garden. It probably did
more than any other building to move the 100 block of West 45th Street
from its low-down, nineteenth-century past to its buttoned up, early
twentieth-century future. Even with the Astor's hulking, middle-class presence on the opposite side of Times Square, however, the case-study swath
of West 45th was never entirely free of streetwalkers. Prostitution dwindled
gradually as each new hotel or theater of the 1910s and 1920s required the
demolition of old row houses, tenements, or carriage houses standing in
their path. This left madams and molls with fewer safe havens. In other
New York City neighborhoods, the idea that hotels and theaters of this ilk
could flourish without entirely eradicating the ladies of the night from their
surroundings was laughable. Times Square, however, was a different beast.
Indeed the historian Elizabeth Blackmar identifies the space as the first in
the city to sustain high real estate values without first being wiped clean of
its rough-and-tumble past.[8]

Other than being an exception to this unwritten rule of real estate, the
theaters and hotels that showed up on the 100 block of West 45th after
1890 or so are no great surprise. This midtown block simply got its share
of the performance halls and hotels that were taking over the district. What
is quite surprising, however, and indispensable for understanding how this
block lost its luster, was how many theatrical craftspeople and administrators worked on the block or nearby. None of them was as well known or
visible as an arrested madam or an arresting performer, but they were
definitely present, with increasing frequency, throughout the 1910s and
1920s.

They worked directly above or behind theaters such as the Hudson and
the Lyceum on West 45th Street. In the case of the 1902 Hudson, the rear
of the theater had an oversized door for loading in backdrops and scenery,
which was still visible at the time this book went to press. When Ethel
Barrymore took the Hudson's stage in *Cousin Kate* in the fall of 1903 or

when the drama *Camille* opened the following spring, this stage door would have been swarming with stagehands busy loading in racks of costumes, lights and trusses, and the backdrops or three-dimensional scenery pieces needed to bring these shows to life. Audiences may have leisurely entered through the well-manicured facade on 44th Street, arriving at 8:00 P.M. for their evening entertainments, but the 45th Street side of the house was all business, all day, for the entire duration of each show's development, construction, and rehearsal period. Given that the Hudson hosted six different plays in 1904 and eight in 1905, the earliest years of this stage door would have been quite active indeed.

Across the street at the Lyceum, this craft and consumption layout repeated, with the audience entrance fronting on 45th and the more functional spaces sitting closer to 46th Street. Even with the craft portion of the building on 46th, the 100 block of 45th Street still got more out of this building than a handful of ticket takers, box office clerks, and the 8:00 P.M. throng. Above the structure's finely sculpted, columned facade, the producer Daniel Frohman had created a copious administrative space, where he and his staff could work, hold meetings, store documents, and write correspondence.[9]

Behind the stage of the Lyceum, Frohman's seven-story craft and construction tower ensured that this facility would be much more than just a palace of consumption. Inside the tower as many as fifty-five designers, seamstresses, beaders, and cutters toiled away on costumes, while other craftspeople worked within a "warren of spaces" for music rehearsals, scenery construction, and stage properties.[10] These workrooms, occupied during daytime hours with experts in sewing, painting, or administration, are excellent examples of how there was much more to this stretch of midtown than met the eye. Even the interiors of the theaters themselves, generally known after World War II as hallowed sanctuaries of performance and consumption, had a surprisingly diverse functionality during this era. In the first few decades of the twentieth century, the spatial boundaries dividing construction and consumption were less stark. This was certainly true at both the New Lyceum and the Hudson; at each the owner of the building and the producer of shows within it were one and the same. When Daniel Frohman or the Hudson's owner, Henry B. Harris, wanted to develop new products, they used their own theaters as much as possible, holding auditions, running rehearsals, and testing costumes and scenery under the lights in slack times when any prior shows were not using the spaces for performances.

Figure 19. Oversized stage door of the Hudson Theatre as it opens onto the south side of West 45th Street, east of Broadway. Photo by the author, 2010.

Indeed most theatrical producers flooded their theaters with a dizzying mishmash of activities in the early twentieth century, in ways that would give conniptions to even the most serene of twenty-first-century house managers. They allowed their music arrangers, lyricists, and comedic writers to plunk down pieces of wood on top of plush velvet seats to create makeshift desks in the "orchestra" sections, and they let carpenters hijack the main stages even if the sawdust might fly. In swirls of methodical madness, dancers, singers, and craftspeople often rubbed elbows, working in the same building at the same time. While a painter touched up scenery in the wings stage left and dancers drilled choreography center stage, a singing chorus might rehearse songs near an upright piano parked in the wings stage right. Above them electricians might climb ladders to rig lights onto the proscenium or the balcony boxes, even while dramatic leads ran their lines in the aisles.

A great analogy for the functionality of theaters in this era is the full-sized dinner party in a pint-sized city apartment. Anyone who has lived through this harrowing experience will immediately recognize the similarities. When hosting "dinner at eight" in such a space, one does not have the luxury of keeping food preparation spaces entirely separated from formal dining spaces. Instead every available counter and work space tends to be taken over by meal preparation. Food, cutting boards, mixing bowls, and kitchen appliances make pit stops in the most unlikely of places, atop desks and bookshelves, as hosts struggle within the limited space to bring the meal to fruition. Arrive too early, and all would appear to be mayhem and madness. Arrive on time, however, fashionably late at 8:15 or 8:30, and one would find the table set, the kitchen cleaned, appliances put away, and the food ready to serve.

Turn-of-the-century playhouses, such as the Hudson, the Lyceum, and the Olympia, benefited from this sort of dynamic and practical functionality. Producers such as Frohman, the Shuberts, and David Belasco developed their products in-house and then sold them within the very same building for as long as they were profitable. Once attendance for a play or musical flagged, each decided what was next, ordered the "strike" or disassembly of the old show, and used the facility to develop the next piece. Neither union rules nor the pressures of weekly operating expenses prevented these practices, as they would after World War II.

In these myriad ways, the first theaters to arrive on the 100 block of West 45th Street were far more than sites of theatrical consumption. Each brought tremendous amounts of theater-related craft, construction, and administration to the block, attracting dramatis personae of every conceivable blue-collar stripe. Joining them as regular daytime workers on the block were the bellhops, concierges, and middle-class guests of nearby hotels. By the mid-1920s the Hotels Knickerbocker and Jackson had joined the still-operational St. James and Belmont, for a total of four hotels on the block. In 1928 the Belmont was renovated and renamed the Hotel Peerless. Although city visitors and tourists were the most common inhabitants of these hotels, it is important to point out that this was also the era of the extended stay, when many hotels would offer reduced rates to actors or craftspeople in town to work on shows. These hotels therefore had a more intimate connection to those people than they would in later decades. These connections were also visible on the ground level of several hotels, which became the sites of small, theater-related shops.

In addition to craftspeople and hotel employees, theatrical agents became a natural part of the West 45th Street habitat during this era. By 1903 agents such as Alfred E. Aarons, L. E. Lawrence, and Edward E. Rice had opened offices just south of 45th and Broadway. In their work spaces at the 1512 Broadway building, they were well situated to wheel and deal for the actors, playwrights, or songwriters they represented. Their colleague Jules Murry shows up in the 1903 *Business Listings* at 1520 Broadway, just north of the same intersection. Given that dozens of other agents had offices right on Times Square, on West 42nd, and on West 44th, and that they all worked in an age of frequent face-to-face communication, it is reasonable to conclude that the dramatic agent was indeed a common sighting on the block.[11]

As theater became a major growth industry during the first thirty years of the twentieth century, other satellite businesses appeared. Lane Costume, Mendelsohn's Textile, specialized makeup supplier M. Ducore, and a generalized theatrical supplier named Philip Roman had all opened shops on the block by the end of the 1920s. Adding to this mix in 1924 was the Loew's State movie theater, which occupied the northwest corner of West 45th and Broadway. Granted, a movie house was certainly no site of craft work or show development, but the facility did reinforce the block's middle-class character through the constant presence of employees and patrons.

Even during the lean 1930s, when many midtown blocks suffered crime problems and even more businesses went belly up, the 100 block of West 45th was able to sustain a supplier of ballet toe shoes and three different costume shops. Among the costumers were designers Helene and George Pons, who opened a full-service shop, survived the Depression, and then went on to outfit prominent Broadway musicals, including *Kiss Me, Kate* and *My Fair Lady*.[12] More typical of the block and the larger city, however, were business closures and the occasional demolition. The grizzled Olympia, for example, after hosting film, vaudeville, and many other forms of entertainment for forty years, finally succumbed to the wrecking ball in 1935. In its place arose another movie house, first named the Criterion and later called the New York, which bolstered the block with middle-class movie-going until resuming live stage shows in 1989.[13]

By the 1940s West 45th Street's costumers and show suppliers were joined by entrepreneurs in music arranging and publishing operating out of the mid-rise buildings at 115 and 145 West 45th. At the 115 address, the entire second floor became the home to Tams-Witmark, a music publisher with one of the largest sheet music libraries in the entire nation. Measuring by the 1940s Yellow Pages, this block retained no fewer than fourteen theater-related shops similar to Tams-Witmark, including the surviving costume shops and ballet shoe supplier of the 1930s, four music publishers, one music arranger, one wig maker, two ticket sellers, one theatrical agent, and a seller of Stereophonic tape recorders.[14]

When woven together with the still-operational Hudson and Lyceum Theatres, these shops demonstrate a compelling thread of theatrical craft work and administration from one end of the block to the other. The mix of shops on the block did change from decade to decade, because these were trades characterized by frequent relocation and turnover.[15] The tasks performed in these shops also changed, because the mix of art and craft in show building was constantly in flux. But there is no denying that theater craft and administration had a strong and long-standing place on the block for over fifty years.

Like the two movie palaces on the western end of the block, there were of course plenty of other businesses here by the 1950s with no connection to theater making.[16] Yellow Pages and classified ads from this decade feature a luggage salesman, two jewelry stores, a handful of rare coin and stamp dealers, a kosher restaurant, a supper club, and a "Gypsy" restaurant. Though none of these establishments was a supplier of specialty goods for stagehands or electricians, they were relatively innocuous neighbors, doing nothing to hinder local craft work. As daytime businesses the luggage, jewelry, and coin shops also did their part to anchor the block with commercial activity many hours before audiences filled the sidewalks on their way to and from shows.

Most of the theatrical action on West 45th moved indoors at 8:00 P.M., but there was one television show on the street that actually moved onto the sidewalk, albeit briefly and only on occasion. It was called *The Tonight Show*, and it taped before a live studio audience in the Hudson Theater between 1954 and 1962. During these years the hosts Jack Paar and Steve Allen ran a popular segment called "Man-on-the-Street," utilizing the theater's loading door on the south side of West 45th. When producers opened this door (see Figure 19), *The Tonight Show*'s mischievous hosts could grill pedestrians with easy questions, in the hope that they would flounder under the glare of the lights and cameras. Much to the delight of the studio audiences and those watching at home, many did. Certainly if the street life and pedestrian mix behind that steel door had been troublesome, the show's producers would have steered clear.[17]

Individually any of the television crews, shops, theaters, or restaurants of West 45th Street was in a weak position to discourage or combat crime. Collectively, however, proprietors and employees could make their presence felt. George and Helene Pons, for example, could easily call the police from their costume shop if they witnessed criminal behavior during the day. In the late evenings, as theaters and movie audiences headed home, employees of late-night establishments such as supper clubs could keep their eyes on the street and casually police sidewalk behavior. In multistory buildings on the block, law-abiding tenants such as Tams-Witmark had a vested interest in keeping other floors clear of illegal uses, while landlords had their own incentives to maintain respectable buildings. The net impact of this multilayered business activity, both during the day and late into the night, was to preserve the overall safety, legality, and cleanliness of the street throughout the first half of the twentieth century.[18]

In terms of crime, it is true that three brothels plagued the block in 1901, and there is some evidence, albeit unsubstantiated, that organized gambling flourished at 117 West 45th beginning in 1907.[19] It is almost guaranteed that during the 1920s some of the watering holes and restaurants on the block served up illegal liquor, and prostitutes undoubtedly utilized some of the street's hotel rooms during the Depression. There is no evidence, however, that the crime problems of this block were ever anything more than average prior to the 1960s. It seems that there was not enough space, either physically or culturally, for criminal users to become dominant. Even the brashest of broads or most pronounced of pimps could not dominate a block that was otherwise filled with productive and active businesses. Culturally West 45th was already dominated by different breeds of hustlers, including the theatrical agent, the Broadway hoofer, the beader for hire, and the stage producer. These dynamics would change dramatically by the 1970s, but there is little evidence that in the mid-century era pimps, prostitutes, or drug pushers had a strong presence on West 45th Street.

These dynamics, of relatively safe sidewalks and law-abiding businesses, stemmed from more than just the businesses operating precisely on the 100 block of this midtown street. They were also reinforced by major businesses operating across the avenues in both directions. Brooks Costume, for example, just across 6th Avenue on West 44th Street, was a major player in Broadway costuming. Considering how the theater industry functioned in the 1940s and 1950s, Brooks employees would have definitely been frequent visitors to West 45th Street. Just as the Hotel Astor had factored into the equation from across Times Square in earlier decades, so did Brooks have its influence. West 45th was a direct route from most Broadway theaters to the celebrated costume firm, which routinely nabbed Broadway contracts. Because the bustling, multistory center of Broadway costuming pulled a steady stream of actors, designers, directors, and producers to and from its building on foot, it multiplied the stabilizing impact of law-abiding pedestrians on the block.

One of these pedestrians was Emma Z. Swan, featured earlier for her work on the musical *Oklahoma!* This Brooks seamstress was just the type of person one might find walking down the 100 block of West 45th at mid-century. Though there is little historical record of Ms. Swan beyond her work as a Brooks employee, she was, according to a friend, a "tall, elegant gal," and there is little chance that this stage professional would have tolerated drug pushers, pimps, or prostitutes near her workplace without calling the police. Emma commuted five days a week from Hoboken to her job at Brooks, where she worked closely with Broadway's top designers. There was a good chance she even did some shopping on behalf of her firm at the Stage Fabrics Corporation, when the loft space was actually filled with fabrics rather than murder suspects.[20] As an expert working on the fit and draping of costumes, Emma Swan can easily be pictured traversing West 45th to go fit actors during their rehearsals at various Broadway houses. When Brooks did the costumes for a Broadway show, seamstresses such as Swan could expect to make at least one or two trips to the theater in which the show was rehearsing.

This would have certainly been true in 1949 when Brooks became the costumer of choice for *Death of a Salesman*, fine-tuning its costumes at the Morosco Theatre on 45th Street between 7th and 8th Avenues. In the case of *Salesman*, which rehearsed on the same side street, the use of the 100 block of West 45th Street by Brooks employees was almost scripted. These employees were equally likely to traverse the block in 1951, when the firm costumed the musical *Guys and Dolls*. Their destination, the 46th Street Theater, was just one block north at the Morosco, and the sidewalks beneath the Stage Fabrics Corporation and Tams-Witmark were likely routes. When costuming these shows, there would have also been some instances when it made more sense for performers to come to Brooks. In these cases, when Broadway performers left rehearsals briefly to appear at Brooks for fittings, they too contributed to the theater-related character of the block.

Joan Roberts and Celeste Holm, the leading ladies of *Oklahoma!* in 1943, were two such performers. Both Roberts and Holm shared their impressions of Times Square's sidewalks in interviews.[21] They walked back and forth between Brooks Costume and the St. James Theatre on 44th Street for fittings on several occasions between January 15 and March 31, 1943, and told no tales of criminal activity or dangerous conditions. Although their particular route may have been the 100 block of West 44th rather than 45th, these women were only two out of the entire cast of fifty people. Surely a good number of these fifty, along with the costume designer Miles White and the show's producers, Helburn and Langner, would have walked the rather innocuous gauntlet of West 45th during *Oklahoma!*'s rehearsal period.

Another candidate for the casual enforcement of sidewalk safety on West 45th was Madame Barbara Karinska, a costumer in Times Square until 1963. Her West 44th Street loft was just around the corner, and as she explained in interviews, Karinska often walked the district to shop for fabrics from the 1930s through the early 1960s.[22] With the major suppliers of specialty dance fabrics not to the south, in the garment district, but to the north, on the 100 blocks of West 46th and West 47th, it is highly likely that the distinguished, elderly costumer treaded the block just as her colleagues did.[23]

There is little reason to doubt that until the early 1960s any of these highly skilled women of the theater industry would have had trouble walking alone across West 45th Street, especially during daytime hours. It was

probably more likely for them to bump into colleagues they knew personally than hostile strangers. As the 1960s progressed, however, the number of
theater-related businesses on the block plummeted, while crime and adult
entertainment flourished. After having held strong at more than ten
throughout the mid-century period, the total number of theater-related
shops on this block dropped to only five in 1966. By 1970 only three
remained, and by 1990 not one business of this sort remained on the block.
Within the low-rise buildings of West 45th Street, new tenants arrived to
take their place, and they were nothing like those whom Broadway's crafts-
women were accustomed to seeing. Some of these new tenants sold their
bodies by the hour, others presented brief peep shows for quarters, and still
others sold pornographic magazines. Beginning in the mid-1960s, they
filled buildings once populated by agents and costume rental clerks, bringing unprecedented levels of instability, uncertainty, and crime to the block.

Across the avenues, on both sides of West 45th, there were similar
changes that had considerable bearing on this little slice of midtown.
Brooks Costume, the hefty, theater-related anchor on the eastern side of
6th Avenue, had abandoned ship long before the storm, choosing a site
near Columbus Circle back in the 1950s to be closer to its customers in
television broadcasting. On the opposite side of the block, the distinguished
and storied Hotel Astor, just to the west of Times Square, was dismantled
by wrecking crews and razed flat in 1966. Neither business was replaced by
anything that could infuse West 45th Street with the same levels of theater-
related business activity or foot traffic.

When faced with these changes, many of the proprietors on West 45th
chose to relocate or retire. Rather than attempting to apprentice themselves
to the older shops on this street, younger craftspeople tended to find positions within the ever-expanding network of regional theaters outside of
New York City. As a case study of local theater craft, West 45th Street
therefore provides a road map as to how the era of theatrical supply goods
and specialty shops came to a close within the larger district. On this block,
and throughout Times Square, the shop owners who closed down in the
1960s were not replaced by any young turks in costuming or theatrical
supply. Considering the dwindling number of shows per year on Broadway
after 1960 and the fact that anyone who made a go of theater-related work
on West 45th had to share their block with the likes of the bank robber
Donald Wasp and the murder suspect Roy Hogan, this is hardly surprising.
Although the last of the theater-related proprietors on the block did work

cheek to jowl with prostitutes and peep shows for several years, the larger trend was for these craft shops to disappear altogether, and for a wild mix of criminal activities to flourish in the urban vacuum they left behind.

Crime on West 45th Street

An incident within the Tilmar building in the spring of 1968 perfectly illustrates how this block began to spin out of control after losing several layers of theater-related activity. The soaring, lofted Tilmar had been chock-full of craft shops and theatrical agencies well into the 1950s.[24] By 1968, however, it had no such tenants to speak of and was filled instead with a hodge-podge of transient jewelry, coin, and stamp dealers. On March 9, 1968, dwindling rent rolls became the least of the building's problems when a group of "bandits" shot a jewelry business owner on the eleventh floor, leaving him in critical condition. For five thousand dollars in cash, the robbers had tied up proprietor A. Gonzales and his employees at gunpoint, only to shoot Gonzales as some sort of "warning" on their way out the door. Although it is tempting to write off this violent robbery as an unfortunate anomaly, it was, sadly, part of a larger pattern.[25]

On a block with a history of newspaper coverage focused on theater and real estate, holdups, robberies, criminal hideouts, and even cold-blooded murders began to nab headlines with alarming frequency after 1960. As early as 1963 the clerk of a brand-new parking garage on the southwest corner of 45th Street and 6th Avenue was held up at gunpoint and relieved of the cash within his kiosk. Just across the street, on the northwest corner of the same intersection, gun-toting bandits plundered Daniel J. Lander's small jewelry store in 1965.[26]

The block's hotels, especially those offering single-room occupancy (SRO), were especially vulnerable to this rising tide of criminal activity. In the 1960s the old Belmont, despite a 1928 renovation and an assertive new "Hotel Peerless" moniker, had devolved into a low-rent dive. In June 1964 three of its more nefarious male guests along with their lady accomplice were arrested for having committed almost forty burglaries and assaults in just eighteen months. In the same hotel in 1967, the NYPD hunted down and arrested its lead suspect in the cold-blooded murder of a midtown rare-book dealer. By 1968, around the time that Gonzalez and his staff were tied up at the Tilmar building, the Peerless had become one of the more foolish hiding places on the block, given the slew of recent arrests within the building. This did not stop Donald Wasp from renting a cheap room in the building and getting arrested there in April 1968 on the charge of robbing a bank in lower Manhattan.[27]

By the turn of the 1970s, this upsurge in crime had spread to the block's theaters, sidewalks, and saloons, and its low-down reality was rapidly conforming to the harsh image of Times Square suggested by films such as *Midnight Cowboy* and *Taxi Driver*. When the producer Michael McAloney rented the Lyceum Theater for his 1970 play *Borstal Boy*, he must have known there was some risk that his actors and audiences would get mugged or assaulted, but he probably assumed that such incidents would be few and far between. Indeed, IATSE stagehands completed the "take in" of the scenery, and performers skirted past the seedy Peerless en route to rehearsals in March, all without incident. As the play continued into the hot weeks of July, however, the changing character of West 45th Street caught up with its crew. In a single three-week period, six people who worked on the production were mugged on that street when trying to return home after an 8:00 P.M. performance, while a seventh individual was jumped near his home on the Upper West Side. With thirty actors and about ten crew members traveling to the Lyceum eight times a week, the occasional mugging was to be expected. Seven incidents within three weeks, however, was a true aberration, earning both the theater and the production some unwanted publicity.[28]

One year later the increasing lawlessness of the block actually caused the sidewalks to run with blood. On a cold December evening in 1971, teenagers outside of a bar began fighting, and the situation escalated so badly that an eighteen-year-old boy from New Jersey was shot and killed. He died right on the West 45th Street sidewalk just a few yards from the old Hudson Theater stage door where Jack Paar and Steve Allen had once conducted their delightful "Man-on-the-Street" interviews.

Only steps from where this youth from New Jersey was shot, another man was gunned down in 1973, this time inside a dingy saloon called the Broadway Pub. When detectives arrested the assassin, they were able to link him to the Mafia.[29] This and other events generated considerable media coverage, making it increasingly difficult for building owners on the block to keep law-abiding tenants of any kind, let alone theater-related businesses. New York City's newspapers had given the block a reasonable amount of attention prior to 1960, but most headlines dealt with theatrical

matters and real estate. After 1960 papers such as the *New York Times* began
to mention "West 45th Street" as a site of robberies and killings in a way that
was entirely new. Granted, the style and content of newspapers was changing
in the 1960s, tending toward the sensational, but this does not negate the fact
that horrific incidents were actually taking place on the block.[30]

As it turned out, shootings and holdups and robberies were only the tip
of the iceberg. Just as landlords were becoming desperate to secure tenants, a
perfect storm of cultural change, Supreme Court rulings, and organized-
crime initiatives gave adult entertainment a major leg up on the block as well.
Though "the deuce," a notorious stretch of 42nd Street between 7th and 8th
Avenues, got more of these racy establishments than any other block, the 100
block of West 45th certainly got its fair share of smut. On the northwest
corner of 45th and 6th, for example, the M & M Bookstore replaced Daniel
J. Lander's jewelry shop in the mid-1960s. An actual bookstore or another
jewelry store would have been fine, but the M & M's proprietors had other
jewels in mind. They filled their racks and shelves with a provocative mix of
print pornography, on sale for tired businessmen, tourists, and local miscre-
ants alike. At some point around 1970, the M & M at 101 West 45th added
to this mix by debuting the very latest in libidinous consumption: two porn-
film vending machines. For a mere quarter, patrons could view two minutes
of any pornographic film that tickled their fancy.

City leaders were nowhere near as amused as M & M's customers. In
July 1971 Mayor John Lindsay joined forces with the district attorney and
the NYPD to organize raids on this shop and eight others like it in the
Times Square area. "Sweating policemen" rolled the heavy vending
machines out of the M & M shop in the August heat, while their colleagues
arrested the store's employees on obscenity charges. One year later this
same law-and-order coalition succeeded in declaring the "sleazy" Peerless
Hotel a "public nuisance," closing it down and even sealing its entrance
with bricks. By the end of 1972 the powers-that-be who organized these
raids and closures might have thought that they had nipped their city's
porn problems in the bud.[31]

They would have been wrong. The pornographic parade that began in
the late 1960s was just hitting its stride in the early 1970s, and dozens of
other adult bookstores, massage parlors, hot-sheet hotels, topless bars, peep
shows, and criminal hideouts quickly followed in the footsteps of the Peerless and the M & M. They were especially likely to appear in the small,
underutilized buildings left behind after the great collapse of Broadway's

production infrastructure. With relentless efficiency and alluring profitability, they sprouted like Hydra's heads throughout the theater district. Jane Jacobs's famous "street ballet" quickly became a bump and grind. After the 1972 city crackdown, the Peerless Hotel did disappear from West 45th Street, but prostitution most certainly did not. There were simply too many other SRO places ripe for the picking on the block. Indeed within months of the Peerless's closure, the run-down Knickerbocker Hotel immediately next door had become overrun with hookers, pimps, "johns," and purveyors of the "rub and tug." By January 1973 the Mayor's Office had singled out the Knickerbocker as a place "frequently used by prostitutes," and those charged with eradicating vice from Times Square undoubtedly fretted over the question of how, exactly, such a herculean feat was to be accomplished.[32]

Pornographic bookstores such as the M & M were an even bigger burr in the saddle of city leaders than SRO hotels, because the city could force only temporary closures while bookstore proprietors worked through their arrests and paid their fines. Once these men had successfully navigated the city's legal system, their profitable, smutty magazines could once again exit their stores in discreet brown paper bags. Despite several closures, the M & M bookstore was not fully dislodged from the northwest corner of 45th and 6th Avenue until 1988, when a massive office tower began to take shape on the site, displacing all small buildings in its path.

What of the theater-related shops so effective in anchoring the 100 block of West 45th Street with legitimate business activity and law-abiding pedestrians for so many decades? Few stayed until the bitter end, but those that did coexisted with adult shops for a period of several years. Despite the undeniable presence of peep shows, topless bars, and hot-sheet hotels in the 1970s, the block was still the site of three costume shops, several Broadway rehearsals, and, most surprisingly, Fanny Violino's hat shop. In the eye of the storm, in the midst of the squalor of Times Square in 1970, there sat Fanny Violino, making of all things, hats.[33] Seemingly unaware of the crushing local, regional, and even national forces dictating that shops such as this no longer had a place on West 45th Street, Violino and her two compatriots, the proprietors of the Chenko[34] and Universal Costume companies, simply soldiered on. Eventually, though, by 1990, not a single theater-related business of any sort remained on the block.

Figure 20 depicts these dramatic changes, using Sanborn insurance maps as a baseline. In 1966 the only traces of adult or criminal uses were

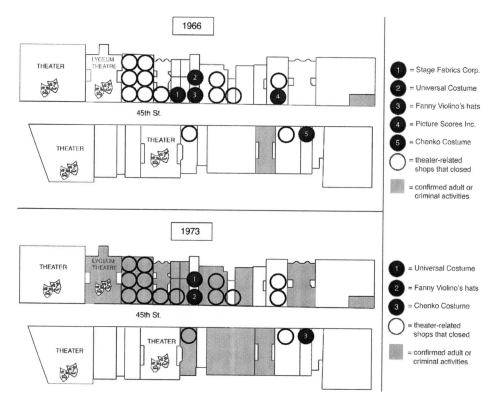

Figure 20. Maps of West 45th Street between Broadway and 6th Avenue showing
the evolution of the block from 1966 to 1973. These two maps clearly show the
decline of theater-related businesses along with the proliferation of crime and adult
entertainment. Building shapes are based on Sanborn fire insurance maps. Illustrated
by Manuel Barreiro.

the aforementioned Hotel Peerless and the pornographic bookshop on the
corner of 6th Avenue, both marked in gray. Though there are a considerable number of hollow circles, signifying prior theater-related shops that
had disappeared, and a few numbered locations signifying the remaining
shops of 1966, the urban mix of the block appears to have been sound. As
this same methodology is applied for 1973, however, many more of the few
remaining theater-related businesses were closed. Even more striking are
the number of buildings marked in gray, denoting some type of trouble
with crime or adult entertainment. This 1973 map clearly shows that the

slow creep of crime and adult shops on the block was intimately related to the demise of craft businesses.[35]

"Block-Matching" the Slide from Craft to Crime

As a case study, the 100 block of West 45th Street illustrates in no uncertain terms that there was a direct correlation between the dwindling craft activities of the stage and the surging criminal and adult activities of the "new Times Square" in the 1970s. On this particular block there were at least five buildings that lost craft tenants and then suffered criminal incidents soon thereafter. This chapter's theory of craft displacement and neighborhood transition, however, does not need a stockpile of buildings with a similar one-to-one correlation in order to be compelling. It is entirely reasonable to track these changes on the block level, just as it makes sense to look at the same trends within the larger district. Through a process that this author will refer to as "block-matching," historians can track a similar slide from craft to crime on the 200 block of West 49th Street and also on the 100 and 200 blocks of West 42nd Street.

West 49th Street just east of Broadway was similar to West 45th in many respects and is an excellent candidate for block-matching. In 1902 this block became home to St. Malachy's Church, which was quickly dubbed the "actors' chapel" after becoming the house of worship for performers such as George M. Cohan and Rudolph Valentino. Joining St. Malachy's on the 200 block of West 49th were the Ambassador and 49th Street Theatres in 1921, the Forrest Theatre in 1925, and several small hotels in the late 1920s. With the 1925 version of Madison Square Garden rising just across 8th Avenue to the west and the music-filled Brill Building appearing on the northeastern corner in 1931, this block was positively inundated with entertainment-related activity, even before counting theater-related shops.

These shops appeared on the block as early as the 1920s, when Ringle rehearsal studios, Textos costumes, and Francesca costumes all opened for business. The 1929 *Business Listings* also reveal Morris Orange's costume rental shop just across Broadway, one ticket seller at 8th and 49th, and two more ticket sellers across 49th Street at 7th Avenue. Even during the troubled 1930s, when many shops disappeared, the block held on to its theatricality through the Federal Theatre Project. This project of the WPA not only produced three plays at the Forrest Theatre but also booked Ringle studios for rehearsals, according to the FTP business records on file in the Library of Congress.[36]

Though this swath of urban space lost the Forrest Theatre to demolition in 1940, it did gain three new costumers and a shoemaker by 1950. These included Follies Costume, Vilical, and Max Vilner costumes, all at 254 West 49th, and La Mendola shoes, just across 8th Avenue, under the business listing of "theatrical footwear." Given that most of these shops were highly mobile and short-lived, it is not surprising that Follies Costume was the only craft firm left on the block by 1960. What is surprising, however, is that no new shops appeared to take their place. The closest that any shop got to this block after 1960 was just around the corner. Ingerid's Hair Design did have a brief run at 1595 Broadway, but this was closer to 48th than 49th.

Shops disappeared, but most of the block's small, walk-up buildings did not, at least not initially. They sat underutilized and ripe for the plucking, like so many others in the district. Just as they did on West 45th Street, pimps, prostitutes, and proprietors of adult bookstores and movie houses weaseled their way into these buildings during the 1960s, right under the noses of the New York City leaders charged with urban renewal and city development. Two hotels immediately next door to St. Malachy's Church, for example, the Byron Hotel at 249 West 49th and the Ramona at 253 West 49th, were "frequently used by prostitutes," according to a mayor's report from 1973. Just across 8th Avenue, two pornographic bookstores claimed the western edge of the block in the same year.[37]

At the eastern side of this block, the 49th Street Playhouse consistently showed "hard-core" films, while adult books and magazines were readily available at both 1605 and 1595 Broadway, just around the corner. A few feet farther east, at the intersection of 7th Avenue and 49th, Ellwest Stereo sold similar print pornography, while the Mini Cinema screened "hard-core pornographic films." Several of these sites, investigated by the city in 1973, were noted for having peep machines or for staging live sex shows. As a block-matching case study, the 200 block of West 49th Street is just as effective as West 45th Street in demonstrating a compelling correlation between dwindling theatrical craft work on the one hand and escalating sex work and crime on the other.

Another nearby stretch of the city, 42nd Street between 6th and 8th Avenues, provides a similar stockpile of evidence to support the idea that these spaces devolved directly from craft to crime. These two blocks famously became home to an unusually large number of theaters in the first half of the twentieth century, but they also hosted plenty of satellite businesses and related shops. In the city's 1903 *Business Listings*, the 100 and 200 blocks include the offices of the theatrical agents Felix Reich, Hurtig & Seamon, Joseph Brooks, and Klaw & Erlanger, of Theatrical Syndicate fame.[38] Joining them in theater-related work in 1922 was the 33 West 42nd Street building, which had become the work space for not one but twelve different singing teachers. By the end of the 1920s, Longacre Scenic Studios had opened an office at 220 West 42nd, while the theatrical supplier M. Bell was operating at the intersection of 42nd and Broadway. Clearly these blocks were thoroughly theatrical in ways that went far beyond performance halls.

If "theater-related businesses" include all shops working in direct support of the theater industry, as they have been defined for the purposes of this book, then ticket sellers can also be counted as part of this theater-related mix. They abounded on West 42nd between 6th and 8th Avenues, totaling twelve by the end of the 1920s.[39] Though ticket sales offices dwindled in the years following, these two midtown blocks continued to take on other theater-related tenants in their stead. In the 1940s, for example, the scenic painter Robert Bergman opened an office at 229 West 42nd where he could meet with producers or directors. So too Barney's Theatrical Shoe Co. and Ben & Sally Dance Footwear Inc. opened on the same block in the 1940s, while another shoemaker, Michael Savino, sold ballet toe shoes just to the west on the same street, at 342 West 42nd. In a scenario that may now sound familiar to readers, these shops began to vanish in the 1950s, and only one new shop cropped up in their place. It was the work space of the costumer Gertrude Cornell, a veritable flash in the pan at 140 West 42nd. After appearing in the 1950s listings, Gertrude's shop was already gone by 1960.

Throughout the 1960s, when this section of Times Square famously sank into a mire of prostitution, drugs, and peep shows, the only shop here even remotely related to Broadway was Jack Schaller's theatrical supplies, far to the west at 442 West 42nd. With ruthless efficiency, entrepreneurs of adult entertainment quickly snatched up the available walk-up buildings on these blocks in the 1960s, 1970s, and 1980s. In doing so, they created one of the most famous, well-studied stretches of adult entertainment and crime in the history of urban America.

Writing About Times Square

Stories about adult and criminal shenanigans in Times Square during this era are legion. It is widely known that this space mutated into an adult playground, a center of cultural mixing, and a crime problem during the 1970s and 1980s.[40] Less well known, however, and vitally important is the history of Times Square, and the larger theater district, as an American production center on the wane. By filling this gap in our understanding of the midtown economy, we can recognize that the space was so much more than just the sum of its naughty parts.

Identifying the layers of economic activity that disappeared from Times Square in this era will also help scholars more fully explain why crime and adult entertainment festered in this particular neighborhood more than in any other. Many talented academics have investigated this question, fleshing out the historical layers of the district in admirable detail. Mary C. Henderson's iconic *The City and the Theatre*, for example, explains these changes in terms of changing "sexual mores" and Supreme Court rulings. While these aspects of history were undoubtedly important in Times Square, I assert that they do not explain the more profound economic shifts of the district. Henderson writes of adult proprietors "renting empty stores," for example, without asking why those stores were empty in the first place.[41]

Her fine book, of course, was not designed to address the backstage businesses of Broadway, just as the insightful essays in William R. Taylor's *Inventing Times Square* were not explicitly devoted to this purpose. Taylor's edited volume, however, gets much closer to addressing the issue of midtown craft and construction firms. In his introduction Taylor suggests that many businesses of this type departed because of exorbitant rents after World War II.[42] This is of course true, but high midtown rents were only one piece of a much larger puzzle. Another author in this volume, the theater historian Brooks McNamara, specifically addresses the prominent role of "costume houses, scenery shops, and manufacturers of properties" in the theater district, but his analysis focuses intensely on the late 1930s. When McNamara looks at the transformations of Times Square after World War II, he acknowledges that "traditional entertainment-related businesses were leaving the neighborhood, and new—and often undesirable—businesses were swiftly taking their places."[43] Yet he offers no answer as to why or how this dramatic transition occurred.

The most compelling answers to these questions thus far have come from the sociologist Samuel R. Delany and the historians Alexander Reichl and Lynne Sagalyn. Delany released the fascinating *Times Square Red, Times Square Blue* in 1999 after having interviewed and interacted with the men of Times Square's prurient subculture. Diving headlong into the realms of pornography and homosexual prostitution, Delany discovered a flawed yet humane Times Square, offering an important corrective to the critical, alarmist narratives of a space in crisis. While the urban space that Delany chronicled was aggressively sexual, it was hardly the cesspool of villainy and decay painted by Times Square's critics.

Even more critical of the myths that have circulated about Times Square was Alexander Reichl's *Reconstructing Times Square*, also published in 1999. Reichl not only argues that the critiques of post–World War II Times Square unfairly targeted men of color engaging in lawful leisure but also suggests that the efforts to "renew" the space in the 1970s and 1980s were designed explicitly to make the sidewalks safe for the white middle class. Reichl deftly shows how simplified and nostalgic portrayals of Times Square as a theatrical "Great White Way" helped planners to justify bold and aggressive steps of demolition and reconstruction, and how these steps came at the expense of racial, ethnic, and socioeconomic diversity.

Lynne Sagalyn's *Times Square Roulette*, a masterful history of the office towers shoehorned into Times Square during the 1970s and 1980s, strikes a similar tone about the misuse of history and nostalgia. Sagalyn documents the ways that city planners wielded history as a weapon when fighting for redevelopment, and she explains real estate and governmental efforts to reclaim the space after 1965 in impressive detail.

One of her most important contributions is her explanation of land assemblages, development plans, and their powerful impact on pornographic and adult Times Square. In Sagalyn's telling, many of Times Square's tiny, underperforming buildings became home to shops such as porno bookshops only after a development plan or land assemblage had cast their future into doubt. Sagalyn explains that many landlords took on temporary, highly profitable tenants such as peep show operators as a way to "milk" a building before its demise by wrecking ball. Because Times Square redevelopment sputtered and stalled in fits and starts from the 1960s to the early 1980s, this libidinous limbo phase dragged on far longer than any developer or renewal bureaucrat ever imagined. Sagalyn finishes her narrative by explaining how these fits and starts ended in 1982, when the

New York City Board of Estimate "up-zoned" most of the theater district between 6th and 8th Avenues. Between 1980 and 1990 developers succeeded in erecting nearly a dozen towers in and around Times Square, obliterating some of the last vestiges of midtown theater craft in the process.[44]

Sagalyn's book is similar to Reichl's in that it emphasizes developer duplicity. Both books argue, quite convincingly, that developers cloaked their redevelopment agenda with nostalgic pleas to restore the Times Square of yesteryear. What this book does differently is to look at practices of cloaking and disguising, but as they were utilized by theatrical producers and advertisers in decades prior to those studied by Reichl and Sagalyn. Many years before Mayor Ed Koch and the developer John Portman smothered Times Square with nostalgia-infused blueprints and massive schemes for malls and office towers, an earlier generation of New York power players told tall tales of their own about the day-to-day life of the theater district.

They were the producers, press agents, and boosters of Broadway, and they worked tirelessly throughout the twentieth century to convince audiences that commercial stage shows were not products of careful craft but rather delightful concoctions of talent, whipped up by artists on the fly. Actors and designers were equally complicit in this grand deception, because nine times out of ten, it served their interests. Rather than admitting the truth about the dull humdrum of nine-to-five labor and grueling rehearsals, many stage professionals have told white lies about stagecraft for generations, often in ways that bolstered the mystique of their work.[45] These show folks did their job far too well, however, because no one seems to have understood, in any decade, just how much backstage work was being done in the district. There is little evidence to suggest that theatergoers ever understood the vast amount of skilled labor that went into the shows they consumed.[46] Even more to the point, there is virtually no evidence to suggest that New York City's planners, mayors, or other political leaders ever understood or cared about these aspects of stage production.

If these individuals had truly understood or cared about such matters in the mid-twentieth century, when craft jobs were leaving New York City for the regional theaters in droves, they may have recognized that such an exodus would deprive the smallest and most low-profile of the district's buildings of stable, law-abiding tenants. Such recognition, however, would have mucked up many of their fantasies of urban renewal. If this exodus had been noticed at the time, city leaders of the 1970s and 1980s would have been forced to realize just how foolhardy their nostalgic visions of reclaimed theatrical greatness in Times Square really were. One cannot build a restored theater industry without the vital foundation stones of costume shops, scenic painters, and rehearsal spaces, but this is precisely what developers such as John Portman sought to do. It was as if they were bulldozing automobile factories to build automobile showrooms without giving thought to where or how their new cars would be assembled. If the Broadway product were a meal, the analogy would be that these developers obliterated kitchens and pantries to build ever more lavish dining rooms without giving thought to where the next meal, or show, would come from.

By emphasizing the kitchenlike work spaces that rapidly disappeared from Times Square after 1960, the section on government below will document a decline in economic diversity, an issue that has yet to be addressed in major academic studies of the space. The works of Taylor, Delany, Reichl, Sagalyn, and others are excellent on the motivations, agendas, and class biases of redevelopment, but they do not dwell on the question of why it was possible for developers and politicians to target this particular swath of the city in the first place. Within the impressive body of knowledge about Times Square, no book, chapter, or article fully accounts for what happened in this district's smallest buildings. It was within these structures, such as the Tilmar building at 135 West 45th, that economically diverse activities in craft and theater administration had flourished.

It was also within these structures that the collapse of craft firms became a direct catalyst for the weedlike growth of crime and adult entertainment during the 1960s and 1970s. Historians and sociologists have long wrestled with the causes of this troubling Times Square flora, identifying everything from pornography to real estate values as wellsprings of change, but none has taken a long, hard look at what happened inside the district's buildings before they went to seed. City leaders produced reams of reports on the challenges in Times Square as they were unfolding, and the scholars who have looked back on these years have dissected every conceivable sociological trend and layer of sidewalk use in a changing neighborhood. Yet none of these chroniclers, either at the time or after the fact, has written about the veritable throng of craft workers right under their noses.

For the academic studies of Times Square, this oversight has much to do with the nature of theater-related shops. They were small, mobile, and hard to recognize as major players in the midtown economy. For the government studies completed in the 1960s and 1970s, this oversight probably stemmed from the fact that planners and mayoral aides tended not to spend their time fretting about massive, decades-long shifts from a producer to a consumer economy. They were also not in the habit of seeking out profound trends of geographic dispersion or decentralization in stagecraft. They were not studying the New York of the 1960s and 1970s; they were living it.

The Lefkowitz Hearings

Some government leaders did study Broadway's business practices in detail during the 1960s, but not in a way that producers welcomed. They were the state investigators of the 1964 Lefkowitz hearings, and they exposed scandal after scandal on Broadway, each more sordid and embarrassing than the last. This was not the first time that New York City leaders took a keen interest in Broadway, but it was certainly one of the more damaging cases. When city leaders such as Robert Moses fought to remake midtown Manhattan for the automobile, undercutting Broadway's operations in unexpected ways, no one directly attacked the theater industry. Even when city elites barreled ahead with the Regional Plan of 1929, municipal parking garages, and decontrolled commercial rents, no one explicitly attacked Broadway.

This certainly changed in 1964, when New York state attorney general Louis J. Lefkowitz spearheaded an initiative to investigate Broadway corruption. Though the year had begun auspiciously, with Barbra Streisand selling out the Winter Garden in *Funny Girl* and Carol Channing playing to packed houses at the St. James in *Hello, Dolly*, it took a dark turn in May when the hearings began. Casting a pall over the season, the Lefkowitz hearings exposed wide-ranging corruption on Broadway in everything from ticket sales to scenery construction. As it turned out, a scandalously high number of the theatergoers flocking to hit shows such as *Funny Girl* and *Dolly* were buying their tickets from scalpers. Equally surprising, and perhaps even more damaging to the Broadway industry, were the Lefkowitz reports on stage construction and capitalization. State investigators accused several theater producers of demanding bribes before awarding scenery contracts, while others were condemned for bilking investors out of investments into shows that had never existed. In the most flagrant and audacious cases, producers publicly boasted that major stars had committed to doing their shows when the stars in question had not even heard of the projects.

It seems that the primary concern of these hearings was scalpers, who had of course been selling tickets to hit shows at inflated prices and for immense personal profits since the days of Edwin Booth. The difference between 1864 and 1964, however, was that by the latter year the practice had become big business, especially when Broadway's own ticket sales-people got involved. If a unionized ticket seller set aside top-notch tickets for a "digger," as many did in the early 1960s, this digger could scalp them at a hefty markup and then cut his ticket-selling partner in on the profits. Such skulduggery was nearly impossible to track at the industrywide level, and it was rampant by the time the Lefkowitz hearings convened. These shared, off-the-books profits, known in Broadway parlance as "ice," were so ubiquitous by 1964 that the Lefkowitz legislators estimated their total value at ten million dollars.[47] Even if only half that much money was circu-lating in the black market for tickets, this was still a serious problem for the beleaguered industry. None of these dollars could be rolled back into the Broadway feedback loop for continued research and development (that is, new shows), because they were falling into the hands of third-party speculators.

To combat the practice, state investigators suggested that Broadway crack down on its scalpers while also introducing stringent standards for its unionized ticket sellers. The League of New York Theaters took them up on both suggestions, temporarily curbing scalpers and "ice" profiteers, but they could not buck the trend for long. These characters were almost as tenacious as New York City's proverbial rats and roaches, and the craftiest among them found ways to circumvent the new rules within just a few years.

Also surfacing during the Lefkowitz hearings were sordid stories of kick-backs and corrupt capitalization among Broadway's producing and con-struction teams. Kickbacks and bribes became more problematic as "the pie" of available construction contracts shrank every year. Because the industry generated an ever-dwindling number of new shows, the stakes went up on each competitive bid for a new contract. This was especially true in the scenery trade. Apparently the stakes were high enough for David Steinberg, the proprietor of Imperial Scenic Studios, to succumb to bribery demands from the general manager of the 1963 musical *Tovarich*. Lefko-witz's state investigators accused a Mr. Monty Shaff of demanding (and

receiving) seventy-five hundred dollars from Steinberg in return for awarding the lucrative fifty-seven-thousand-dollar contract for scenery to Imperial Scenic. Also falling victim to these shakedowns was a highly respected
scenic proprietor named Fred Feller, who was extorted by Robert Alex
Baron to the tune of fifty dollars a week. Both Shaff and Baron were found
guilty of "commercial bribery," scandalizing both the scenery trade and the
industry as a whole. In response the League of New York Theaters imple-
mented a more transparent bid system, helping to regulate and monitor
the interactions between producers and the firms they hired to build
components.[48]

While significant, none of these transgressions in scalping or kickbacks
was as ruinous as the Lefkowitz findings on Broadway capitalization, which
the committee found especially troubling. Many a producer, of course, had
defrauded commercial theater investors in the past, or at least attempted to
do so. In 1949 Broadway angels had been subjected to one of the industry's
most egregious violations of investor confidence. Ned J. Warren and William B. Steur had promised the red-hot stars Lucille Ball and June Allyson
as their leads in a musical, and for this reason they had little trouble wran-
gling a total of thirty-nine thousand dollars from the bank accounts of
forty different Broadway angels. Two decades before Mel Brooks created
his classic film *The Producers*, these two gave his character Max Bialystock
a run for his money, as neither Ball nor Allyson had even heard of the
project. By the time this little detail was discovered, the two producers had
fled to San Francisco, where they were arrested on charges of grand larceny.
Similar stories of producer duplicity were legion in the early 1960s. This
type of fraud was precisely the reason that the Lefkowitz Committee went
after unscrupulous producers with a new set of regulations, which went
into effect in June 1964.[49]

Press coverage about bribes and scalpers had been bad for Broadway,
but the Lefkowitz rulings on theatrical investing proved positively crippling.
After June 1964 people interested in "angeling" Broadway shows had to
prove that their investments would not put them at risk financially, via
documentation about the investments as a percentage of their net worth.
Though written into law with the best of intentions, to prevent the producers of make-believe musicals from bilking New Yorkers, these cumbersome
new rules put an unfortunate damper on theatrical investing.

Leading Broadway producers complained vociferously in 1966, con-
tending that "financial geniuses of Wall Street . . . had stolen millions"

while "the two states where Wall Street securities are sold by the millions [New York and New Jersey] have practically forbidden the sale of theatrical interests."[50] Just when regional performing arts centers were launching capital campaigns across the nation, the strict new Lefkowitz rules gave even the most devoted angels reason to doubt the wisdom of investing in Broadway.

In historical terms, the Lefkowitz hearings brought city government into its most intimate relationship yet with the Broadway industry. By the time John V. Lindsay began to poke his rather well-shaped, patrician nose into Broadway's affairs, albeit with the best of intentions, the Lefkowitz Committee had already established a strong precedent of government regulation of the theater industry.

The Mayor of Broadway

When John V. Lindsay was elected mayor in 1966, he became the most enthusiastic Broadway booster to have ever won New York City's highest office. Jimmy Walker had shown considerable attention to Broadway's chorus girls, and Robert F. Wagner had attended more than a few Broadway opening nights, but Lindsay's interest was more than cursory. During his two terms in power, from 1966 to 1974, this mayor with matinee-idol looks was concerned with everything from ticket sales to the construction of new playhouses. In what was truly a City Hall first, Lindsay made a seven-minute appearance onstage at the struggling musical *Seesaw* in March 1973 to help boost the show's profile.[51]

His administration also promoted a unified half-price ticket system for Broadway, called TKTS, even going so far as to donate an old campaign trailer to serve as the first sales center.[52] In June 1973 this trailer showed up smack-dab in the middle of Times Square, close to the spot where discounted tickets are still on sale today. Despite all of these efforts, however, Broadway producers still faced a reduced number of new shows per year by the time Lindsay left office in 1973. The industry was struggling, and city efforts to shore it up were ultimately more sound and fury than substance.

How is it possible that such a supportive mayor was unable to halt Broadway's slow decline? For one thing, the planners and elites who worked with Lindsay to reinvigorate Broadway consistently overlooked the issue of show construction, doing little to underpin craft work spaces or theater-related businesses. In this way the failures of both governmental leaders and city planners in regard to Broadway were failures of conception rather than implementation. It was not that property owners, business proprietors, governmental leaders, and city planners made allowances for show building and failed to follow through. Rather these people never recognized its importance in the first place. No one in a position of prominence seemed to realize that cost-effective and artistically coherent show building on Broadway was as important to city tourism as "I Love New York" commercials and half-price tickets at TKTS.

Even if Robert Moses, John V. Lindsay, and subsequent mayors such as Abe Beame and Ed Koch had gained insight into the all-too-important process of making theater, it is unlikely that any one of these leaders could have done much to keep the businesses doing this work in midtown or to keep adult and criminal businesses out. This was particularly true for Lindsay, who got the keys to Gracie Mansion just as Times Square was becoming the scummy place that Travis Bickel in the film *Taxi Driver* hoped would be washed clean by a "real rain." Some have gone so far as to call New York during the Lindsay years the "ungovernable city." This is not a stretch, considering that the city as a whole and its quintessential public space at 42nd Street were both in dire straits at the time.[53]

Clearly even the most powerful of New York City's leaders were not solely responsible for the crime and smut of Times Square, any more than they could be blamed for the mass exodus of craft activities featured in Chapter 5. They did, however, do much to speed up these changes, and they had a hand in making them more complete. This is especially true for real estate developers such as Seymour Durst, who amassed real estate assemblages in Times Square with the goal of creating lucrative office towers. Equally influential were the governmental leaders who promoted tax deals and zoning allowances for developers and the planners who picked up where Robert Moses had left off, cooking up ways for midtown to be made more convenient for motorists.

Visions of massive office towers in Times Square had been dancing in the heads of New York City elites since the lofty days of the 1910s and 1920s. Back when the distinctive Candler Building reached twenty-four stories on 42nd Street in 1914 and when the Paramount Building capped off at thirty-three stories in 1926, the sky really did seem to be the limit in Times Square. These pinnacles of volume and height, however, were far more the exception than the rule in the district, at least until the early

1960s. In 1961 the city of New York famously amended its zoning laws to promote office towers throughout Manhattan, even in predominantly low-rise, walk-up districts such as Times Square.

Influenced by the designs of the Swiss architect Le Corbusier and by the "super-block" concept in vogue at the time, the 1961 ordinances made it possible for developers to build bulky and voluminous towers so long as they provided sufficient park or plaza space around them. Encouraging "tower-in-the-plaza" and " tower-in-the-park" designs on super-blocks and land assemblages, these laws enabled developers to break the four-or five-story plane that had dominated Times Square from the turn of the century. In the same year that he won his mayoral contest, John V. Lindsay gave an interview to *Realty* magazine demonstrating that he was not only aware of these trends but also a champion of them. He commented as follows in 1966: "The grid-block system, impressed upon New York by the demands of the earlier technology, is today wasteful, obsolete, and inade-quate. . . . If the depressed areas . . . are to be revitalized, an essential first step is to break up the grid-block system and create super-blocks which combine work-residence complexes."[54] In print Lindsay was on to some-thing, because viable midtown work spaces were indeed a pressing issue for theater craftspeople at the time. In practice, however, these types of work spaces did not materialize during his administration, at least not on a scale that could slow the departure of theater craft from New York City.

By endorsing newly zoned super-blocks as the preferred method of development and by promoting projects such as the Minskoff Tower, the Uris Theatre, Manhattan Plaza, and the Marriott Marquis Hotel, Lindsay and like-minded leaders embroiled government in the affairs of Times Square like never before. These entanglements accrued on top of the already expanded relationship created by the Lefkowitz hearings, which had brought government into the theatrical equation as both regulator and ref-eree. In terms of theatrical buildings and business practices, this new rela-tionship put a damper on the chaotic, ad hoc patterns of Broadway, which had lit up the Great White Way so brightly since the turn of the century. In their place, new patterns of heavily planned and regulated theater emerged in Times Square, with consequences that no one could anticipate.

Towers in Times Square

As early as the 1940s, midtown developers and city planners had enter-tained notions of demolishing the troubled, aging Astor Hotel to make room for a bold new office tower. Nothing came of this idea until the 1960s, when new zoning laws and a robust economy made the project both practical and attractive. By the time the Minskoff development team was ready to move ahead on plans for a tower on the site, city voters had chosen John V. Lindsay as their new mayor. A well-known champion of Broadway, Lindsay could hardly bring a jarring office tower and parking garage hybrid into Times Square without making concessions to the theater community. These concessions came in the form of a "Special Theater District," which stretched from 40th to 57th Streets and from 6th to 8th Avenues. It was announced in October 1967 after a Gracie Mansion meeting between the Minskoff team and the Lindsay administration. Conceived as a way to preserve theatrical uses in and around Times Square, this compromise also allowed developers to maximize the size and profitability of their towers.[55]

As applied at the intersection of 45th and Broadway, the Special Theater District allowed the Minskoff team to pile 20 percent more bulk onto their new 1515 Broadway building as long as they set aside space for "legitimate" theater in the tower. When "wreckers in red and yellow safety helmets" began to dismantle the Astor at the end of 1967, the theater community had guarantees that a state-of-the-art playhouse would be included within the new tower.[56] Though some wanted more, specifically the preservation of the grand, storied, beaux arts hotel, the historic preservation movement was too incipient to save the structure. The City Planning Commission staunchly supported demolition, and the Sam Minskoff & Sons development team had neatly dispatched the lovely old hotel and cleared the rubble by 1971. The engineered steel frame of 1515 Broadway quickly rose in its place.

When the Minskoff team cut the ribbon on their new tower in 1973, the 1,621-seat Minskoff Theatre stole most of the headlines. Designed with considerable input from city government and heavily regulated in everything from fire safety to bathroom capacity, the Minskoff Theatre arrived as a supposed savior or Broadway, at least according to the Lindsay administration and several reporters at the New York Times. In the grand scheme of commercial theater in Times Square, however, the Minskoff playhouse was not the real story. The major development here in regard to theater craft was the opening of the Minskoff rehearsal studios, a series of eight brand new, comfortable, copious, and centrally located studios totaling fourteen thousand square feet.[57]

From their opening in 1976 to their unexpected closure in 1989 when their rent suddenly tripled, these studio spaces were a major life raft for commercial theater in midtown. Whether the Minskoffs helped to create this rehearsal center begrudgingly or willingly was beside the point; it was by far the largest generator of local craft work, and those businesses that managed to stay open in Times Square past 1970 undoubtedly owed many contracts in costuming, shoe making, and design to these rehearsal studios. Major musicals such as *Evita* utilized these studios for everything from auditions to dance rehearsals in ways that were crucial for the successful creation of new stage shows. Even as such spaces were becoming scarce and were increasingly considered a "precious commodity" by Broadway insiders, they were not prized or even much considered by most midtown developers and property owners.[58]

Midtown theater owner Paul Vroom was precisely this type of property owner in 1968; he owned several theaters but did not seem to understand the vital role that rehearsal spaces played in his bottom line. When asked about the construction of the Minskoff and Uris Theatres, this owner of three playhouses was bullish about the prospects of these newcomers in Times Square. He was concerned, however, about the productions available for upcoming seasons, adding this caveat: "[W]hether we'll have enough good shows to fill them, only God knows."[59] Rather than recognizing rehearsal studios and craft shops as the vital venues that they were, generating new products for him in his own backyard, Vroom attributed new shows to some higher power. If the owners of General Motors and Ford showrooms had thrown up their hands in this way, asking the very heavens above what products they might be selling next, one would hope that a 1968 journalist would have the sense to put them on the phone with Detroit posthaste. On Broadway, however, for myriad reasons that have been outlined throughout this book, ignorance about one's supply chain was not only common but almost expected.

Those who sold Broadway products, within the brand new Minskoff and within dozens of older, dilapidated playhouses, did not take enough care to understand how these products were generated during the late 1960s. Many seemed willing to let the theater artists spread their pixie dust as they would, hoping that something substantive would materialize. While plenty of show ideas have sprung from inscrutable seeds of divine inspiration, the mundane reality of the finished Broadway show is far less glamorous. Every single show to have raised its curtain on Broadway was crafted through a long, sometimes painstaking process of rehearsal and construction within workshops and rehearsal studios. Even the most well-conceived show must be built to exist, and it must be built by craftspeople.

As this urban historian sees it, the provenance of good shows on Broadway had nothing to do with matters heavenly or profound and everything to do with composers spending careful hours in music rooms, with directors helping to craft performances in rehearsal studios, and with costume seamstresses showing up at these studios to take measurements and discuss aesthetics with production teams. Good shows have been inspired by everything under the sun, but none of them could be performed until they were built. When it came to the new towers of Times Square, which began to arrive in the late 1960s, only the Minskoff building made any allotment for this type of work.

Another Times Square tower, built around the same time as the Minskoff, allotted generous space for parking and a grandiose lobby but none for craft or rehearsals. This second tower proposed under the guidelines of the Special Theater District was a project of the Uris Corporation and would rise on the northern reaches of Times Square, at 50th Street. Hot on the heels of Sam Minskoff & Sons, the Uris Corporation had pitched its tower soon after learning of the city's new zoning allowances through the "builders' grapevine."[60] It was approved in 1967 and took shape with the cavernous Uris Theatre (now the Gershwin) at its base, along with a parking garage and a smaller theater in the basement level. Given that the basement space became home to the Off-Broadway Circle-in-the-Square company, which originated new plays, one could argue that Broadway show development did occur downstairs. But upstairs, when the building was finished in 1971, all spaces were devoted unequivocally to tickets, performances, parking, and the consumption of theater.

Although those behind this 50th Street tower had followed the trail blazed by the Minskoffs in the planning stages, the Uris Corporation's leaders beat the Minskoffs to the finish line by opening their theater a full five months earlier. With much anticipation theatergoers thronged to the opening night of Broadway's newest playhouse in November 1972 only to find that the theater had booked a spectacularly awful rock musical called *Via Galactica* as its first tenant. Critics and audiences panned the troubled show, and it closed after only one week. When the Minskoff Theatre opened in March 1973, its managers did much better with more traditional fare, serving up a revival of *Irene*, a little-known musical from the early 1920s. With Debbie Reynolds of *Singin' in the Rain* fame as its leading lady, *Irene* pulled off a respectable six-month run, despite the rather gaping nature of the super-sized theater.

Although both playhouses would go on to host a number of long-running hit musicals in the 1980s and 1990s, neither was particularly well reviewed as an auditorium when it opened. Writing in June 1973, the *New York Times* critic Walter Kerr took issue with the way the spaces were disconnected from the surrounding neighborhood, protesting that "they have entrances hidden in wind tunnels, they have lobbies reached by escalators, they are *indoor* houses."[61] Other critics found them too cavernous, too reliant on amplification, and lacking in theatrical intimacy. As consumption spaces, however, many found them a welcome relief from the cramped and dilapidated old playhouses that dominated Broadway for decades. Audiences were particularly grateful for the ample legroom, generous aisle spaces, and copious bathroom facilities they found once they were inside.

No matter how much legroom they may have, however, audiences will still squirm if the show they are sitting through is boring, nonsensical, or just plain awful. To protect against this, industry leaders such as director Harold Prince, actor Angela Lansbury, composer Stephen Sondheim, scenic designer Neil Mazzella, and civic activist Fred Papert did everything they could to keep live theater as lively as possible in the 1970s. Their struggle was assisted by innovative projects in housing and off-Broadway production, but even the successes at Manhattan Plaza and Theater Row were not enough to reverse many decades of decline in Manhattan-based theater craft.

Manhattan Plaza and Theater Row

If the Minskoff and Uris theater-in-a-tower projects were products of careful governmental intervention, the Manhattan Plaza project was more a happy accident. By far the most ambitious super-block project in Times Square, Manhattan Plaza was taken over by the city in the late 1970s only after it stalled as market-rate housing. There was much talk on the Great White Way that the two gargantuan towers at 43rd Street between 10th and 9th Avenues could be a major source of Times Square revitalization, but it was not until 1977 that anything came to fruition. Mayor Abe Beame not only orchestrated a city takeover of the towers but also guided a plan through the City Planning Commission in which 30 percent of the apartments would be set aside for low-income, elderly, and disabled tenants

while the remaining 70 percent would be saved exclusively for theater artists, musicians, performers, craftspeople, and other people working actively
in the performing arts. The plan worked even better than most had
expected. When the towers were ready for occupancy, their managers
famously nabbed playwright Tennessee Williams and actress Angela Lansbury as high-profile tenants and developed an impressive wait-list for people in performing arts jobs who yearned to live in the low-rent, centrally
located apartments.[62]

Though the "gaffers, electricians, wardrobe people, designers, casting
agents," musicians, singers, and actors who moved into the facility at the
end of the 1970s did have a small number of rehearsal rooms at their disposal, these were not big or numerous enough to give any significant boost
to Broadway show building.[63] They were wonderful for artists looking to
hone their crafts, but they were hardly the kind of spaces that could accommodate the entire cast of a big-budget Broadway musical. In order to truly
turn back the clock on the national dispersal of theater craft facilities to the
regional theaters, Manhattan Plaza would have needed to be twice as big,
with tremendous square footage for scenery, costumes, wigs, shoes, lighting, and rehearsals. Even if that had been the case, such a facility might
have been bypassed nonetheless. Theater craftspeople in 1978 and 1979
did gain a vitally important, visionary, overwhelmingly successful housing
project in which they could lock down affordable leases, but they still had
fewer and fewer job opportunities in a city of dwindling theater-related
firms.

Directly across the street from Manhattan Plaza, on the south side of
West 42nd and on a much smaller scale, the project that would later become known as Theater Row began to take shape during the 1960s. In
rough and inhospitable urban terrain on the 400 block of West 42nd Street,
the realtor Irving Maidman gambled on converting a series of run-down
walk-up buildings into theaters. He did succeed in creating several new Off-
Broadway houses, and it was also to his credit that each of his converted
row houses had been retrofitted with "rehearsal halls and workshops for
building and storing sets, props, and costumes." The historian Lynne Sagalyn acknowledges that at the time of Maidman's project, rehearsal halls and
workshops were "critically important space in short supply throughout the
entire Theater District."[64]

Fred S. Papert brought a similar vision of craft spaces to West 42nd
Street when he followed up on Maidman's row-house theaters with a much

larger, even more successful collection of his own. He spearheaded a project called Theater Row in 1978, succeeding through "dogged persistence." Like Maidman, this leader had the vision to include twelve stories of space, in several of the old row houses, devoted to scenic construction, costuming, rehearsals, and storage.[65] Both Maidman and Papert obviously knew the theater well and had the insight to set aside space for the crucial backstage work of the stage.

Despite these admirable steps, neither of them was able to make much of a dent in the larger dispersal trend, which was at once citywide and national. At a micro level, Maidman and Papert were able to ensure that costumes could be fitted in the same building where rehearsals took place, but the bigger story in Times Square was that of theater-craft dispersal. In the same year that Theater Row's second phase opened with its new crop of workshops (1982), the crew at the Bagley Wright Theater polished up sprawling, state-of-the-art workrooms in Seattle, unequivocally dwarfing the good work being done on West 42nd Street.[66]

It is also important to point out that these Theater Row work spaces were limited by more than just their size. While it was true that the super-sized construction and rehearsal activities of a Broadway show were unlikely to fit in Papert's pint-sized buildings, the more important detail was that these makeshift shops were nonunion and therefore strictly off-limits. Any leader of beleaguered Broadway who tried to utilize them would have quickly run afoul of union regulations. In this way there was still little to no space for Broadway craft on West 42nd Street even after these new spaces opened. The Manhattan Plaza project had preserved affordable housing for theater artists and probably did more than any other single project to keep skilled labor and artistic talent in the city. The builders of Theater Row had forged rehearsal, construction, and performance spaces out of the very dilapidated row houses that had become so troublesome on 42nd Street. Both projects were admirable, successful, and popular, but neither could buck larger trends.

If the leaders of the Broadway industry wanted to compete against the formidable regional theaters that had sprouted nationwide, with enviable facilities and workshops to spare, they could no longer look to the streets surrounding Times Square as their go-to sites of construction, their fertile sources of new material, or their cauldrons of culture. Instead they had to look across state and even national boundaries for alternative sources of inspiration and sites of construction. Innovative producers such as Harold

Prince and Cameron Mackintosh did precisely that, fabricating new models of globalized production through shows such as *Evita*, *Cats*, and *Les Misérables*. As these globally produced shows took Broadway by storm in the 1980s and 1990s, their producers unwittingly accelerated the already advanced trend of deindustrialization in Times Square. They did so each time they brought components with them across the Atlantic from London or ordered special audio equipment from San Francisco. They continued to contract with specialty firms for "Broadway" components, but these firms were doing their construction farther from the actual Broadway district than ever before.

"When the Money Keeps Rolling in You Don't Ask How"

Broadway Craft in a Globalized Industry

A T THE END of 1976, Andrew Lloyd Webber's musical *Evita* began to enthrall American theater enthusiasts, but only via vinyl. Though there would be no U.S. production until 1979, the storied "British invasion" of the American musical stage pressed on through a popular studio recording.[1] That the disembodied voices of singers such as Colm Wilkinson were the first components of the musical to arrive in America was entirely appropriate for an industry that was rapidly going global. The generation of performers who came of age during and after *Evita* routinely slipped into costumes sewn half a world away, sang harmonies created in countries they had never visited, and danced in shoes crafted as far away as Brazil. The globalized theater was the only theater they ever knew. As it was designed to do, the London recording of *Evita* was a "bestseller throughout Europe" and then hit the U.S. market, although it was not yet a best seller until the opening of the U.S. production. The album was hardly a global phenomenon on the scale of *The Phantom of the Opera* or *Les Misérables*, but it did cross national boundaries and permeate several corners of the globe. By the summer of 1979, when a fully corporeal *Evita* finally arrived stateside, some of its potential audience members already had their appetites whetted by the dramatics of the recording.[2]

This fleshing out of this famous musical, however, did not occur within New York City, at least not originally. The first American performances of the controversial, historical "rock opera" based on the life of Eva Peron were actually out west in the city of angels and later in the city by the bay. Though the musical was auditioned, cast, and rehearsed in New York, the producer Harold Prince chose Los Angeles and San Francisco for out-of-town tryouts. Producers had utilized similar "tryout" performances to fine-tune shows for many decades, and it was not all that unusual for a tryout to occur in a city far from New York. The producer Robert Whitehead, for example, routinely used Chicago and Detroit for these tryouts in the 1940s and 1950s.

What did make the *Evita* development process unusual, however, was the way that Prince's team gathered components for the show from so many different locations. Producing mavericks in the early twentieth century had done this sort of thing before, purchasing the occasional batch of costumes from Paris or London.[3] But the disparate nature of stage components in the 1970s, 1980s, and beyond was entirely unprecedented. Leaders of the ever-expanding multitude of regional theaters and performing arts centers had built their own components in cities nationwide throughout the 1950s and 1960s, but only on the rarest of occasions would these components make it to Broadway. During the same decades, Whitehead purchased costume sketches and muslin fabric patterns from Paris for a 1958 musical called *Goldilocks*, while David Merrick broke new ground in 1962 by holding his *Oliver!* rehearsals in Los Angeles. Even Prince had gotten into this game relatively early, contracting with a London-based scenery builder for his 1970 musical, *Company*. Despite a frustrating delay in the scenery due to a British transit strike, he was not discouraged with internationally built scenery.[4]

Much to the contrary, Prince doubled down on this idea with *Evita* in 1979, contracting with craftspeople in several different cities. Having already pulled together a first set of artistically coherent components in London, he was undoubtedly less jittery about the chemistry of his American production. He could rely on exacting blueprints and the expertise of his London production team, who traveled stateside to create the show anew. For these reasons Prince was confident that the crafted components of America's *Evita* could be unloaded at the Dorothy Chandler Pavilion in the summer of 1979 without ever having been in the same room before. Costumes from Manhattan, stage properties from upstate New York, projection equipment from London, and audio equipment from San Francisco arrived at the pavilion in a legitimately transatlantic, if not fully global fashion. They "met" for the first time in Los Angeles during technical rehearsals.

Such moments of actualization, when stage components are first revealed to the production team in their physical form, are fraught with tension. As the designers Tazeena Firth and Timothy O'Brien opened their freight boxes, what were they to do if the aesthetic of Nino Novellino's properties did not match those in London? What if they did match the London show but somehow clashed with the American costumes, which had been laboriously handcrafted and fitted to each actor? As nerve-racking as these moments may have been for Firth and O'Brien, they were probably the least of Prince's worries when the components converged in Los Angeles. *Evita* was a real beast of a show compared to *Oklahoma!*, with its painted backdrops or its surrey with the fringe on top. To portray Argentina in the age of fascism, the London designers had created an elaborate moving screen, a video projection system, a custom Formica floor with built-in floodlights, and an intricately amplified stage capable of reverberation during key moments in the show. None of the original London components were available stateside, because *Evita* was still running in the West End, and yet all of these effects were vital to the U.S. production.

Prince had to ensure that the new components congealed in time for his U.S. opening in September 1979. Several instruments suffered complications in the weeks leading up to this opening, namely the elaborate sound equipment and the overtaxed vocal cords of leading lady Patti LuPone.[5] Overall, however, the show's many pieces merged quite well. The *Evita* production team ironed out most of the show's kinks in Los Angeles and San Francisco and then succeeded in bringing another hit musical to Broadway. By 1980 *Evita* had joined the ranks of several "standing-room-only" shows, giving every appearance that America's commercial theater was booming. While it is true that long-running hits such as *A Chorus Line* (1975), *Evita* (1979), *Cats* (1982), *Les Misérables* (1987), and *The Phantom of the Opera* (1988) energized theater tourism in New York City, it is not true that these shows created the same bumper crop of local craft work as had earlier shows such as *Oklahoma!* Because so many of these new hits took shape through components built outside New York, they accelerated the centrifugal tendencies of the rapidly globalizing industry.

As the producers of global blockbusters in the 1980s and 1990s enjoyed unprecedented publicity and profits, the Times Square district lost more of its rehearsal and craft space with each passing year. An even more ominous trend of this era, for those working in wig making, scenery, costumes, and other related trades, was the undeniable contraction of the number of new shows per year. Granted, the shops that did survive amidst these dwindling work opportunities did benefit from the "arms race" in high-tech scenery and production values, and many did secure lucrative contracts for computerized and automated scenery. But this famous escalation of theatrical technology also left smaller, low-technology shops in the lurch, unable to secure contracts.

Other than the occasional *New York Times* or *Playbill* journalist who drew attention to these issues in the 1980s and 1990s, no one seemed to be speaking up about the precarious position of theater craft in New York City. When leading costumers such as William Ivey Long did beat the drum about issues of disappearing craft-work spaces and workshops, their suggestions went largely unheeded by city leaders. Instead mayors such as Ed Koch sang the praises of each hit show on Broadway, perked up by a hot flash of commercial success in a troubled Times Square district. None of these Broadway boosters seemed to recognize that the industry was rapidly losing its capacity to reproduce within its traditional womb, midtown Manhattan.

Rather than exploring the image and reality of "crisis" and crime in Times Square, this chapter will explore the deeply rooted, structural problems of Broadway craft and construction as they existed underneath a veneer of wildly successful Broadway musicals. Fewer craft shops survived in the 1980s and 1990s than during any other decade of the twentieth century. Rehearsal studios that survived, especially those within the Minskoff tower and at 890 Broadway, served as vital surrogates for an aging industry. Producers succeeded in incubating new shows within these spaces, but the far more dominant trend after 1990 was for Broadway shows to be built elsewhere. Measuring by the Broadway box office, by city tourism, or by the number of Americans who paid eighty or ninety dollars a ticket to see dancing cats, this menopause metaphor fails to compel. By these measures Broadway closed out the 1980s stronger than ever, propelled by the box-office power of spinning Parisian revolutionaries, amplified phantoms, and descending helicopters. As sites of craft and show development, however, the avenues and streets surrounding Times Square in the 1980s and 1990s came closer to being barren than ever before.

Audition and Rehearsal Spaces

In early 1979 the singer-actor Peter Marinos hopped on a graffiti-ridden train on the Upper West Side to travel down to Minskoff studios, where he would audition for the much-anticipated American company of *Evita*. Within the convenient and centrally located Minskoff tower, Marinos shared his impressive tenor voice with music director Paul Gemignani and nabbed a coveted spot in the ensemble. Within this craft oasis, dozens of other hopefuls joined Marinos to audition for the new tuner by Andrew Lloyd Webber, but only forty-five were cast. To audition the lead characters, theater insider Prince secured daytime use of the Shubert Theatre, which was sparsely adorned for the long-running, minimalist *A Chorus Line*. Walking up to the very line where characters such as Cassie and Paul sang out their nightly dramas at 8:08 P.M., LuPone delivered what she described as a "defiant" performance of "Buenos Aires," "Don't Cry for Me, Argentina," and "Rainbow High," nailing the part. She was joined by the triumphant auditioners Mandy Patinkin and Bob Gunton, who also won their roles at the Shubert. If a different show with more elaborate scenery had been playing there, it is unlikely that this high-octane audition space would have been available, even to Prince.[6]

Evita's casting process was more or less standard for Broadway, except for Prince's use of the Shubert. Most active playhouses, occupied by show in performances, were simply off-limits for this sort of use by the 1980s. Efficient layering of daytime and evening uses had been common through the 1960s, but it was fading quickly by the time LuPone stepped up to the white line at the Shubert. Only one generation earlier, performers could take it for granted that many of their auditions would take place within a dormant theater or during the day in an otherwise occupied playhouse. This was even true for rank-and-file ensemble players and dancers. Throughout the 1960s and into the 1970s, director and choreographer Bob Fosse used such arrangements routinely to audition dancers and actors for shows such as *Little Me*, *How to Succeed in Business Without Really Trying*, *Pippin*, and *Chicago*.

Fosse's use of the Lunt-Fontanne Theatre in June 1962 perfectly illustrates the efficiency of this practice. *The Sound of Music* was still going strong at the Lunt-Fontanne, playing to full houses nightly, but Fosse and his assistants were able to colonize the space for a string of afternoon auditions over several days. They saw performers for the touring company of

Fosse's recent hit musical *How to Succeed . . .* , while simultaneously considering these same members of Actors' Equity for Fosse's new show, *Little Me*. Fosse's audition schedules reveal that on one particular Wednesday, which appears to have been March 14 1962, he and his team ran auditions from 11:00 A.M. until well after 5:00 P.M. Booking this same span of time in any of the local rehearsal studios would have cost a pretty penny, but here the team was able to use the Lunt-Fontanne for what appear to have been minimal costs or no costs at all.[7]

The situations at the Majestic Theatre in December 1971 and at the Imperial in 1972 were even more copacetic. Both theaters were occupied by shows produced by Stuart Ostrow, who just so happened to be producing Fosse's next musical, *Pippin*. Fosse's auditions could therefore take place in these theaters with no favors owed and certainly without money changing hands. On various afternoons in December 1971, Fosse auditioned leads for *Pippin* at the Majestic, before the cast and crew of Ostrow's musical *1776* took the stage in the evenings. At the Imperial in 1972, Fosse simply used the stage of the original Broadway *Pippin* as a site of afternoon auditions for the show's national touring company. This convenient arrangement was facilitated by *Pippin*'s scenery. It was minimal and did not take up much of the stage, as would be the case for *A Chorus Line* several years later.[8]

Not all of Fosse's auditions during these years were free from studio rental fees, however. Just as the Stigwood Group had to pay for its *Evita* auditions at the Minskoff studios in 1979, so producers Cy Fueur, Ernest Martin, and Stuart Ostrow had to pony up for audition studios on several occasions in the 1970s. Fueur and Martin rented space at the Variety Arts studios for Fosse's *Little Me* auditions in November 1963; it seems that they did not have suitable space within the theaters they were already renting that particular month. A similar situation arose in July 1972, when Ostrow rented studio space for *Pippin* auditions at Studio 58, 150 West 58th Street. These nonplayhouse auditions were the exceptions rather than the rule, however, at least for a leading talent such as Bob Fosse. Another interesting exception, which speaks volumes about the increasingly tight restrictions placed on theater buildings by local unions, was the stagehands' strike of September 1975. This definitely put a cramp in Fosse's style. In order to bargain successfully over their contracts during performances, the stagehands' union thought it necessary to keep all theaters locked during the day as well, with no exceptions. Apparently this lockout applied even to the great impresario Bob Fosse, who was scheduled to hold auditions, presumably at the Imperial, and had to cancel them.[9]

Striking a similar sour note in the archival record are the details of *Pippin* when it moved to the shiny new theater at the base of the Minskoff tower for its last few months on Broadway. During their three-month run at the Minskoff, Fosse and his merry bands of dance captains and audition assistants were banished from the Minskoff main stage during daytime hours. In the eyes of the building's owners, this brand new space was simply too valuable to be handed over for something as irrelevant as auditions, free of charge. Instead, Fosse had to pay for Minskoff rehearsal studio number 4, right downstairs. The building owners did not seem to realize that supporting or subsidizing auditions and rehearsals could be an investment that kept their theater booked with hit shows.[10]

Based on the copious documentation left by Fosse and held in the Library of Congress, it is no exaggeration to say that legions of chorus dancers and singers, the hard-working rank and file of Broadway, auditioned for Bob Fosse within "double-booked" Broadway playhouses before the daytime ban on the Minskoff became the new normal. In doing so they tapped a rich legacy of multilayered efficiency dating back to the early twentieth century. For generations of performers, from the 1910s to the 1960s, auditions on Broadway stages were just business as usual. For performers auditioning after about 1980 or so, however, such chances were rare privileges.

Several pressures emerged to restrict the practice after the 1970s. First and foremost, the scenery and costumes of the 1980s had become far more intricate, delicate, and expensive than those of earlier decades. Second, many of Broadway's historic theaters were plagued with deterioration, and building owners had to be more careful than their predecessors about who might be dancing up against the prosceniums or romping in the wings. Last but certainly not least, unionized craftspeople such as stagehands and costume managers kept their work spaces under lock and key in ways that had not been as necessary at mid-century, when Broadway's unions occupied a less precarious place within the city economy.

For all of these reasons, ferocious gatekeepers kept most theaters on lockdown until performance time, in order to protect a mix of wildly expensive handcrafted costumes, fragile hand-painted backdrops, carefully calibrated scenery, crumbling prosceniums, and regulated union work spaces. Scenery was an especially sticky issue in this era, when audiences began to expect sets to glide seamlessly in and out of view. Even something as small as a bracelet, coin, or bobby pin could monkey up the computerized, gliding scenery of the 1980s and 1990s. Theater owners and producers did not ban auditioning hordes of hopefuls from their stages in selfishness or short-sightedness but rather out of necessity. One does not invest hundreds of thousands of dollars in a computerized or hydraulic scenery track only to have legions of auditioners fouettéing and emoting all over it.[11]

In this way *Evita*'s leading players, LuPone, Gunton, and Patinkin, were doubly lucky in February 1979 when they auditioned at the Shubert Theatre. They got the chance to audition on the storied, charming, and energizing stage of a historic theater from 1913, and they also landed meaty roles in a musical that would play to packed houses for many months. These three talents joined the highly skilled American ensemble to form an *Evita* "company" in the summer of 1979. Not all of the performers at the first rehearsal were American, however. The show's producers, David Land and Robert Stigwood, had flown three British dancers over from London to drill the U.S. ensemble, with the goal of making the Broadway production as much of a facsimile of the West End hit as possible.[12]

Under the vigilant surveillance of the British dancers and director Harold Prince, the crew of performers rehearsed for about four weeks at King's Studios, on the far west side of Manhattan near 11th Avenue. These rehearsals were crucial opportunities for the cast to work together before boarding planes for Los Angeles. At King's, *Evita*'s company drilled music harmonies with Paul Gemignani, got fitted for costumes by Eaves Costumes, and learned their lines for book scenes. Paul Huntley traveled down from his Upper West Side work space to fit several of the women for wigs, especially LuPone. Though King's was not exactly at the pulsating center of theatrical activity at Times Square, its location was certainly close enough for satellite proprietors to travel to rehearsals. It was close enough for performers to leave rehearsals for fittings at the Eaves Costume facility at 423 West 55th Street, and it was reasonably close to Barbara Matera's shop at 311 West 43rd, where LuPone's costumes were crafted.

To travel from their homes to and from this King's Studios rehearsal location, cast members certainly had to "hoof it" if not provided with cab fare, as LuPone, Gunton, and Patinkin were. The nearest subways were at 7th and 8th Avenues, several avenues away. Though cast members did not recall incidents involving members of their troupe getting mugged or assaulted when walking to this facility, they did have to travel a considerable

Figure 21. Director Harold Prince (left) looking on as actress Patti LuPone is fit into a costume for the Broadway production of the musical *Evita*, 1979. Courtesy of Martha Swope. © Billy Rose Theatre Division, The New York Public Library for the Performing Arts.

distance.[13] As they walked back and forth to the decidedly nonglamorous 11th Avenue on a daily basis during rehearsals, these *Evita* players were actually among the luckier performers in the city. Prince was a well-established, well-funded director in 1979, known at the time as one of the best in the business. Some still consider him the best director to have wielded a clipboard in the 1970s. A producer as often as he was a director, Prince certainly had the funds and contacts to secure one of the precious few craft spaces left in an increasingly white-collar Manhattan. Rookie producers had fewer choices for rehearsal and development spaces, because they could not pull strings as Prince did. In particular, Prince's success in auditioning his principals at the Shubert during underutilized daytime hours was a major coup.

Other than a dormant Broadway theater, the Minskoff building, or King's Studios, the only viable options for auditions and rehearsals in early 1979 were the hodgepodge of makeshift spaces surrounding Times Square.

Prince's favored space for developing shows during the 1960s and 1970s had been the American Theater Lab on 19th Street and Broadway. According to Ted Chapin, who worked as an assistant to Prince in the space during rehearsals for *Company* in 1970, it had "one large rehearsal room big enough to represent an entire Broadway stage, a second room half its size, large enough for dance rehearsals, and a third one even smaller, for music." Unfortunately this valuable institution folded at some point in the mid-1970s, yet another casualty of the ever-diminishing number of new Broadway shows per year. There were of course smaller music rooms, mirrored dance studios, and spaces for orchestrating music peppered throughout the city, but by 1979 precious few were large enough to handle the full pageantry of a big show in rehearsal. Available evidence suggests that the slightly larger King's Studios was about as far from a first choice for Prince as it was from 7th Avenue. Despite the increasingly sparse landscape for theatrical development, not all was lost in 1979. New York City was about to get a towering new oasis for theatrical development, courtesy of a master showman by the name of Michael Bennett.[14]

In 1979 Bennett was reaping a fantastical financial harvest from his 1975 megahit, *A Chorus Line*. Like a theatrical George Lucas, Bennett had built himself into the profit structure of *A Chorus Line* after having originated the idea for the show down at the city-sponsored Public Theater in the Village. When the show hit pay dirt, however, Bennett did not run off to Rio with Max Bialystock. Instead he poured his windfall profits right back into the industry by purchasing 890 Broadway, a commodious loft building just north of Union Square. His chosen location was in the same section of town that had brimmed with theatrical satellite businesses one hundred years earlier, back in the days of "the Rialto" at Union Square. It is possible that Bennett was aware of this historical symmetry, but the determining factors seem to have been the usual suspects: price, layout, and availability. When he completed his purchase of 890 Broadway, at some point in 1978 or 1979, he set aside most of the space for theatrical craft and rehearsals, creating an indispensable oasis for development work. There had been one theatrical supplier in the building prior to this, in the 1970s, but the space that Bennett created was far more sweeping.[15] He deliberately recruited craftspeople at the top of their field, roping in the costumer Barbara Matera, the shoemaker Jacob Citerer, and all of their assistants as tenants.[16]

Under Bennett's stewardship, this band of highly skilled craftspeople assisted in the creation of iconic musicals such as *Cats, Les Misérables, The*

Phantom of the Opera, and *Miss Saigon*. Considering how threadbare all of these shows would have been without proper rehearsals, fittings, and design collaboration, it is no stretch to say that 890 Broadway was *the* most important theater-related building in New York City during the 1980s. Despite the undeniable success of Bennett's ark at 890 Broadway, he did not have enough space to save all of Broadway's talented craftspeople and proprietors from the flood of rising rents and evictions they faced in the increasingly white-collar city. Rather than giving up, a thoughtful group of these individuals, not under Bennett's umbrella, organized themselves for negotiations with the city of New York.

They recognized a crisis in their respective trades and pleaded with city leaders for organized assistance, hopefully in the form of a city-sponsored building purchase. One of the leaders of this effort, William Ivey Long, explained how craftspeople pooled their money to build a "war chest" for buying a building, only to see the fund drained by a lawyer's self-interest and duplicity. Unbeknownst to the craftspeople involved, this lawyer attended droves of meetings with the city regarding the idea, logging his time as billable hours all the while. Given that skilled artisans and shop proprietors tended not to have the deep pockets of a corporation, it did not take long for this single lawyer to gobble up most of the war chest with his antics. The effort stalled, and Long has explained how by the late 1980s a new crop of blockbuster shows had divided the craftspeople among themselves. Those who did secure contracts to work on shows such as *The Phantom of the Opera* and *Miss Saigon* found themselves flush with work and no longer needing quite so much help in finding affordable work spaces.[17]

Those not lucky enough to be swept along by this the surge in megamusicals struggled mightily to stay solvent; many dozens simply closed up shop and disappeared altogether. Although the ample Minskoff studios continued to operate at Broadway and 45th Street until 1989, hosting many important rehearsals and auditions, no theatrical craftsperson was ever invited to set up an in-house costume-making, dying, beading, shoe-making, wig-making, or hat-making operation. In this case there was no Bennettesque impresario to recognize the towering importance of theater craft. Much to the contrary, the building's managers seem to have only tolerated the rehearsal studios. They certainly did not behave like landlords who had a genuine interest in cultivating new shows. Their treatment of the studios in 1989 is a case in point.

After securing a place in the building through the special zoning laws of the early 1970s, which required that at least 5 percent of new theater-district towers be set aside for "theatrical uses," the proprietors of the Minskoff Rehearsal Studios got a rude awakening in the spring of 1989. Demand for their space had changed markedly since 1974. There were now many more high-end companies willing to pay top dollar for the space. The building's owners knew this, but according to the special district law they could rent it only for "theatrical" uses. They figured out that if they shoe-horned the live broadcasting of MTV Studios into the space, they could technically meet the letter of the law even while blatantly violating its spirit. In 1989 MTV Studios had no relationship to the Broadway stage whatso-ever. Though MTV programming did have its own sort of theatricality, it was cynically disingenuous to claim that these broadcasts met the zoning requirement. Many of the people who had fought for this zoning had retired, and the building's owners got little guff when they gouged the rehearsal studios with a 150 percent rent increase, effectively kicking them to the curb. The studios closed, and the space quickly filled with MTV's media moguls and music video producers.

Show Construction in the Era of *Evita*

While the Minskoff and similar craft spaces struggled with extinction in a city of rent hikes and building demolitions, facilities such as the Dorothy Chandler Pavilion in Los Angeles succeeded as luxurious digs for technical rehearsals. Once the professionals of the *Evita* company, components and all, landed in Los Angeles in late summer, 1979, they benefited from the newness and spaciousness of their new way station. Their primary task was not so much to shape characters or scenes, as they had done in New York, but rather to make the fully realized production take shape. This required far more than the occasional fitting at Eaves Costume or Paul Huntley wigs. As explained in the introduction to this chapter, *Evita* was not just a show, as *Oklahoma!* had been; it was a *production*, in every sense of the word. Although the precise definitions of a "show" and a "production" are diffi-cult to pin down, even when limiting one's discussion to 1979, a basic working definition would be as follows: a show is any musical or play for which stage components are replaced, repaired, or replicated with relative ease; and a production is one for which crafted components are either too elaborate or too expensive to be replaced quickly or easily.

Defined in these terms, *Evita* was certainly no "show." It was amplified, projected, reverberated, and automated. When Prince and his team created the American version in 1979, their vision for the physical components exceeded most of what had come before on Broadway. For a mix of reasons involving union rules and practicality, they could not simply import a set of duplicate components from England. They had to re-create a new set of specialty components stateside. The vendors and proprietors they used, as listed in *Playbill*, are listed in Table 2.

Getting these items along with the cast, crew, and production team under one roof at the Dorothy Chandler Pavilion was only half the battle. Prince and his designers then had to weave their rather involved collection of finished components together with each other and with the show's players. This process of weaving was not without its challenges.

At the easy end of the technological spectrum, *Evita*'s designers had to make sure that each actor had at least one costume and proper shoes. Most had several costumes, and many also had wigs, hosiery, and gloves. The designers Timothy O'Brien and Tazeena Firth had already selected and fitted all of these components during rehearsals back in New York before the company schlepped out to Los Angeles. Jessie Zimmer, a go-to contractor for most Broadway musicals in the 1970s, was easily able to supply the cast with all necessary gloves and hosiery prior to their departure. At Newel Art Galleries, Firth and O'Brien were able to handpick important pieces of antique furniture, such as the Perons' bed, without leaving the island of Manhattan. To complete the authentic 1940s look of their ensemble, they bought vintage polyester dresses, achieving the right cut and design at a minimal cost. When female cast members began to dance vigorously in their dresses, however, under the hot lights of dress rehearsals in Los Angeles, they unleashed an unforeseen, rather disgusting mélange of odors. Apparently polyester as a fabric is quite the repository of body odor, in ways that defy even the most fervent washing or dry cleaning. According to a firsthand witness, Peter Marinos, who shared the stage with these unexpectedly stinky starlets, the dresses were malodorous enough to bring even Broadway's notoriously tough and professional dancers to tears.[18]

Thankfully the remaining costumes were mercifully free of funky smells. To outfit the character of "Che" in military authenticity, Firth and O'Brien sent Mandy Patinkin to shop at a local army-navy surplus store (probably

Table 2. Contractors Credited for *Evita* in *Playbill*

U.S. Contractor	Components Supplied	Location
Theatre Techniques Inc.	Scenery	Cornwall-on-Hudson, NY
Nolan Scenery Studios	Scenery painting	1163 Atlantic Ave., Brooklyn, NY
Eaves Costume	Costumes executed	423 W. 55th St., New York, NY
Barbara Matera Ltd.	Evita's costumes	311 W. 43rd St., New York, NY
Paul Huntley	Wigs	124 E. 84th St., New York, NY
Four Star Stage Lighting	Lighting equipment	68 E. 153rd St., Bronx, NY
David Hersey Associates	Lighting equipment	London
Harry McCune Sound Service Inc.	Sound equipment	San Francisco
Bran Ferren Video Projection	Projection equipment	London
I. Weiss & Sons	Draperies, upholstery	445 W. 45th St., New York, NY
Nino Novellino Properties (c/o Costume Armour)	Effigy of Evita	Stewart Airport, Newburgh, NY
Newel Art Galleries	Antique furniture and furnishings	883 2nd Ave., New York, NY
Capezio	Dance shoes	1612 & 1855 Broadway, New York, NY
G. Bank's Theatrical Footwear	Men's dance boots	320 W. 48th St., New York, NY
Gladstone	Fabrics	16 W. 56th St., New York, NY
Jessie Zimmer	Hosiery and gloves	Unknown

Sources: Contractor and component information is from *Evita Playbill*, NYPL-BR; location information is from New York City *Yellow Pages*, 1980, NYPL-MRR.

Kaufman's on 42nd Street). He returned with baggy garments that would keep him cool, inspiring no small amount of jealousy among his more constricted, overheated cast members. In addition to these prefabricated garments, the costumes consisted of many made-to-order pieces. Firth and O'Brien relied on Louis Gladstone, at 16 West 56th Street, to supply the specialty fabrics needed for these exacting projects. The fabrics for ensemble costumes went to Eaves, and those for Eva's costumes went to Barbara Matera's shop. Once all costumes had been crafted and fitted, O'Brien and Firth had them freighted off to Los Angeles, where they would lie in wait for the tense beginning of dress rehearsals.

Supplying Firth and O'Brien with what they needed in 1979 was easy enough for Gladstone and Eaves, but both firms were actually imperiled in the era of *Evita*. Louis Gladstone had operated on 47th Street and 6th Avenue for many decades, but as the 1960s came to a close, his building was obliterated to make room for an office tower. Rather than closing for good, Gladstone found rental space at 16 West 56th, keeping his firm open for just a few more years before finally giving up the ghost altogether in the late 1980s. Eaves Costumes had relocated from 46th Street to the far west side in the 1970s, reducing its rent and weathering the drought in new Broadway shows, but even this survival strategy was not quite enough. In order to stay open, the storied costume house finally agreed to a merger with its top competitor, Brooks, to form the Brooks-Eaves Costume Company in 1981. After the merger, the proprietors of the amalgamated firm took their rental costumes and expert craftspeople and plunked them down in Long Island City, Queens, avoiding the increasingly exorbitant rental costs of a facility in Manhattan.

When these firms had created costumes for *Evita*, they were still part of a midtown supply network, but the ground under them was shifting rapidly by the turn of the 1980s. Manhattan's economy was undergoing a structural transformation of seismic proportions, causing all who worked with their hands, with fabrics, or with anything that was not "white collar" to scramble for space. *Evita*'s wig maker Paul Huntley demonstrated ingenuity in the face of these challenges when he took the same tack as the costumer William Ivey Long and secured extra space in his residence to use as a workshop. Both experts used their Manhattan homes as studio spaces in the 1980s, cleverly avoiding the overhead costs of midtown work spaces.[19]

While costumes and wigs could emerge from the smallest of work spaces, *Evita*'s oversized draperies, banners, and effigies most certainly

could not. In order to supply these components properly to Firth and
O'Brien, firms such as I. Weiss & Sons and Nino Novellino Properties had
to work off-site, in concert with the show's designers, and then unveil their
finished products after they were shipped to the Dorothy Chandler. In the
case of I. Weiss, the supplier of the black fabric panels used to present and
frame *Evita* in all three of its venues, the firm was able to cut, measure, and
sew their specialty "soft goods" to fit the exact measurements of the Dorothy Chandler in Los Angeles, the Orpheum in San Francisco, and the
Broadway Theatre in New York. Compared to the technologically advanced, expensive, and geographically disparate components of light,
sound, and video that converged for *Evita*'s opening, the I. Weiss draperies,
crafted at 445 West 45th Street, were almost quaint. An old stalwart of the
drapery trade, the firm had survived at its far-west-side location from the
1940s through the 1980s. When the *Evita* team hired I. Weiss in 1979, it
was one of only two surviving firms in the drapery trade. A little more than
a decade after *Evita*, when I. Weiss finally shuttered for good in the 1990s,
the firm Dazian's Theatricals was the only theatrical soft-goods/drapery
supplier left in all of New York.

     Nino Novellino's most important contribution to *Evita* was his effigy
of the deceased first lady of Argentina, used as she lay in state for her
"descamisados." He crafted this and other stage properties in his workshop
in Newburgh, New York. This was not as far removed as London or San
Francisco, but it still meant that Novellino's props would not be in the
same room as the costumes or tapestries until the entire kit and caboodle
arrived in Los Angeles for dress rehearsals. Similar geographic challenges
existed for the scenery pieces constructed out at the Nolan brothers' shop
in Brooklyn. They were close enough for Firth and O'Brien to inspect but
not so close that all of the crafted components could be built within walking
distance of one another. Thankfully none of the documents in the Harold
Prince Collection indicate that any of the stage props or scenery pieces was
mismatched or out of step with the aesthetic of the overall production. The
success of this process undoubtedly stemmed from consultations with both
O'Brien and Firth.

     How did these London-based designers ensure that their American
batches of props, costumes, and draperies matched the show and each
other? They saw to it themselves, personally. As part of their contracts with
the Stigwood Group, both designers had agreed to be physically present
during rehearsals and technical rehearsals; they had also won the right to

have their round-trip airfare costs covered. These contracted travel reimbursements, a sharp new wrinkle in 1970s production costs, also applied to *Evita*'s sound and lighting designers. None of these theater artists settled for "coach," or for economy class, either. Contracts such as that signed by the lighting designer David Hersey clearly stipulated that he would be reimbursed for "first-class round-trip travel and transportation expenses."[20] His lighting design fee was par for the course in 1979, but the airfare costs of his contributions to the show were unprecedented. He was one of four contracted designers based outside of New York. By way of contrast, *Oklahoma!*'s producers had no lighting designer at all and had to contract with only two local scenic and costume designers.

Even if first-class airfare for a swollen creative team was simply part of the cost of doing business in the globalized musical theater in 1979, it still took a bite out of *Evita*'s budget. Adding to this expensive mix, Robert Stigwood and his business partners also had to pay for the many flights of director Harold Prince as he ricocheted between London, New York, and Los Angeles. With Prince and other members of the creative team flying back and forth between New York and London during the show's development period and making many trips to the try-out theaters in Los Angeles and San Francisco, the *Evita* operation became a dizzying and expensive crisscross of first-class air travel.

Luckily, other than Novellino's upstate effigy, every other thread of *Evita*'s costumes, fabrics, and draperies came from a relatively concentrated district within New York City. The show's third-party contractors were still able to collaborate on these particular components in a traditional Broadway style, assembling them close to rehearsals during the summer of 1979. Though each of these firms had fewer shows to work on per year, they at least enjoyed the convenience of working in close collaboration with their colleagues. When Firth and O'Brien were in town, they could look over all of their work, cut through design challenges, and manage problems in a hands-on fashion.

Compared to the challenges of making effigies or obtaining specialty fabrics, the task of outfitting the entire cast in proper dance shoes from Capezio and G. Bank's Theatrical Footwear would seem to have been simple enough. But this too became complicated when the *Evita* creative team mashed its finished pieces together during dress rehearsals. The shoes selected by O'Brien and Firth had worked well enough at King's Studios, but at the Dorothy Chandler they became a threat to dozens of ankles.

Evita was to be played on a custom-made masonite floor that was punched through with floodlights. Worst of all, it was raked. A raked stage tilts at an angle toward the audience so that theatergoers can more easily see the entire cast at once. Unfortunately for dancers, it also tilts away from one's ankles, in a way that is tricky and often injury-inducing. The cast member interviewed for this book, Peter Marinos, remembered a steady trickle of dancers injured on this raked and floodlight-lit stage, above and beyond the normal afflictions of a show with vigorous dancing. In this way even something as seemingly innocuous as the floor became a source of agita and injury for the actors in *Evita*.

As a fully realized production, *Evita* called for far more than just authentic 1940s dresses, wigs, and dance-ready shoes. Higher up the technological chain, and above the actors' heads, was the show's moving screen and its oversized tapestries. Some of these tapestries unfurled from above the stage or were carried onstage by actors, but others actually framed the proscenium on both sides, inspired by a recent visit to Mexico City by Prince. During the climactic final scene of act 1, the ensemble supplemented all of these visual components with an abundance of open-flame torches, which they carried by hand onto the stage. When the show finished its Los Angeles and San Francisco tryouts and opened in New York, the theater critic Martin Gottfried singled out the visual elements for praise. Gottfried suggested that "the show's power is in its production concept, its fabulous imagery." It is possible that the ensemble found this moving screen, the oversized tapestries, the lit torches, and the other sources of imagery to be "fabulous," but that would probably depend on whether they had recently been smacked upside the head by the moving screen or whether they were among the unlucky few to have their torches burn out of control, forcing them to run offstage and douse them. According to cast member Peter Marinos, both of these mishaps befell members of the beleaguered ensemble on more than one occasion.[21]

Amplification and Projection

There were, of course, plenty of additional layers to this show, each equally fraught with possible complications. *Evita* was an elaborate stage production booked into relatively large theaters, so microphones were a must. At the "cavernous" Dorothy Chandler, at San Francisco's Orpheum, and at the Broadway Theatre in New York, *Evita* absolutely needed amplification to succeed. Performers could not, however, simply utilize amplification as their forebears had from the 1940s to the 1960s. The first microphones on Broadway had been site specific, rigged at the foot of a stage amid the footlights or within a "box set" portraying whatever bedroom, nightclub, or porch might be needed in the show. In 1949's *Kiss Me, Kate*, for example, the characters Fred Graham and Lilli Vanessi sang their charming "Wunderbar" duet within Ms. Vanessi's dressing room, never leaving the imaginary box that framed the room. Because the actors stayed in the room, the microphone picking up their voices could stay too. When performers needed to be amplified from outside a box set in this or other musicals, stage technicians would discreetly dangle microphones from above. For "11 o'clock numbers," leading actors could step right up to the "foot mikes" at the foot of the stage, providing their audience with maximum audibility.

This amplification game changed dramatically in the 1960s with the advent of body microphones. Carol Channing is usually named as the first big star to wear this type of microphone, for the 1964 musical *Hello, Dolly*.[22] By the end of the 1970s, body mics were de rigueur for all leading actors on Broadway, who had no choice but to wear them. Only for a play in an intimate theater could an actor hope to be heard sans microphone, through the power of her or his own voice and technique. By the time *Evita*'s sound designer, David Hersey, flew over from London to rig up LuPone, Bob Gunton, and Mandy Patinkin with their body mics in Los Angeles, San Francisco, and New York, the practice was a well-established part of professional theater.

With body microphones readily available, it was no longer necessary to constrict actors within box sets or to require them to step up to the foot mikes for their big soliloquies or solo numbers. Scenic designers on Broadway were well aware of this liberating detail, and they responded with all manner of abstracted and minimalist designs. *A Chorus Line*, in 1975, enabled its actors to roam the stage singing, acting, and dancing in abstracted spaces. *Evita*'s stage was similarly bare, relying on the most minimal of scenery. The young Eva Peron met the singer Augustin Magaldi amidst nightclub tables on an otherwise bare stage, rather than within a box set portraying an actual nightclub. Later in the musical, the characters of Eva (LuPone) and Juan Peron (Gunton) conversed in a bed rather than a bedroom. Although scenic minimalism and abstraction were certainly not utilized in all 1970s musicals, they were au courant at the time, and they certainly defined *Evita*.[23]

They also created rather thorny sound problems for *Evita*'s creative team. To amplify the show, sound designer David Hersey recruited San Francisco contractor Harry McCune, who supplied the American company of *Evita* with all of its speakers, microphones, amplifiers, and cables. Amplifying the leading actors and adjusting their volume levels were the easy parts for Hersey and McCune. This was especially true because in many of *Evita*'s crucial scenes, characters such as Eva, Magaldi, or Peron were giving speeches or recording within radio sound stages. Because microphones were part of the story on many occasions, Hersey could let these scenes *sound amplified* and did not have to worry about tricking the ear of his audiences. The transparency with which the *Evita* creative team used microphones, reverberation, and obvious amplification became one of the most defining features of the show in Broadway history. According to the choreographer Larry Fuller, "Evita was one of the few times it was legitimate to have voices miked . . . amplification and echoes are thematically justified, an organic part of the show's style."[24] This was certainly true for the principals.

For the orchestra and the elaborately choreographed, mobile ensemble, however, Hersey and McCune faced a bigger challenge. Both needed to be amplified within *Evita*'s gaping playhouses but without sounding obviously amplified. McCune had agreed to "assemble and test the equipment in our San Francisco shop, and deliver [it] to the Dorothy Chandler Pavilion for installation."[25] This gave Hersey and Prince precious few days to try out the equipment with their ensemble and orchestra during "tech week." These components had not been assembled and tested in midtown or taken out of town for a brief tryout in a nearby place such as New Haven and then brought right back to the space where they had been fine-tuned. They traveled from San Francisco to Los Angeles, back to San Francisco, and then to New York City. When installed at the Dorothy Chandler during tech week, they were in the same room as the cast and the orchestra for the first time.

Happily none of the reviews in either Los Angeles or San Francisco harped on the sound design. When Harry McCune's sound equipment arrived at the Broadway Theatre on 53rd Street in midtown Manhattan, however, the stars did not align for Hersey, Prince, and the rest of the creative team. New Yorkers lined up to get tickets to the much-anticipated show, but from day one the New York production was hamstrung by intractable sound problems. As Prince prepared for the Broadway opening, he scrambled to fix the sound, even hiring the leading New York sound designer Abe Jacob to fix McCune's and Hersey's work.[26] In the experience and opinion of the theater critic Frank Rich, even Jacob was unable to salvage the compromised sound: "As one wades through the intermission crowd at the Broadway Theater, one hears many theatergoers asking one another the same thing: 'can you understand the words?' The answer, far too often, is no. 'Evita' now has severe audibility problems. Paul Gemignani's band and the performers are too frequently out of balance, and the amplification system (designed by Abe Jacob) hisses and pops. Most of the ensemble singing is mushy."[27] Despite this rather embarrassing review, Evita's creators were offering their audiences far more than an auditory experience.

They also utilized video footage in ways that broke new ground on Broadway. On the aforementioned screen, moving over the heads of ensemble dancers and occasionally bonking them in their noggins, historic video footage of the actual Eva and Juan Peron appeared at various points throughout the show. When combined with the well-reviewed lighting and Prince's Brechtian staging, this displayed video footage intensified the overall sensory experience of Evita's audiences. The lights projecting up from beneath the feet of the cast may have been a bit rough on the occasional ankle, but they succeeded in giving much of the show a dark, dramatic, and even haunting aesthetic. The rest of the show's lights were hung from trusses on all sides of the stages and along the various balconies at the show's three U.S. playhouses.

Shipping, Rentals Costs, and the "Feedback Loop"

For many of these components, such as the vintage dresses, the shoes, the specialty fabrics, and the moving screen, the Stigwood Group simply purchased the items and added the charges in with the other costs of Evita's development, such as Prince's airfare or Fuller's choreographer's fee. These up-front capital outlays were unavoidable for a big Broadway musical in 1979, and they created an increasingly steep entry barrier for new producers. This was especially true for Evita because many of its components were custom-built. All told, as a percentage of the show's budget, Evita's scenic, audio, video, projection, and lighting components were certainly more of a burden than the painted backdrops and surreys of Oklahoma! had been in 1943.

Purchased components and up-front costs were the least of Robert Stigwood's worries in 1979, however. Items such as the masonite floor, custom-
built by Theatre Techniques, Inc. or Nino Novellino's finely crafted effigy
of Eva Peron may have been expensive as onetime purchases, but an even
bigger challenge to the *Evita* team was the show's weekly rental costs.[28]
These costs created a steep threshold, which Stigwood had to climb, like
Sisyphus pushing a boulder, each week his show was open in the United
States. Any theater producer worth his or her salt, whether in 1929 or 1979,
would have been well aware that the weekly operating costs of one's cast,
crew, and stagehands were a make-or-break detail of a show's profit mar-
gin. Weekly salaries were an unavoidable part of doing business on Broadway. What producers such as Stigwood did not necessarily know in the
era of *Evita* was exactly how much each cable, lighting truss, amplifier,
or microphone would cost them as weekly rentals. Weekly bills from the
contractors Harry McCune Sound Service, Four Star Stage Lighting, and
Bran Ferren Video Projection were gifts that kept on giving for the duration
of the show's run. They encumbered *Evita* with an entirely new layer of
weekly operating costs.

Purchasing expensive, high-tech equipment such as the "mounting and
railing system" for the screen or the custom-built projection lenses was
simply out of the question. *Evita*'s managers could not afford to purchase
even half of the audio, video, and lighting equipment they needed, even
with their impressive capitalization, a successful cast recording, and buzz
from the West End. They simply had to rent. Stigwood did manage to
wriggle free from one of these weekly rental costs by allying himself with
director Harold Prince. Tiring of having to pay exorbitant rental fees on
the same electronic lighting console for each of his shows on Broadway,
Prince had dramatically burned through eighty thousand dollars of his own
money to buy his own console just a few years before *Evita*.[29] He was able
to loan it to the electricians at 53rd and Broadway, knocking out at least
one of the show's weekly costs. Other than this valuable component, however, the Stigwood Group was stuck with rentals. Each projector, slide
carousel, specialty bulb, speaker, cable, and amplifier had a weekly fee,
which impinged on the ability to keep *Evita* open without packed houses.

In addition to these rental fees, which rose every year in predictable,
arms-race fashion, late-1970s shows such as *Evita* struggled to cover
mounting shipping and freight expenses. These included the costs of shipping all of the projection equipment, including the slide carousel and the

video projector, from the Bran Ferren shop in the United Kingdom.[30] Within the United States these costs mounted not only when the show's components were transported to California and back again for a New York opening but also when they were sent up from Los Angeles for a brief stint in San Francisco. In the grand saga of American stage components, the costumes, sets, speakers, and wigs for *Evita* were far more disparate in their origins than these had been for most prior shows. They were not yet the fully outsourced components of the 1990s, global in every sense of the word, but they did emerge from several far-flung locations. They certainly generated more shipping costs than had the railroad or trucking fees of the *Oklahoma!* era.

Back at mid-century these fees kicked in only twice, for the back and forth of an out-of-town tryout in Boston or New Haven. As the case of *Oklahoma!* demonstrated, every thread and swath of the mid-century Broadway show first emerged from a shop in Manhattan and therefore had no original shipping or transport costs. In rare cases specialty costumes did arrive by steamship from London or France, but these more global moments in mid-century stagecraft were always the exception. By comparison the costumes, scenery, and other components that traveled to and from Broadway after the turn of the 1980s were wildly global, zigging and zagging to the very ends of the earth.

Despite the shipping costs of its disparate components, the airfare costs of its transatlantic creative team, and some unfavorable reviews, the American production of *Evita* was an undisputed triumph in financial terms. The show did have ambitious technical requirements, a high up-front capitalization, and burdensome weekly operating costs, but it also had tremendous buzz and media attention. It ran for five years, allowing its backers to recoup their investments and profit handsomely. Whether this was due more to choice casting, the infamy of Eva Peron as a historical character, or the Andrew Lloyd Webber score is best debated by theater critics and music scholars. The international hit song "Don't Cry for Me, Argentina" is certainly tuneful, and the performances by LuPone, Patinkin, Gunton, and the rest of the cast do seem to have been thrilling, at least as they have been captured on the cast recording. But the author's aim in this book is not to address such questions of artistry and performance but rather to analyze the show as a collection of finished components, as the product of highly skilled craft work, and as a financial vehicle designed to make a profit.

In these terms *Evita* was a smash hit. Despite this, the profits of the show did not flow directly back to Broadway via the "feedback loop" that defined so many hit shows from decades past. In 1943 *Oklahoma!*'s original backers had included many Broadway insiders, who fed their profits back into future Rodgers and Hammerstein productions. *A Chorus Line* had unleashed a windfall of profits for Michael Bennett in 1975, which he rolled back into the industry through his purchase of 890 Broadway. In stark contrast to this long-standing pattern, most of *Evita*'s investments came from London. The musical had first opened at London's Prince Edward Theatre in 1978, with Harold Prince at the helm as director but not as lead producer. It was the Stigwood Group, under the leadership of British Robert Stigwood, that put up most of the money. When *Evita* made it to New York, the production did gain support from several New York City "angels," including Prince and his business partner Ruth Mitchell. Most of the people with a stake in the 1979 Broadway production, however, lived across the Atlantic.[31]

Perhaps this divide between the show and its absentee investors was just an inevitable step toward the truly global capitalizations of the 1980s and 1990s. But on the streets near Times Square, the decline in local investments did have a noticeable impact. Though Prince and Mitchell had invested in *Evita*, local costume firms, actresses such as Rosalind Russell, and theater-loving angels such as Howard Cullman were no longer investing in Broadway as they once had. In order for the Broadway feedback loop to work effectively, the profits of hit shows needed to be rolled right back into the industry. There had always been a mix of non-Broadway investors on the Great White Way, some even from London, but such investors had always been secondary players in an insider's game. In the 1970s and 1980s the proportions of insider and outsider investors flipped, and all sorts of movie studios, multinational entertainment conglomerates, and other non-Broadway investors essentially took over.

These power players in the commercial theater, such as Columbia Pictures and Clear Channel Entertainment, brought new motives to the theatrical investment landscape. When a local proprietor such as James E. Stroock of Brooks Costume invested money on Broadway, as he did throughout the 1940s, his motives were probably to make money and to invest in his industry. When the commercial theater flourished, so too did his costuming business. Stroock was certainly as free as any 1979 Londoner to take his profits and run for the hills. But there is considerable evidence in the financial records of producers such as Harold Prince and in the publication *Angels* that investors such as Stroock routinely rolled their profits right back into Broadway. In 1979, however, when dividends began to flow from the hit New York production of *Evita*, they flowed right across the Atlantic Ocean. The recipients of *Evita* profits in England may have been devoted to the theater or even worked in the theater themselves, but they had loyalties to the West End, not just to Broadway. There was little chance that any *Evita* backers in London would be moved to buy a Manhattan building, open rehearsal studios, and rent space at cut rates to craftspeople, as Michael Bennett did. To the knowledge of the author, none did.[32]

Global Theater in the 1990s and Beyond

From the moment the London cast recording arrived stateside to the final mailing of investor dividend checks, the U.S. production of *Evita* was a fascinating product of modern Broadway. Of all the hit shows from the 1970s and 1980s, this musical is one of the stronger markers of the trends that were revamping commercial theater. While *A Chorus Line* and *Annie* were more famous and plays such as *Bent* and *On Golden Pond* garnered more critical acclaim, the composer Andrew Lloyd Webber's *Evita* was the perfect product of its time. It straddled two eras of craft history, with one foot in the concentrated, walkable Manhattan workrooms of decades past and the other striding confidently toward the globalized future.

Within a few short years of *Evita*'s triumph, the next generation of globalized musicals stormed the barricades of a previously insular and local Broadway, making *Evita* look almost provincial. In 1983 the British producer Cameron Mackintosh marked his territory on Broadway with the musical *Cats*, which featured scenery built in both London and, of all places, Columbus, Ohio.[33] In 1987 a British costume house named Bermans and Nathans Ltd. did every garment for the U.S. production of *Les Misérables*. Much to the chagrin of local costumers and their union, the whole tattered kit and caboodle arrived en masse from England; not a stitch of costume was crafted locally. Though this show did provide jobs to American performers, it did little for craft workers, who continued to dwindle in New York City. The costumer Carrie Robbins lamented in 1989 that she could not find the right local experts to make dance shoes for *Jerome Robbins' Broadway* and therefore had to resort to suppliers in Brazil. The 1993 production of *Show Boat* utilized lighting equipment from Winnipeg, Canada, while a 1994 production of *Medea* imported every last one of its scenic components from the United Kingdom. The trend continued unabated into the new millennium. In 2005 the musical *Dirty Rotten Scoundrels* displayed scenery built in San Diego on a Broadway stage.[34]

There were other important, qualitative differences in these productions besides their globalized sites of construction. Especially in the 1990s, new Broadway shows began to arrive in New York as the spawn of corporations and international conglomerates. Although *Cats* and *Les Misérables* had relatively traditional backers, subsequent productions such as *The Lion King, Ragtime*, and the revival of *42nd Street* had a dizzyingly international financial structure. Of all the corporations to stake territory on Broadway in this era, Disney was the most famous.

In a series of events so ingrained in the narratives of Broadway and Times Square that they have inspired an entire lexicon (Disneyfied, Disneyfication), the Walt Disney Company landed on Broadway in the 1990s with its stunning renovation of the New Amsterdam Theatre and its opening of a Disney Store nearby on 42nd Street. Although the opening production of *King David* in the reclaimed space was a flop, the second was a smash. *The Lion King*, which was a blockbuster hit and the winner of six Tony Awards, was produced and capitalized entirely by Disney Theatrical Productions, a subsidiary of the Walt Disney Company.

This iconic development, the first of many high-profile, corporate capitalizations in the 1990s and 2000s, ushered in several qualitative changes in the way theater got produced on Broadway. The first, least surprising outcome of the new corporate age was that show choices became more conservative. As Steven Adler wrote in his notable and revealing *On Broadway: Art and Commerce on the Great White Way*, concerns grew that "large bureaucracies cannot generate the passion and vision of the individual producer."[35] In the case of Disney's *The Lion King*, the musical was certainly original, especially in its puppetry, but the source material most certainly was not. Hot on the heels of the company's 1994 animated film *Lion King*, Disney took only a calculated risk.

This conservatism in show choices also manifested through revivals. Back in 1980 when the maverick producer David Merrick brought *42nd Street* to Broadway, it was an original musical. Though based heavily on a novel and a 1933 film, it was still the daring vision of Merrick and director-choreographer Gower Champion, with investors who had little to no artistic input. When *42nd Street* was revived at the turn of the millennium, however, it was a safe choice made by committee. By 2001 the beloved tap show was well known and had become a staple of high schools and community theaters nationwide.

It was safe also because of the massive mix of corporate backers, who divided up the risk of investment. The 1980 capitalization had been only Merrick and individuals he could convince to write him checks. For the 2001 revival, the United States–based Dodger Theatricals joined forces with the Stage Holding Company, run by Joop van den Ende out of Holland, while the theater was the newly christened Ford Center for the Performing Arts, which was also "an SFX Theatrical Group Venture." The corporate presence on Broadway had become dizzying.

The revival of *42nd Street* was doubly conservative if one considers its intended market. Van den Ende was primarily a producer of European tours and productions who likely wanted the well-known show to run just long enough to gain Broadway credibility. He could then send out global tours. This shift in emphasis, in which Broadway runs mattered less than national and international tours, is well documented, especially in Adler's *On Broadway* (2004). It was yet another facet of the larger shift toward relatively corporate, conservative decision making.

To some extent the music of Broadway got caught up in these trends. From the days of syncopated jazz to big bands, Broadway music had always moved in step with national trends. At mid-century a distinctive, orchestra-based Broadway sound had emerged only to be challenged quickly by the unfamiliar sounds of rock 'n' roll. Although the dynamic between these bodies of music was incredibly complex, for this project it is important to focus on the effort made by Broadway producers to stay relevant through rock musicals and their closely related cousins, rock operas.

Beginning in the late 1960s, amplified rock music stormed Broadway through musicals such as *Hair* and *Jesus Christ Superstar*. Although the music styles and subject matter for both shows were anything but conservative, the producers' impulse to stay current with popular music most certainly was. The earliest musicals in this mold featured electric guitar prominently, but synthesizer and even disco sounds crept in through the late 1970s and the 1980s.[36] The corporate, even cynical conservatism of these amplified musicals was especially apparent when "juke-box musicals" such as *Mamma Mia* (2001), *Movin' Out* (2002), and *Jersey Boys* (2005) began to arrive on Broadway. In these most recent cases, the "score" was nothing more than a playlist of popular music's most known and beloved songs.

With conglomerates such as Clear Channel Entertainment, Disney, and Livent at the helm of many Broadway plays and musicals from the 1990s forward, the cultivation of local craft spaces was hardly an agenda item. Indeed these corporate conglomerates not only compiled show components from anywhere and everywhere but also ushered in subtle changes in the meaning of the spaces traversed and inhabited by theatergoers. Some of the most interesting works on this topic, by Michael McKinnie and Maurya Wickstrom, emphasize the slippery slide of contested public sidewalks and theaters into spaces of pure consumption and displays of "urban affluence." McKinnie, writing on Toronto in ways quite relevant to Times Square, notes that the city's downtown became "theatrical" in the sense that audiences were performing their own affluence and sophistication as theatergoers. When applied to Times Square in the late 1990s, McKinnie's arguments help us to understand how scenic construction work on the sidewalks, load-ins, and other evidence of theater making did not mesh with the new vision for the Great White Way.[37]

Such displays of theater making can kill the glamour of theatergoing in Times Square, which had less conceptual and physical space for craft and construction with each passing year after 1990. New York City, especially Times Square, had long been highly theatrical, but craft workers and their materials had been part of the show. In the "new Times Square" after 1990, such people and goods entered the space like contraband, not meant to be seen by the theatergoing public.

Maurya Wickstrom's work on Disney in Times Square reinforces and enriches the idea that a more corporatized Times Square has far less space for theater craft. Wickstrom highlights the ways that consumers experience and perform the Disney brand by putting on princess costumes in the Disney store or by shopping in the *Lion King* gift shop immediately before or after seeing the musical. Noting that the show's advertising encourages theatergoers to "enjoy your audience with the King," she explains how the commodification of Broadway and Times Square is therefore masked by a focus on experience and interactivity.[38]

Theater professionals had long made efforts to keep their backstage craft and rehearsal work hidden, so as to preserve the "magic" of their trade. In the 1990s and beyond, corporations such as Disney joined them in the overall effort to infuse theatrical consumption with a "magical" or otherworldly quality. Theater craft was not a part of the experience they were selling, in the same way that one never sees staff carting boxes of supplies or loading up food carts at a Disney theme park. In this way the overall impact of the corporation on Broadway was to reinforce the ongoing dispersal of theater-related craft work out of New York.

The globalization trend did have centripetal aspects to counteract the otherwise centrifugal trend; sometimes theater-related businesses in New York City, or at least those nearby, got to build for shows in other cities. When the successful Broadway opening of the musical *Miss Saigon* was followed by duplicate productions in Toronto and Stuttgart, Hudson Scenic Studios in Yonkers got to build several of the show's famous helicopters. When the popular Broadway production of *The Lion King* was parlayed into facsimile productions in several international cities, the firms that did the original production got to craft all of the touring scenery and costumes. Also counterbalancing the dispersal effect more locally, several top theater-related firms near New York City continued to make costumes and scenery for national touring companies even into the 1990s.

Internationally, however, the pattern of New York–area firms building scenery for export was more the exception than the rule. Most international producers of Broadway shows were entirely free of union jurisdictions and could hire anyone. When the production team for *The Phantom of the Opera* brought their smoke machines, their falling chandeliers, and their elaborate costumes to cities such as Berlin, Singapore, and Stockholm, no components were built in the United States, let alone New York. Ultimately the advent of a truly globalized musical theater did more to break up New York City's craft dominance than it did to reinforce it.

No firm better represents the globalization trend in commercial theater than the Production Resource Group (PRG), founded in 1982 in Westchester County, New York. Jeremiah Harris, the founder of PRG, had deep roots on Broadway through his family's storied history and through his employment in scene shops and with theatrical management companies. When he founded his own firm, originally called Harris Production Services, he did so in a traditional, site-specific, Broadway fashion. He and his crew worked on New York City shows from an oversized workshop in Westchester. As they finished scenery pieces for shows such as *The Phantom of the Opera*, they were able to truck them down to midtown in just one day.

As the firm continued to secure work on both Broadway and non-Broadway projects, however, its ties to Gotham faded. A high-tech, groundbreaking show that Harris and his team crafted at the MGM Grand Hotel in Las Vegas put them at the head of the scenery-building pack in 1995, and in subsequent years the firm was easily able to acquire specialty firms in lighting, sound, and technology.

By 2011 this stage production behemoth had offices in eleven U.S. states, Toronto, Buenos Aires, London, Birmingham, Maidstone (United Kingdom), Hamburg, Cologne, Frankfurt, Munich, Berlin, Dusseldorf, Brussels, Tildonk (Belgium), Paris, Utrecht, Madrid, Zurich, Cape Town, Tokyo, Shanghai, Sydney, Melbourne, and Adelaide. The problem for anyone tracking craft work in midtown Manhattan is that this multinational corporation was, in essence, everywhere and nowhere at the same time. The name PRG appears in countless *Playbills* from throughout the 1990s and in even more after the year 2000. A cursory examination of the author's own *Playbill* collection reveals credits for the PRG octopus in almost half of the shows on Broadway after the turn of the millennium. Yet the company's only presence in west midtown was a small office for meeting with industry professionals at 9th Avenue and 45th Street. Is PRG a highly skilled, invaluable conglomerate of some of the industry's finest talents, keeping commercial theater going through their craft and construction work? Undoubtedly it is. Is it also an unmoored umbrella of an organization, compared to the old Nolan Bros. and Feller firms, lacking deep roots in New York City? This too is true.

In 1975 or even 1985 one might have lamented the fact that theater craft was so rapidly migrating and consolidating toward a handful of multinational corporations such as PRG. It was possible to argue that these trends left the smaller manufacturing buildings of midtown in the lurch, bereft of a once-thriving industry. By the time of PRG's founding in 1995, however, theater craft in midtown was a shadow of its former self. Had Jere Harris felt nostalgic in 1995 and sought to wedge his massive scenery operation into Manhattan, he would not have been doing any favor for the city. He would have been competing for space, expensively, with information-based corporations such as Conde Nast and Ernst & Young. At this point in Times Square's history, there were plenty of white-collar operations clamoring for a foothold in western midtown real estate.

By the 1990s PRG towered on Broadway not through a tenancy in a local skyscraper but through the ubiquity of its components, on local stages and around the world. The dominance of this multinational firm in component construction is not surprising when one considers the structural changes of both the city and the theater industry. The latter continued to

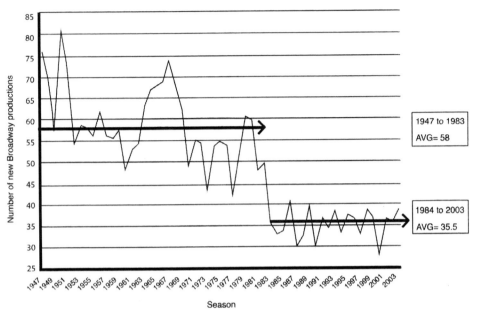

Figure 22. The precipitous decline in the number of new shows on Broadway. Based on statistics from www.ibdb.com, accessed June 6, 2011. Illustrated by Manuel Barreiro.

generate work through the late 1980s but at a new average of about thirty-five new shows per year. With fewer contracts available, the costume houses, scene shops, and other theater-related businesses of midtown gradually closed or consolidated. It was never the job of producers such as Harold Prince and Cameron Mackintosh to keep them open; their mission was only to create quality theater and make money for their investors. Theater craft in this age did not disappear so much as it contracted, consolidated, and ultimately survived under the umbrella of organizations such as PRG. It was uprooted from midtown Manhattan but by no means destroyed.

Broadway's craft work was not the only part of the industry to become uprooted and unmoored in this era. Much of the advertising of the 1980s and 1990s, especially for musicals, broke free of former attachments to famous composers and famous performers, featuring instead a series of easily recognizable icons. Through cats' eyes, orphans, phantom masks, and helicopters, advertisements clued their audiences in to one of the most profitable and unconventional features of modern Broadway. These were shows that could be enjoyed in any language.

Consider, for example, the many thousands of theatergoers who applauded wildly beginning in 1983 when Grizabellas worldwide began to belt out the song "Memory" before being lifted up to theater ceilings by automated cherry pickers. At this defining and celebrated moment in the musical *Cats*, it mattered little what language the surrounding chorus of "cat" singers used to serenade her ascendance. Americans could see and enjoy the German-language production in Berlin just as international tourists could enjoy the U.S. show at the Winter Garden regardless of their mastery of English. Through iconography and spectacle, these blockbuster musicals gave the old British navy a run for its money in terms of imperial dominance. For those who loved these musicals, Cameron Mackintosh was a post-Broadway genius, a global pied piper of family-friendly high drama on the musical stage. For those with a less positive memory of the years when the grand old dame that was Broadway surrendered to *Miss Saigon*, Mackintosh and his ilk have been cast as grand villains, as purveyors of slickly packaged tripe devoid of any real substance.

History, of course, loves its villains. It is far easier to stomach the sharp growing pains of an industry, or a district, if there are people to blame. Members of the Broadway community have been casting about in search of villains for as long as these immense structural changes have been wreaking havoc on their industry. For some, there were no characters more lamentable than the pimps, prostitutes, and drug dealers mentioned in Chapter 6. Others found their villains in modern producers, such as Robert Stigwood and Cameron Mackintosh, who pushed commercial theater in a global direction. Still others enjoy blaming union leaders for saddling Broadway shows with high labor costs through stagehands' salaries or painters' pensions.

When viewed through a historical lens, however, none of these characters has really earned the heaps of blame being dumped upon them. To blame them would be to assume that they had more mastery of the district than anyone else did. The industry moved, shrank, modernized, and evolved from the 1970s to the turn of the new millennium, just as the district had transformed to the point of becoming almost unrecognizable. In the era of PRG, it was no longer necessary for scenery or costumes to emerge from a tightly concentrated Manhattan district. Harkening back to the Armbruster studio discussed in Chapter 1, which had once dominated scenic painting from Columbus, Ohio, firms such as PRG were free to craft goods anywhere. As long as their work was of "Broadway" caliber, they could build for Broadway without being on Broadway.

When this globalization trend is considered alongside the regional-theater explosion discussed in Chapter 5, it is easy to see how it was so damaging to midtown theater craft. When international shows arrived on Broadway with entire batches of components already constructed abroad, they were as unlikely as a Minneapolis musical to generate work for midtown Manhattan's craftspeople. The epic structural shift in the New York City economy, away from craft and light manufacturing and to white-collar, information-based activities, was not so absolute as to obliterate theater craft from the five boroughs entirely. From the late 1980s to the first years of the new millennium, there were always a handful of shops keeping a local presence on the far west side, or near Times Square.

Most theater construction work after 1990, however, occurred among a postindustrial network of skilled craftspeople not tied to any particular work space or workshop. When PRG opened a show on Broadway, the firm would send necessary experts down from Westchester County or perhaps fly them in from Brussels or Shanghai. They arrived in a district known in local parlance as "Broadway" without maintaining any permanent brick-and-mortar presence there. This was an era in which theater craft had been lifted like a web above and around the harsh, boxy new towers of the new Times Square. People still gather in the district to do theater craft, but like the performers they support, most do so only in sporadic bursts of temporary tenancy.

Scenery shop proprietors such as Fred Feller, Pete Feller, Neil Mazzella, Fred Gallo, and Leo B. Meyer all somehow managed to keep their businesses afloat in the 1990s, despite working in an industry in which it was assumed that they would be lucky to break even.[39] Crafting components to exact specifications for theaters many miles away, suffering from complications and technical difficulties, and working in an industry with few new shows, only a handful of these scenery workers managed to maintain their businesses into the twenty-first century.

Some of their collaborators in costuming, shoes, lighting, and wig making also maintained shops near Times Square, but few were able to work exclusively in the theater after 1980. The designers of recent decades have built their careers through a gypsylike existence, globetrotting through film, stage, television, and convention work in the United States and across the

Atlantic. Try as they might, developers, planners, property owners, and others advocating the "highest and best use" for Times Square real estate were unsuccessful at completely snuffing out these types of businesses.

Rehearsal space also survived into the twenty-first century but only through the aggressive interventions of Broadway leaders who knew that such space was vital to their industry. Gathering $33.7 million through the mechanism of the nonprofit New 42nd Street organization in 2001, industry leaders finally succeeded in opening an eighty-four-thousand-square-foot, state-of-the-art rehearsal center, complete with fourteen rental spaces, on 42nd Street between 7th and 8th Avenues. Although there are no affordable work spaces for costume, wig, shoe, lighting, or scenery specialists in the Times Square of the new millennium, the rehearsal center at least affords these craftspeople the opportunity to meet their casts for design consultations, fittings, and rehearsals at "the crossroads of the world." Noting that while "everything else on this street is about consumption . . . this is about process," Cora Cahan of the New 42nd Street organization was quite aware that the new studios there were something special. To this day the space is an invaluable, sought-after island of craft and show development in a sea of consumption.[40]

This success came just in time. By the late 1990s the reliable 890 Broadway rehearsal center of the 1980s had become overcrowded with dance companies and troubled with its own rent pressures, with little to no help from the city to stay viable.[41] Despite the economic benefit derived by all New Yorkers from a booming Broadway economy, city leaders and policy makers failed to value spaces of craft and construction. One can only hope that the producers, property owners, city leaders, performers, and landlords of twenty-first-century New York City give more thought to the craft behind the Broadway shows they enjoy. Only through the preservation of the skills, work spaces, and collaborations of its craftspeople can the theater move forward with any semblance of artistry. In the words of the late, great playwright Arthur Miller, "[A]ttention must be paid."

Introduction

1. The most comprehensive work on this subject is Mary C. Henderson, *Theater in America* (New York: Harry N. Abrams, 1986). Regarding London's West End, Tracy C. Davis chronicles and analyzes nineteenth-century industrialization in British theater; see Davis, *The Economics of the British Stage* (Cambridge: Cambridge University Press, 2000). No scholar, however, has asked similar questions of Broadway. In this book "Broadway" will serve as a general synonym for the commercial theater in America.

2. Many U.S. cities had an electrified boulevard as their "great white way," but New York's has been the most famous. For this book, the "Great White Way" will serve as a synonym for the Broadway theater industry.

3. This invisibility applied equally to New York and London. Davis, *The Economics of the British Stage*, argues the following about late nineteenth-century theater-making: "[T]he work itself and the personnel who carried it out were invisible, both to audiences and to the historical consciousness of the era" (314).

4. For the purposes of this book, a "theater-related business" is defined as one engaged in significant supply or construction work for commercial stage shows.

5. Evidence of rehearsals from "July 1936 Schedules, Fed. Music Dept.-NYC 9B-5," folder 6, administrative files box 967, Library of Congress, Federal Theatre Project (hereafter LOC-FTP).

6. Manhattan Classified Telephone Directory, 1940, New York Public Library, Microform Reading Room (hereafter NYPL-MRR).

7. With a September 1936 opening for the play and a standard six-week rehearsal, the Ambassador would have become a site of rehearsal, sewing, rigging, and lighting in August.

8. Manhattan Classified Telephone Directory, 1960, NYPL-MRR.

9. Ibid.; *Simon's Theatrical Directory* (New York: Package Publicity Service, 1966).

10. Shubert Archive, *100 Years of Spectacle* (New York: Harry N. Abrams, 2001), 214.

11. "Tin Pan Alley in Distress," *New York Times* (hereafter *NYT*), April 11, 1976, 233.

12. According to Lynne Sagalyn, the tower was completed in the late 1980s and purchased by Morgan Stanley in 1993; see Sagalyn, *Times Square Roulette* (Boston: MIT Press, 2003), 317–18.

13. See Davis, *The Economics of the British Stage*.

Chapter 1

1. *OSU Theatre Collection Bulletin*, no. 12 (1965), Armbruster Scenic Studio, clippings, New York Public Library, Billy Rose Theatre Division (hereafter NYPL-BR). For 1904 claims that it was the second largest in the United States, see Robert S. Joyce, "The Armbruster Scenic Studio," *OSU Theatre Collection Bulletin*, no. 12 (1965): 7. For drop details, see Allan S. Jackson, "The Artistic Practices of the Armbruster Scenic Studio," *OSU Theatre Collection Bulletin*, no. 12 (1965): 20.

2. For Union Square agent and broker history, see John W. Frick, *New York's First Theatrical Center: The Rialto at Union Square* (Ann Arbor, MI: UMI Research Press, 1985). *Business Listings* from NYPL-MRR, 1896, "Scenery," show C. L. Hagen at 536–42 W. 26th St. Hagen was no East Coast version of the long-lived Armbruster's, however. The firm appeared in listings several times in the 1890s but then quickly disappeared.

3. For an interesting comparison, see Davis, *The Economics of the British Stage*, especially chap. 9, "Labour and Labourers," 319. Despite the robust development of London theater in the 1890s, Davis cites a limited count of roughly fifty businesses supplying for the theater, as listed in the post office *Directories*.

4. Alfred Bernheim on stock: "Each theatre with its company was an independent entity for there was . . . no inducement for it to establish a business relationship with other theatres. Having its own permanent, resident, producing organization it had nothing to gain from an alliance with other theatres or other producing organizations, and in turn, it had nothing to offer. It was entirely self-sufficient. It had its own actors and such mechanical force as it needed. . . . It owned its own sets and drops and other equipment, its properties and its wardrobe. While these might have been inadequate judged by present standards, they were not questioned by the unspoiled playgoers of those days"; see Bernheim, *The Business of the Theatre: An Economic History of the American Theatre, 1750–1932* (New York: Benjamin Blom, 1932), 30–31.

5. Ibid., 32.

6. For nineteenth-century components as worn and ragged, see William Zucchero, "The Modern American Theatrical Stock Company," *OSU Theatre Collection Bulletin*, no. 12 (1965): 34.

7. For plays advertised "Direct from New York," see Henderson, *Theater in America*, 24, 59.

8. Daly's Denver tour is detailed in "Special Through Timetable," folder "Other states [*sic*] programmes 1880s," box "Small programmes 1880s," New-York Historical

Society, Quinn Collection (hereafter NYHS-Quinn). For the quip on parody, see Law-rence Levine, *Highbrow/Lowbrow: The Emergence of Cultural Hierarchy in America* (Cambridge, MA: Harvard University Press, 1990), 3.

9. Henderson, *Theater in America*, 218.

10. Otis Skinner, *Footlights and Spotlights: Recollections of My Life on the Stage* (Westport, CT: Greenwood Press), 42–43.

11. Folder "Academy of Music," box "Small programmes 1880s," NYHS-Quinn.

12. Henderson, *Theater in America*, 193.

13. For muslin drop, see Jackson, "The Artistic Practices of the Armbruster Scenic Studio," 23.

14. Many decades later the producer Harold Prince quipped that he had "never seen a show that was made a hit by its scenery or costumes . . . however, I have seen shows that were seriously injured by the wrong production"; see Prince, *Contradictions: Notes on Twenty-Six Years in the Theatre* (Cornwall, NY: Cornwall Press, 1974), 35.

15. Frick, *New York's First Theatrical Center*, 15.

16. During the 1920s design was specialized and separate credits for costuming and scenery appeared. See Bobbi Owen, *Scenic Design on Broadway: Designers and Their Credits* (New York: Greenwood Press, 1991), xiv.

17. "Niblo's Garden," *NYT*, January 1, 1878, 5.

18. In his review of Raymond Knapp, *The American Musical and the Formation of National Identity*, John W. Frick explains that the Kiralfy Brothers were the "kings of spectacle" and that they "staged massive productions like *Around the World in Eighty Days*, *The Siege of Troy*, and *Constantinople*, or *The Revels of the East in the 1870s and 1880s*" (Frick, "Review: Raymond Knapp. The American Musical and the Formation of National Identity," *American Historical Review* 111 [January 2006]: 515–16). For more on the Hanington Brothers, see Henderson, *Theater in America*, 230.

19. For catalog and custom order history, see Joyce, "The Armbruster Scenic Studio," 15.

20. Two examples include John H. Young, who had a drafting table and book-shelves above the now defunct "Broadway Theatre" in 1903, and Albie McDonald Sr., who drafted above the Grand Opera House on 23rd St. in the 1890s. For Young, see M. G. Humphreys, "Scenery: Painting," *Theatre Magazine* (August 1903), clippings, NYPL-BR. For McDonald, see "Building upon the Sand," *NYT*, February 23, 1936, X3.

21. Many of these practices continued until 1919, when the Actors' Equity strike brought them to an end.

22. Mary C. Henderson, *The City and the Theatre* (New York: J. T. White, 1973), 120.

23. Henderson, *Theater in America*, 229.

24. Henderson summarizes electricity's impact this way; see ibid., 221.

25. One of the most famous cases of this was Eugene O'Neill's father, who played Cyrano de Bergerac for many years. O'Neill wrote about this in *A Long Day's Journey into Night*.

26. In his introduction to his *Tragic Drama & Modern Society* (Totowa, NJ: Barnes & Noble, 1981), the scholar John Orr makes a case for Ibsen as the first major realist playwright (xvii–xviii).

27. "Notes of the Stage," *NYT*, November 10, 1889, 13.

28. The Broadway League's Web site (http://www.ibdb.com, accessed April 21, 2008) lists eight versions of *A Doll's House* in this era, but the 1902 "Mrs. Fiske" version was "revived" only one week after closing, so it should not count twice. A more accurate count would be seven stagings from 1889 to 1908.

29. From stage directions, original manuscript by Henrik Ibsen, published in Norway in 1879.

30. Used scenery did find its way to community theater and Off Broadway but almost never to Broadway.

31. Search "Hedda Gabler" at http://www.ibdb.com.

32. Ibid.

33. *Hedda Gabler*, original stage direction from the first edition, published in Norway in 1890.

34. Nora leaves her husband and slams the door behind her; Hedda commits suicide by shooting herself.

35. For the star system and combination companies, see Zucchero, "The Modern American Theatrical Stock Company," 30.

36. Ibid.

37. For example, see Marlis Schweitzer, *When Broadway Was the Runway: Theater, Fashion, and American Culture* (Philadelphia: University of Pennsylvania Press, 2009), 16: "By the 1880s, as result of panic of 1873, 282 combination companies were touring but only 8 stock companies remained" (Schweitzer cites Bernheim, *The Business of the Theatre*); Jack Poggi, *Theater in America: The Impact of Economic Forces* (Ithaca, NY: Cornell University Press, 1968); Peter A. Davis, "From Stock to Combination: The Panic of 1873 and Its Effects on the American Theatre Industry," *Theater History Studies* 8 (1988): 1–9; and Benjamin McArthur, *Actors and American Culture, 1880–1920* (Iowa City: University of Iowa Press, 2001), 5, 9.

38. Bernheim, *The Business of the Theatre*, 32–33.

39. Mary C. Henderson counts fourteen Broadway playhouses by 1870; see Henderson, *The City and the Theatre*, 116. Supplier counts are from 1879 *Business Listings*, NYPL-MRR. Listed are twenty-seven costumers and four other suppliers, including two calcium light suppliers on Broome St., downtown.

40. Schweitzer explains that by 1905 there were "over three hundred 'first class' shows touring the nation with an additional one hundred to two hundred 'second-rate' shows originating out of cities like Chicago"; see Schweitzer, *When Broadway Was the Runway*, 9. She draws her data from Philip Lewis, *Trouping: How the Show Came to Town* (New York: Harper & Row, 1973). Henderson locates the "direct from Broadway" advertising trend as being "born" in the era spanning 1870–99, but she

mentions this only in passing, drawing no distinction between "direct from New York" and "direct from Broadway"; see Henderson, *The City and the Theatre*, 116.

41. For Daly "personally directs," see Corinthian Academy of Music, 1880 season advertisement; and for "Direct from the Madison Square Theatre," see Chicago Opera House, 1888–89 season advertisement. Both appear in folder "Other states [*sic*] programmes 1880s," box "1880s," NYHS-Quinn.

42. Schweitzer, *When Broadway Was the* Runway, 22, cites two 1897 examples of tours billed explicitly as "Direct from New York." See also Henderson, *Theater in America*, 24, 59.

43. Chicago Opera House, folder "Other states [*sic*] programmes 1880s," box 1880s, NYHS-Quinn.

44. Dominating vaudeville in the 1890s were the Orpheum Circuit, which tightened its grip on midwestern vaudeville, and the Keith and Albee Circuit, which conquered the Eastern Seaboard.

45. For more on this topic, see Mark Hodin, "The Disavowal of Ethnicity: Legitimate Theatre and the Social Construction of Literary Value in Turn-of-the-Century America," *Theatre Journal* 52 no. 2 (2000): 211–26; and Vincent Landro, "Media Mania: The Demonizing of the Theatrical Syndicate," *Journal of American Drama and Theatre* 13 (Spring 2001): 49–50.

46. For more on "direct from Broadway," see James Traub, *The Devil's Playground* (New York: Random House, 2004), 26; and David Sanjek, *American Popular Music and Its Business: The First Four Hundred Years* (New York: Oxford University Press, 2001), 25. For the Shuberts, see Ken Bloom, *Broadway: Its History, People, and Places: An Encyclopedia* (New York: Routledge, 2003), 452: "For all the companies of *Blossom Time* that the Shuberts sent out on the road, they never redid the sets or costumes. . . . He [J. J. Shubert] would put the touring companies into the Ambassador Theatre for one night, so he could then send them out on the road with the billing 'direct from Broadway.' . . . the Shuberts never had any intention of running Blossom Time—they just wanted to be able to advertise the ensuing tour as 'direct from Broadway.'" This trend persisted well into the twentieth century. See, for example, "Detroit Stage Inc. Bally's Home Talent," *Billboard Magazine*, July 19, 1947, 48: "[I]n contrast to the usual emphasis in theatrical publicity upon 'a show direct from Broadway,' it is the homey angle that is being played up, with stress on the fact that three of the cast . . . are strictly local talent."

47. *Stage Chat*: "the above reproduction taken from an actual photograph showing Maxine Elliott and Mabel Taliaferre in the great scene in the Third Act of 'Hearts Aflame.' Reproduced here Next Week, Mon. Tues., Wed. May, 1914." Stage: Periodicals: U.S. (uncataloged), NYPL-BR.

48. "Haswell, Percy," clipping, *NY Telegraph*, October 25, 1903, Robinson Locke bound notebook, ser. 2, NYPL-BR.

Chapter 2

1. "A Factory for Making Plays," *NYT*, November 25, 1906, SM4.

2. "C. L. Hagen," of 536 W. 26th St., does appear as a separated site of scenery building in the 1902 Manhattan *Business Listings* (NYPL-MRR), but unlike Savage's shop, there is no readily available evidence that Hagen built for Broadway.

3. "A Factory for Making Plays," SM4.

4. "Henry W. Savage, Producer, Is Dead," *NYT*, November 30, 1927, 25. The obituary notes that he produced some of the "best known musical shows of the early years of the century" and points out that he "staged 50 successes."

5. See William Zucchero, "The Modern American Theatrical Stock Company," *OSU Theatre Collection Bulletin*, no. 12 (1965): 28–43, NYPL-BR. See also McArthur, *Actors and American Culture.*

6. Economies of scale are a well-known benefit of economic expansion. More specifically, "agglomeration economies" are a specific type of economy of scale. They kick in when a district accumulates a critical mass of suppliers and laborers within close proximity to one another. The phrase is used frequently in economic analyses of industrial districts. For more, see Brendan O'Flaherty, *City Economics* (Cambridge, MA: Harvard University Press, 2005).

7. "Latest Dealings in Realty Field . . . Times Square Deal," *NYT*, September 8, 1921, 32. Geoly purchased 106, 108, 110, and 112 W. 46th St. The parcels were part of the Astor estate sale of 1921.

8. See Henderson, *Theater in America*, 201.

9. Manhattan *Business Listings* from 1915 and 1922, category of "Theatrical Supply," NYPL-MRR.

10. Grinanger and Cirker were identified as collaborators by "How and When David Belasco Goes 'Hunting' for Atmosphere," *NYT*, October 2, 1904, 25; while Buckland, Gros, and Hartmann were named in Henderson, *Theater in America*, 201.

11. "A. Grinanger, Scenic Designer, 84," *NYT*, March 9, 1949, 25. This obituary mentions that "he was also chief designer and artist at various times for Ernest Albert and Castle & Harvey."

12. "How and When David Belasco Goes 'Hunting' for Atmosphere," 30.

13. Ibid.

14. Belasco earned this nickname because of his peculiar penchant for dressing in a priest's tunic, despite his well-known reputation as a womanizer. His personal life overshadowed his work in scenic design, and it did not help that he seemed to relish his reputation for bedding chorines and leading ladies. Most notoriously, when he built his own theater on 44th St. in 1907, he is said to have installed an elevator near the ladies' dressing rooms, which went directly to his apartment upstairs. For details of the elevator, see Henderson, *The City and the Theatre*, 255.

15. William Morrison, *Broadway Theatres: History & Architecture* (New York: Dover Publications, 1999), 52.

16. Both Cirker and Grinanger earned several credits with Belasco from 1900 to 1913 but also with other producers. See http://www.ibdb.com, accessed September 22, 2008.

17. "Mitchell Cirker, 70, Theatrical Designer," *NYT*, February 6, 1953, 19.

18. Mary Gay Humphreys, "Mr. John H. Young in His Studio in the Broadway Theatre," *Theatre Magazine* (August 1903), "Scenery: Painting," clippings, NYPL-BR. John H. Young's obituary, *NYT*, January 5, 1944, 17, names his sons as John B. Young and Lewis C. Young.

19. These details were gleaned from an image of Young Bros. in Kenneth Jackson and David Dunbar, eds., *The Encyclopedia of the City of New York* (New Haven, CT: Yale University Press, 1995), 1167.

20. "Building upon the Sand," *NYT*, February 23, 1936, X3.

21. Another skilled lighting designer, Wilfred Buckland, would have likely stayed with Belasco as well had he not been hired away by a Hollywood studio in 1913. See Jackson and Dunbar, *The Encyclopedia of the City of New York*, "filmmaking," 404.

22. Display Stage Lighting Co., 1929 Yellow Pages, NYPL-MRR. The history of exactly which third-party contractors Belasco hired for each show is relatively unclear prior to the 1920s, because it was not yet standard for backstage experts and craftspeople to be credited in playbills. Before craft unions demanded that their members be properly acknowledged, credits for scenery and lighting were spotty at best.

23. "A Century of Costumes," *NYT*, March 23, 1941, X3.

24. Henderson, *Theater in America*, 202.

25. Ibid., 201–5.

26. For the rectangle designs in 1914 for *The Man Who Married a Dumb Wife*, see ibid., 204. For the *Hamlet* stairs in 1922, see ibid., 205–6.

27. Henderson, *Theater in America*, 207.

28. Mary C. Henderson, *The Story of 42nd Street* (New York: Back Stage Books, 2008), 170.

29. For some of the earliest images of these stagehands at work at the Wallack's and Hippodrome theaters, see Mary C. Henderson, *Broadway Ballyhoo* (New York: H. N. Abrams, 1989), 73.

30. It is the author's understanding that IATSE Local 1 has no official archive and does not make its papers available to scholars. Limited IATSE correspondence is available in NYPL-BR, and select papers may be available in other archives.

31. *Abie's Irish Rose* playbill, May 2, 1922, NYPL-BR.

32. Physioc correspondence, October 19, 1921, folder 2B, box 3, Wagner Collection 65, Tamiment Library, New York University (hereafter NYU-W65). When he did this, Physioc was no novice. He was credited for designing fifty-nine Broadway shows prior to his 1921 fine (see http://www.ibdb.com, accessed October 16, 2008), including a major roof-top installation in 1905 "over the combined roofs of the New York and Criterion Theatres." Rooftop credit was discovered in a program dated Monday, June 26, 1905, folder "Misc., 1900s," box "small programs," NYHS-Quinn.

33. "6-Story Building Sold for Studios," *NYT*, November 5, 1956, 52. Not long after Nolan Bros. was sold, another scene shop named Triangle Studios moved in. This shop appeared at 533 W. 24th, according to the 1963 edition of *Simon's Theatrical Directory* (New York: Package Publicity Service, 1963).

34. See "Business Properties," *NYT*, October 5, 1923, 31, for details about the building. Vail's chosen location was both savvy and precocious. By the 1950s the W. 40s and 50s, near 9th and 10th Aves., would become home to many Broadway scene shops.

35. *Scenic Artist*, June 1927 (New York: Seaboard Publishing Co., 1927), 27, NYPL-BR.

36. Ibid., 6.

37. "Building upon the Sand," X3.

38. 1902 listings from "Business Directory," NYPL-MRR. For the "every major city" quote, see Henderson, *Theater in America*, 222; and for secondhand dealers, see ibid., 220.

39. 1902 "Business Directory," NYPL-MRR.

40. Bernheim, *The Business of the Theatre*, 75.

41. See "Costumers" in *Business Listings* or later in *Yellow Pages*: 1896, 43; 1902, 75; 1929, 70; 1940, 52; 1950, 41; 1960, 50; 1970, 33; 1980, 14; 1990, 10, NYPL-MRR.

42. Some of the details regarding the early years of Eaves are unclear. The *NYT* obituary for Charles Geoly claims that he began as an "errand boy" in 1896 and then bought the firm in 1909 ("Charles Geoly Is Dead," *NYT*, June 18, 1959, 31). Henderson, *Theater in America*, 223, however, cites the sale as in 1897. Also, Eaves's own advertising booklet from the 1940s names the founding year of the firm as 1863 ("Eaves Booklet," "Production": financing, clippings, NYPL-BR), but Henderson, *Theater in America*, 223, says 1867. The buildings purchased by Geoly in 1921 were 106, 108, 110, and 112 W. 46th, per "Latest Dealings in Realty Field . . . Times Square Deal," *NYT*, September 8, 1921, 32.

43. "A Factory for Making Plays," SM4.

44. This was the "Hippodrome Studio Building," later sold to Vail Construction. See "Business Properties," *NYT*, October 5, 1923, 31.

45. "New Lyceum a Model of Comfort," *NYT*, September 27, 1903, 26.

46. Henderson, *Theater in America*, 221, explains that leading producers "set up their own costume workrooms to reduce costs and, as a result, eventually built up large inventories that could be used to costume touring shows and future productions."

47. Henderson, *The City and the Theatre*, 267.

48. See ibid.; and Henderson, *Theater in America*, 28.

49. See "Dressing Up Broadway," *NYT*, November 5, 1961, X3; and "James E. Stroock, Costumer, Dead," *NYT*, June 23, 1965, 29. The *NYT* Stroock obituary dates Brooks uniforms back to 1908, but Henderson, *Theater in America*, 224, cites 1906.

50. "Costumes—Masquerade & Theatrical," Manhattan Classified Telephone Directory, 1940, NYPL-MRR.

51. Other notable credits include *Death of a Salesman; Mister Roberts; Street Scene; Oklahoma!; Carousel; Finian's Rainbow; The Heiress; Look Homeward, Angel; Guys and Dolls; The Miracle Worker; I Do! I Do!; and No, No, Nanette.*

52. Schweitzer, *When Broadway Was the Runway*, 67.

53. See Henderson, *Theater in America*, 220–30, for details about the costume unions.

54. See "Costumers" or "Costumes": 1902, 75; 1929, 70; 1940, 52; 1950, 41; 1960, 50; 1970, 33; 1980, 14; 1990, 1, NYPL-MRR.

55. Originally from Hopkins's 1937 autobiography published by Doubleday, *To a Lonely Boy*, and quoted in Henderson, *The Story of 42nd Street*, 169.

56. Although it is impossible to know statistically how often this occurred, the fact that Actors' Equity demanded that these practices stop in 1919 is strong evidence that this was not uncommon in the late nineteenth century.

57. 1922 *Business Listings*, NYPL-MRR.

58. Chapter 6 goes into more detail about theater craft and sidewalk safety in the district, following the lead of Jane Jacobs, *The Death and Life of Great American Cities* (New York: Random House, 1961).

59. Details are from Henderson, *The Story of 42nd Street*, 166–68.

60. "Cut Theatre Rates Put Up the Profits," *NYT*, January 15, 1912, 13.

Chapter 3

1. "Sing for Your Supper" was penned by Richard Rogers and Lorenz Hart in 1938 for the musical *The Boys from Syracuse*, and evoked the Depression through lyrics about performers singing to earn their next meal. New shows opening each September, as counted on http://www.ibdb.com, last accessed January 15, 2009, are as follows: 1895, 14; 1900, 22; 1905, 29; 1908, 23; 1910, 17; 1915, 16; 1920, 19; 1922, 24; 1925, 32; 1928, 21; 1930, 24; 1933, 12; 1935, 17; 1945, 15; 1955, 7; 1965, 2; 1975, 3; 1985, 3; 1995, 0.

2. "Gossip of the Rialto," *NYT*, April 12, 1931, X1.

3. "A. L. Erlanger Debts Listed at Hearing," *NYT*, June 22, 1932.

4. "Morris Green Files Plea in Bankruptcy," *NYT*, August 16, 1932.

5. "Theatre League Asks Stagehands Paycut," *NYT*, June 22, 1932.

6. "Membership, 1935–42," February 10, 1935, folder 4, box 4, NYU-W65.

7. "Membership, 1935–42," February 1, 1935, folder 4, box 4, NYU-W65.

8. "Membership, 1935–42," resolution, June 24, 1935: "no member making $90 or more per month shall have his dues advanced," folder 4, box 4, NYU-W65.

9. In 1929 there were 142 theater-related businesses, and in 1940 there were still 126, only an 11 percent drop, as counted in *Business Listings*, NYPL-MRR. Although a listed firm was not necessarily an employed firm, the number of surviving shops is a decent barometer of solvency.

10. Mary C. Henderson, *Mielziner: Master of Modern Stage Design* (New York: Back Stage Books, 2000), 103.

11. "Value Doubled on Lumber Company's Plot Near Eighth Avenue in Two Years, Causing Recent Sale and Purchase of New Site Further West," *NYT*, March 22, 1925.

12. See Robert Fishman, "The Regional Plan and the Transformation of the Industrial Metropolis," in David Ward and Olivier Zunz, eds., *Landscape of Modernity* (Baltimore: Johns Hopkins University Press, 1997), 106–23.

13. Robert Fitch, *The Assassination of New York* (New York: Verso Books, 1994), 60.

14. Ibid., 59.

15. Rockefeller Center was also a capstone for efforts to push the garment industry away from 5th Ave. Although it would maintain a few select spaces for backstage craft work related to live broadcast shows such as *The Tonight Show* at mid-century and *Saturday Night Live* in later decades, these spaces were never as numerous as the lost walk-up rentals.

16. *Damn Yankees, West Side Story,* and *Company* "Capitalization" folders list Prince at "1 Rock.Plaza," Harold Prince Collection, NYPL-BR. Leo Shull, *Angels: The People Who Finance the Broadway Theatre* (New York: Show Business Press, 1946), lists general partners William Weintraub (several shows) and Ralph Neubeger (for the show *Anna Lucasta*) at 30 Rockefeller Plaza.

17. "Radio City Plans New Stage Devices," *NYT*, July 27, 1932. Chapter 2 featured Clark as a partner in the purchase of 534 W. 30th St. with McDonald Construction, a scene shop.

18. Another legacy of Rockefeller Center was to cement the popularity of tower-in-the-plaza redevelopment in midtown. Many planners looking to redevelop midtown after 1940 used Rockefeller Center's clean, stark plaza as a point of reference. Redevelopment schemes for Times Square began with Mayor Robert F. Wagner and were discussed until they came to fruition in the 1980s. Lynne Sagalyn, *Times Square Roulette* (Cambridge: MIT Press, 2001), 45, 193, explains how 1980s developers envisioned a "Rockefeller Center West."

19. The sixty-two other performers in the 1934 production of *Anything Goes* are listed at http://www.ibdb.com, accessed February 26, 2009.

20. Le Corbusier famously commented on New York from atop the Empire State Building in 1935.

21. See Bosley Crowther, "Building upon the Sand," *NYT*, February 23, 1936, X3.

22. Ibid., X3; 1940 *Business Listings* for stage riggers and scene shops reveal Bradford Ashworth at 314 11th Ave. and Centre Studios at 520 W. 30th St., NYPL-MRR.

23. Nicholas Van Hoogstraten, *Lost Broadway Theatres* (Princeton, NJ: Princeton Architectural Press, 1997), 87.

24. Ibid., 87, 144. In Philadelphia a tank "capable of pumping 230 gallons per minute" crashed through the ceiling of the Park theater in 1890. See "The Tumble of a Tank," *NYT*, April 14, 1890. For more on the districtwide installation of water tanks, see "Astor Theatre Gets Its License at Last," *NYT*, September 9, 1906; "Water Tanks,"

NYT, July 21, 1910; and "Water Tanks," *NYT*, August 14, 1910. *Tea and Sympathy* closed on June 18, 1955, according to http://www.ibdb.com, accessed April 2, 2009.

25. Regardless of their thoughts on quality, theater historians uniformly cite the 1920s as a robust and prolific era for stage shows. See, for example, Henderson, *The City and the Theatre,* 168.

26. "Credits on Copyright Music No Longer a Joking Matter," *NYT*, May 15, 1932. E. C. Mills is quoted as follows: "[T]he familiarity of tunes heard so often on the radio caused corresponding shrinkage in the revenue derived from the sale of sheet music."

27. For a WEAF broadcast from the Hammerstein Theatre in August 1931, the composers George Gershwin, Jerome Kern, Richard Rodgers, Cole Porter, and the team of Brown, DeSylva, and Henderson all earned top billing as the starring "stage folk" of a live radio broadcast. See Van Hoogstraten, *Lost Broadway Theatres,* 238; and "To Rename Theatre: Stage Folk to Take Part . . . ," *NYT*, July 27, 1931, 19.

28. For ASCAP commentary on popular songs and the interpolation of popular songs such as "Blue Skies," "Alexander's Ragtime Band," and "I Got Rhythm," see "Credits on Copyright Music No Longer a Joking Matter."

29. For more on radio plays, see "Broadway: The Place That Words Built," in William Taylor, ed., *Inventing Times Square* (Baltimore: Johns Hopkins University Press, 1991), 227.

30. See "Listening-In," *NYT*, June 5, 1932. Wynn's show was original, but he was not the first radio performer to recognize the value of a live audience. New York State governor Alfred E. Smith made an impromptu request in 1932 to give a speech to an audience within a broadcasting studio. See "Now the Audience Joins the Broadcast," *NYT*, April 23, 1933. The *Times* foreshadows television's "laugh track" by noting that recorded laughter bolstered broadcasts.

31. James Baughman explains the iconic place of these broadcasts in radio history; see Baughman, "Take Me Away from Manhattan: NYC and the American Mass Culture, 1930–1990," in Martin Shefter, ed., *Capital of the American Century: The National and International Influence of New York City* (New York: Russell Sage Foundation, 1993), 117–43.

32. "Listening-In," *NYT*, June 5, 1932. Gasoline pumps appeared due to Texaco sponsorship.

33. A list of the full cast is available at http://www.ibdb.com, accessed April 6, 2009.

34. For scenery details of a 1931 roof garden play, *The Cyclone Lover*, see http://www.ibdb.com, accessed April 8, 2009.

35. See Schweitzer, *When Broadway Was the Runway,* 186–88.

36. Susan Murray, *Hitch Your Antenna to the Stars: Early Television and Broadcast Stardom* (New York: Routledge, 2005), 14.

37. "Listening-In" *NYT*, June 5, 1932: "The crowd in the lobby of the New Amsterdam Theatre on Tuesday nights would lead a passer-by to think that the curtain

was about to go up on the Follies. But no, the attraction is Ed Wynn on the roof, where there are 675 seats for radio enthusiasts anxious to see the comedian in action at the microphone."

38. "Premiere of a 'Destiny' Show," *NYT*, March 24, 1935, explains the Bowes debut at Radio City. The move to Hammerstein's and the audience of thirteen hundred are mentioned in "Behind the Scenes," *NYT*, August 23, 1936.

39. "Behind the Scenes," *NYT*, August 23, 1936, shows opera listed for Friday and Saturday evenings on WMCA.

40. A compelling argument to this effect appears in Robert Snyder, *The Voice of the City: Vaudeville and Popular Culture in New York* (New York: Ivan R. Dee, 2005).

41. In Morrison, *Broadway Theatres*, radio tenancy is chronicled from the 1930s to the 1950s at the Playhouse (ABC, 1949–52), Hudson, Maxine Elliott's, Longacre (WOR Mutual), Ritz (1939–69), Royale (CBS radio, 1930s–41), Hammerstein's (CBS, 1936–50), Belasco (1948–53), and Little (CBS Radio) theaters; see especially 39, 59, 136, and 139.

42. *The Jazz Singer* opened at Warners on Broadway at 52nd Street. See *Variety* articles from October and November 1927 for more on the reactions from Broadway leaders. Though not the first movie with synchronized dialogue, *The Jazz Singer* was the first with a wide release and a commercial run.

43. For more on stage producers losing ground with lowbrow audiences and taking their shows in more highbrow, intellectual, and literary directions, see Levine, *Highbrow/Lowbrow*; and the introduction in Craig Morrison, *Theaters* (New York: W. W. Norton, 2004).

44. Whether the collapse of vaudeville was more the result of talking pictures or the crash itself is an interesting and debatable question, but it is not central to this book.

45. An exact count of converted theaters is difficult because many switched readily between film, live theater, and burlesque. Counting from Morrison, *Broadway Theatres*, there were twenty-one that converted: the New Amsterdam, Eltinge, Selwyn, Times Square, Apollo, Victory, Astor, Bijou, Princess, Palace, Longacre, Punch & Judy, Henry Miller, Theatre Masque, Ambassador, Winter Garden, George M. Cohan, Lunt-Fontanne, Gaiety, Lew Fields, and Lyric.

46. "News of the Screen . . . Opens Tonight . . . Midsummer Night's Dream," *NYT*, April 21, 1937.

47. For Paramount in Astoria, see Richard Koszarski, *Hollywood on the Hudson: Film and Television in New York from Griffith to Sarnoff* (New Brunswick, NJ: Rutgers University Press, 2008), 27–28. For Edison in New York, see Jackson and Dunbar, *Encyclopedia of the City of New York*, "filmmaking," 403. For "Film Cutting Room" and "Film Storage," both at 126 W. 46th St., see *Business Listings*, 1922, NYPL-MRR. For Eaves supplying Griffith, see Eaves booklet, Production: Financing, clippings, NYPL-BR. For 1926 films, see Koszarski, *Hollywood on the Hudson*, 9.

48. For types of mid-war shoots, see Koszarski, *Hollywood on the Hudson*, 10–12, 171. For the decisions of many studios to invest in sound equipment only on the West Coast, see Koszarski, *Hollywood on the Hudson*, chap. 5.

49. Career details for Irene Sharaff and Charles LeMaire can be found in Henderson, *Theater in America*, 226. Dazian's stationery can be found in the Museum of the City of New York, Theater Collection (hereafter MCNY-TC), "Dazian's Theatricals," box of clippings and memorabilia.

50. "General Corr., 1947–49," box 2, folder 40, NYU-W65. Several letters from Rudy Karnholt to Hollywood designers implore them to join. There is also a letter from CSU (scenic designers for Hollywood) member Lester Polakov to Rudy Karnholt, June 18, 1947: "things are certainly bleak for the C.S.U. . . . It is my personal opinion that they'll never get back into the studios."

51. Andrew B. Harris, *Broadway Theatre* (New York: Routledge, 1994), 59.

52. Office locations discovered in "Adv. & Publicity, WPA-FTP Presentations, Weekly Schedules—1937," folder 2, and "Caravan Theatre—Posters—Corr. & Publicity," folder 33, both in administrative files box 964, LOC-FTP.

53. For *We Live and Laugh* at Ringle's, see "July 1936 Schedules, Fed. Music Dept.—NYC 9B-5," folder 6, administrative files box 967, LOC-FTP.

54. "Adv. & Publicity, WPA-FTP Presentations, Weekly Schedules—1937," folder 2, administrative files box 964, LOC-FTP. Weekly schedules of the Caravan Theatre document a wide range of venues throughout all of New York City's five boroughs; "Caravan Theatre—Posters—Corr. & Publicity," folder 33, administrative files box 964, LOC-FTP. Correspondence from Charles Platkin, May 21, 1937, to the IND subway explains that FTP's Caravan Theatres had "five traveling trucks convertible into stages . . . some 200 traveling players," and emphasizes that the posters for their shows were seen by two million people in 1936.

55. See Murray, *Hitch Your Antenna to the Stars*, chap. 2; and "News of the Radio: NBC Television Station Plans a Varied Series of Programs for Next 11 Days," *NYT*, August 21, 1947.

56. For broadcast details, see television listings in the *NYT*, August 10, 1947, and September 21, 1948. Interestingly, Berle inherited his *Texaco* show from radio host Ed Wynn. For Ray Bolger's Broadway credits, see http://www.ibdb.com, accessed April 15, 2009.

57. Baughman, "Take Me Away from Manhattan," 124.

58. For more on production numbers performed in full costumes with full dance crews and choruses, see Murray, *Hitch Your Antenna to the Stars*, chap. 2. For *Pal Joey* on *Ed Sullivan*, see http://www.imdb.com, season 5, episode 41, June 15, 1952, accessed April 15, 2009.

59. Baughman, "Take Me Away from Manhattan," 124.

60. Morrison, *Broadway Theatres*, 161, features DuMont at the Craig. For the Ambassador rental, see Maryann Chach et al., *The Shuberts Present: 100 Years of American Theater* (New York: H. N. Abrams, 2001), 214. For television broadcasting at additional theaters, see Morrison, *Broadway Theatres*, 35, 59, 121, 141, 143, 145, 165.

61. Morrison, *Broadway Theatres*, 59.

62. Van Hoogstraten, *Lost Broadway Theatres*, 111.

63. Quoted in the Shubert Archive's newsletter publication, *100 Years of Spectacle* (New York: Shubert Archive, 2001), 216.

64. Yellow Pages reveal that Shubert Stage Costumes operated at 3 W. 61st St. through the 1940s and 1950s, while Veronica Costumes was located at 5 W. 62nd St. in 1950, NYPL-MRR.

65. Letter to Dazian's, November 30, 1948: "we hereby wish to inform you that we propose a 15% raise effective Jan. 1st, 1949 for our member, Miss Gwen Cummings," folder 13, box 3, NYU-W65.

66. Correspondence dated December 8, 1947, announcing the move to 234 W. 56th St., and March 8, 1948, newsletter announcing a raise in dues, both in folder 13, box 3, NYU-W65.

67. Hotel names culled from meeting announcements in newsletters from various folders and boxes, NYU-W65. As a specific example, box 2, folder 41, "General Corr., Misc., 1950–52" has correspondence naming the Claridge Hotel.

68. For Brooks and Eaves quotes, see "Costuming for TV," *NYT*, November 11, 1951. For "T.V. packages," see Rotundo letterhead, folder 41, "General Corr., Misc., 1950–52", box 2, NYU-W65. For Vail, see Vail obituary, *NYT*, November 15, 1952.

69. Nothing came directly from *Pajama Game* except Raitt and the audio track. Viewers of the footage should look for the stone walls of the prison cell, the live horse onstage, several costumes, a painted backdrop of hills and trees, and the interior of a saloon complete with wood paneling, a painted floor in the style of slate stone, free-standing tables and chairs, and nets strung overhead. All of this was crafted just for Sullivan's broadcast. See www.imdb.com, *Ed Sullivan*, episode 49 of season 7, August 22, 1954, accessed April 16, 2009.

70. Milton MacKaye, *Saturday Evening Post*, February 2, 1952, as quoted in Baughman, "Take Me Away from Manhattan," 124.

71. "Brooks Costume Moving," *NYT*, April 30, 1952.

72. For union issues such as triple pay for night shoots and the requirement that producers bringing an L.A.-based crew to work in New York also pay New York union members at scale whether or not they work, see "Unions Seek Rise in Film-TV Jobs," *NYT*, June 2, 1964. For the strike and Brodkin's move, see "Strike Brings Threat to Shift Local TV Filming to Hollywood," May 12, 1964; and "2 Struck TV Series Will Move to Coast," *NYT*, May 14, 1964.

73. "Unions Seek Rise in Film-TV Jobs," *NYT*, June 2, 1964.

74. Baughman, "Take Me Away from Manhattan," 126. *The Tonight Show* had originated at Rockefeller Center in 1950 as a variety show called *Broadway Open House*. When the program moved to the Hudson in 1954, hosts Steve Allen and Jack Paar, along with a staff of roughly fifty people, brought daytime and nighttime productivity to W. 44th and W. 45th Sts. just east of Broadway. During broadcasts the staff would

often open the oversized doors on W. 45th, once used to bring in scenery, so that Steve Allen could conduct his amusing "man-on-the-street" interviews with passersby. For more, see Robert Campbell, *The Golden Years of Broadcasting* (New York: Scribner's, 1976), 240–42.

75. Television-related unions from the Joint Council as of 1964, as listed in "Unions Seek Rise in Film-TV Jobs," *NYT*, June 2, 1964.

76. Examples from http://www.ibdb.com and www.imdb.com, accessed April 20, 2009: John Raitt, Vivienne Segal, Carol Channing, Julie Andrews, and Alfred Drake.

Chapter 4

1. "Priority for Stage Sets Asked," *NYT*, November 11, 1941, 29: "Asserting that 'the entertainment of the public during the present crisis is vital to the civilian morale,' the Vail Scenic Construction Company, 530 W. 47th St., makers of theatrical scenery, announced yesterday it had appealed to OPM's Civilian Supply Division for priorities in necessary materials. Shut down on scenery making would affect employment of 100,000 persons, ranging from ushers to carpenters to actors, the appeal said." See also Tim Carter, *Oklahoma!: The Making of an American Musical* (London: Yale University Press, 2007), 148. In his copiously researched and well-written work, Carter chronicles the difficulties of the *Oklahoma!* team in acquiring shoe leather.

2. See Henderson, *Theater in America*, 134; and Ethan Mordden, *Beautiful Mornin': The Broadway Musical in the 1940s* (New York: Oxford University Press, 1999), 78.

3. Brooks Atkinson, *Broadway* (New York: Macmillan, 1970), 337; Howard Taubman, *The Making of the American Theatre* (New York: Coward-McCann, 1965), 254: "[T]he importance of *Oklahoma!* as a landmark has not dimmed." See also Michael Kantor and Laurence Maslon, *Broadway: The American Musical* (New York: Bulfinch, 2004), 196–205; and Max Wilk, *OK! The Story of Oklahoma!* (New York: Grove Press, 1993).

4. For more on the guild, see Walter Prichard Eaton, *The History of the Theatre Guild: The First Fifteen Years* (New York: Theatre Guild Inc., 1934); and Kantor and Maslon, *Broadway*, 200–205. Rodgers and Hammerstein sessions at the Lamb's Club are credited in *Oklahoma! Playbill*, NYPL-BR.

5. Harold Prince explains fund-raising as of 1954: "[W]e capitalized Pajama Game at $250,000 . . . the conventional way. . . .We auditioned for backers in borrowed living rooms"; see Prince, *Contradictions: Notes on Twenty-Six Years in the Theatre* (New York: Dodd, Mead, 1974), 10. Details of the two pianos at Steinway and multiple backers' auditions in 1942 are from an in-person interview by the author with Joan Roberts, the original Laurey character in *Oklahoma!*, in Rockville Centre, New York, September 2006. Details of the $80,000 capitalization are from *Saturday Evening Post*, January 6, 1945, 21–23, 59–60, folder "1940–1949," Theatre Guild, clippings, NYPL-BR.

6. The budget for *Connecticut Yankee* is from the 1946 edition of Leo Shull, *Angels: The People Who Finance the Broadway Theatre*. The budget for *Salesman* is from *Variety*, May 25, 1949, NYPL-MRR. The *Stalag 17* budget is from *Variety*, May 30, 1951, NYPL-MRR.

7. *New York Post* "Society" column, 1958, Meyer Davis, clippings, NYPL-BR.

8. Ibid.

9. Investments are from Shull, *Angels*, 1963 edition.

10. The named investors are "James E. Stroock," proprietor of Brooks Costume, and "David Steinberg," head of Imperial Scenic Studios; see Shull, *Angels*, 1946, 1955, and 1958 eds.

11. Obituary from *Variety*, April 2, 1996, Leo Shull, clippings, NYPL-BR. In the *NYT* obituary clipping on Shull, April 2, 1996, the *Times* claimed that both Lauren Bacall and Kirk Douglas hawked Shull's wares as aspiring, unknown actors, but this may have been a claim of Shull's and nothing more. The six *Angels* editions listed were the only ones to appear in a national Worldcat library search.

12. Limited partnerships were standard through the 1970s, when the Limited Liability Company became more popular due to tax implications. Steven Adler explains the shift in *On Broadway: Art and Commerce on the Great White Way* (Carbondale: Southern Illinois University Press, 2004), 144.

13. In his 1946 edition of *Angels*, Shull listed $643,199 worth of investments into the twenty shows he found data for in 1943. This sum provides another chance to speculate about the full season's investment. When the published investments are quadrupled to account for the eighty shows of the 1942–43 season, this approximate annual capitalization becomes $2,572,796.

14. Jane Jacobs, *The Economy of Cities* (New York: Vintage Books, 1969), 85–100. Du Pont's president suggested to Jacobs that one in twenty was a typical success rate.

15. See Thomas Gale Moore, *The Economics of the American Theater* (Durham, NC: Duke University Press, 1968), for several case studies that are detailed and yet do not account for development work. The League of New York Theaters and Producers conducted the 1975 study in response to a musicians' strike, while the 1993 study was by the Theatre Development Fund.

16. According to Kantor and Maslon, *Broadway*, 201, the return on each $1,000 invested in *Oklahoma!* was nearly $2.5 million.

17. The book on flops is Ken Mandelbaum, *Not Since Carrie: Forty Years of Broadway Musical Flops* (New York: St. Martin's Griffin, 1992).

18. The subtleties of contractors' payments and fee structures were explained to the author by Neil Mazzella, proprietor of Hudson Scenic, in a phone interview, fall 2005.

19. This often-cited quote about *Oklahoma!* has been attributed to rival producer Mike Todd, but Kantor and Maslon, *Broadway*, 200, cites Walter Winchell's press secretary.

20. "Bizarre History of a Failure," *NYT*, January 12, 1941, X3.

21. For a fascinating discussion of hit/flop percentages, see Prince, *Contradictions*, 231; and Bernard Rosenberg and Ernest Harburg, *The Broadway Musical: Collaboration in Commerce and Art* (New York: New York University Press, 1992), 14–15.

22. Mamoulien, de Mille, and others were announced in "News of the Stage," *NYT*, January 19, 1943, 22.

23. Auditions were noted in "News of the Stage," *NYT*, January 22, 1943, 24. At the time of auditions, according to Morrison's *Broadway Theatres*, the Guild Theatre had no tenant.

24. Ms. Holm tells her audition tale in Myrna Katz Frommer and Harvey Frommer, *It Happened on Broadway* (Madison: University of Wisconsin Press, 2004), 100.

25. See "Brooks Costume Co., 1952," folder 30, box 1, NYU-W65.

26. Joan Roberts, the original Laurey, explained the use of basement-level rooms in an in-person interview with the author, November 2006, Rockville Centre, NY. Another example of double booking was when John Raitt auditioned for the *Oklahoma!* tour in the afternoon at the St. James, a few hours before the stage was used by Alfred Drake, Broadway's Curly. See Frommer and Frommer, *It Happened on Broadway*, 105–6.

27. At mid-century most out-of-town tryouts took place before audiences in New Haven, Boston, or Chicago, enabling creative teams to fine-tune their shows before opening in New York.

28. The theater historian Ethan Mordden has suggested that "part of what made *Oklahoma!* so unusual was its cheap staging, inevitable given the Guild's economic problems and beautifully papered over by the ingenious designers"; see Mordden, *Beautiful Mornin'*, 72.

29. *Saturday Evening Post*, January 6, 1945, 21–23, 59–60, folder "1940–1949," Theatre Guild, clippings, NYPL-BR: "Langner suggested . . . Grant Wood's painting for inspiration." The same clipping also features Langner's phone calls to colleagues. In a 2005 phone interview with the author, Hudson Scenic shop proprietor Neil Mazzella confirmed that this collaborative process was, and still is, crucial for effective stagecraft.

30. The "Business Agent's Report," September 18, 1933, folder 2, "Members Corr., 1933," box 4, NYU-W65, features payable painting days and suggests one or two weeks for most projects, with three to four men per painting or scenic construction project. A folder of 1940s invoices in box 4 had no documents specific to *Oklahoma!*, but others from 1943 suggest that painting days and project lengths were similar to those of 1933.

31. For descriptions of Jud's space, see Kantor and Maslon, *Broadway*, 204. The scholar Bobbi Jones names Robert Edmund Jones as the first designer of the New American Stagecraft; see Jones, *Scenic Design on Broadway* (New York: Greenwood Press, 1991), iiiv.

32. For more on this scenery, including images, see Henderson, *Mielziner*, 168–71. For the anecdote regarding cost savings for Bloomgarten, see Harris, *Broadway Theatre*, 58.

33. See collaboration on *Salesman* chronicled in Henderson, *Mielziner*, 168–71. Details include scenery costs of $11,500, lighting costs of $19,000, and a show budget of $45,000.

34. Searches for *Hedda Gabler* at http://www.ibdb.com (accessed May 5, 2009) include design credits for both the 1924 and 1948 productions. For an analysis of the rise of the lighting designer, see Jones, *Scenic Design on Broadway*, xiv.

35. Jones, *Scenic Design on Broadway*, xv, explains that multitasking in scenery, costumes, and lighting was neither practical nor popular by the 1950s.

36. A memo dated December 5, 1951, notes lighting for *Pal Joey*. For this and other lighting documents, including oversized lighting plots, see folders 1 and 2, box 5, Peggy Clark Collection, Library of Congress.

37. *Saturday Evening Post*, January 6, 1945, 21–23, 59–60, folder "1940–1949," Theatre Guild, clippings, NYPL-BR. Langner sent a 1901 mail-order catalog to White "for ideas."

38. In an in-person interview with the author, Rockeville Centre, New York, September 2006, Joan Roberts explained how this happened after the show had left for New Haven. In her recollection it was Miles White who brought the ribbon from New York for her hair.

39. 1940 Telephone Directory, NYPL-MRR, includes advertisements with claims of "largest stock" and "world's finest." For the details of Eaves's services, see Eaves booklet, 6, "Production": financing, clippings, NYPL-BR.

40. "Union Theatrical Costume Manufacturers and Shops," folder 30, "1945–47," box 1, NYU-W65. One or two of those listed are too small to count as fully fledged shops, so the tally is not exact.

41. For Chrisdie leases, see "Westside Leases Made," *NYT*, June 16, 1942, 37. Building widths and heights were culled from period maps of the Sanborn Company. For details of the shop's final years, see classified ad, *NYT*, June 5, 1962, 81; and Mrs. Chrisdie's obituary, *NYT*, June 14, 1965, 33, which notes the 1963 sale but not the buyer's name.

42. The list of nineteen employees, on file after an attempt by Local 829 to unionize Brooks in 1952, exists in folder 30, "Brooks Costume," box 1, NYU-W65.

43. Tennessee Williams, *The Glass Menagerie*, scene 2, stage directions, 1945.

44. Ballots from the vote on April 7, 1941, exist in folder 57, "Historical, 1941–43," box 2, NYU-W65.

45. "Costumers Local Threatens Stage," *NYT*, August 31, 1950, 34.

46. Resolution dated September 1, 1950, discovered in folder 41, "General Corr., Misc., 1950–52," box 2, NYU-W65.

47. Letter from Dick Jones regarding Emma Z. Swan, January 25, 2001, sent after Jones learned that the Museum of the City of New York was paying tribute to costume workers. See Dazian's clippings, MCNY-TC.

48. See Prince, *Contradictions*, 36. For more on *West Side Story* rehearsals, see Deborah Jowitt, *Jerome Robbins: His Life, His Theater, His Dance* (New York: Simon &

Schuster, 2004), 275–77. For cost implications of improper costumes, see Henderson, *Theater in America*, caption on 226.

49. With its store at 130 W. 46th St., Gladstone's was on the same block as Brooks, also on 46th. Maharam was at 117 W. 47th, while Dazian's was at 142 W. 44th. Correspondence from Local 829 to Maharam Fabric Corp. and Dazian's Inc. reveals exactly one unionized employee each at Dazian's and Maharam. It is likely that these employees kept a watchful eye on who was buying theatrical fabrics and for what purpose. See correspondence folder 13, box 3, NYU-W65.

50. "News of the Stage," *NYT*, January 1, 1942, 36.

51. *United Scenic Artists of America Contract*, Lemuel Ayers, folder 2, box 1, Theatre Guild Collection, Library of Congress.

52. Manhattan *Yellow Pages*, 1940, heading of "Draperies—Theatrical," NYPL-MRR.

53. Correspondence from 1941 reveals the existence and locations of branch offices through letterhead, Dazian's archive, MCNY-TC.

54. Carol Webb, 1943 article, unidentified magazine, "Pg. 16—June Caravan," "A Century in the Theatre," Dazian's archive, MCNY-TC.

55. Advertisement in *Simon's Directory*, 1966 ed. (New York: Package Publicity Service, 1966).

56. Joshua B. Freeman, *Working-Class New York: Life and Labor Since World War II* (New York: New Press, 2001), 12.

57. Budget statistics are from Jackson and Dunbar, *Encyclopedia of New York City*, "budget" entry, 165–67.

58. For productions per year, see *Variety*, June 26, 1966, 64. At www.ibdb.com (accessed May 24, 2009) there are only eighty-three entries for 1942–43, but it is not clear whether this includes shows that were built but never opened. The Broadway "season" in this era ran from September 1 to May 1 of the following year. Scenery details regarding the Atlantic City settings in *The Skin of Our Teeth*, the editor's office in *Lady in the Dark*, and the D.C. living room for Katharine Hepburn's *Without Love* were culled from www.ibdb.com, accessed May 24, 2009.

59. Membership count is from "Minutes," September 15, 1941, folder 57, "Historical, 1941–43," box 2, NYU-W65: "approximately 315 members, of whom some 200 classify themselves as journeymen, painters and around 100 as designers." Scene shop count is from folder 30, "1945–47, Union Theatrical Costume Manufacturers and Shops," box 1, NYU-W65.

60. See Rosenberg and Harburg, *The Broadway Musical*, for the post-1945 data on Broadway.

61. "'Oklahoma!' On Tour: Musical Has Been Seen in All States," *NYT*, February 25, 1951, 92. The railroad tour quote is from Robert Simonson, *On Broadway Men Still Wear Hats: Unusual Lives at the Edges of Broadway* (New York: Smith & Kraus, 2004), 48.

62. For ICC ruling, see Simonson, *On Broadway Men Still Wear Hats*, 48. For the Globe's 1922 advertisement, see *Julius Cahn–Gus Hill Theatrical Guide and Moving Picture Directory*, 1922 ed., uncatalogued, Shubert Archive (hereafter SA).

63. "Midtown Stores Attract Tenants," *NYT*, April 4, 1944, 32: "Kaj Velden Studios . . . two floors comprising about 14,000 sq ft in 545–9 W. 54th St"; "Manhattan Transfers," *NYT*, July 15, 1944, 24, rental listings for "351–55 W. 52nd St." Square footage for the 52nd Street building was estimated from Sanborn insurance maps. For the Fort Lee storage and fire, see "Fort Lee Fire Razes Famed Film Studios," *NYT*, March 24, 1952, 1.

64. For Lee Lash, Eldredge, and J. R. Clancy advertisements, see *Julius Cahn–Gus Hill Theatrical Guide and Moving Picture Directory*, 1922 ed., uncatalogued, SA.

65. *Business Listings/Yellow Pages*, NYPL-MRR, contain theater-related shop totals: 1922, 142; 1940, 126; 1950, 123; 1960, 224; 1970, 220; 1980, 47; 1990, 59.

Chapter 5

1. "Sunrise, Sunset," referenced in the chapter title, was a popular song in the 1964 musical *Fiddler on the Roof*; Barbara Karinska obituary, *NYT*, October 19, 1983, D25; "Life Begins at 40," *NYT*, September 4, 1968, 50.

2. *"Meet Manhattan," Christian Science Monitor*, March 11, 1967, Karinska clippings, NYPL-BR.

3. Phyllis Levin, "Costumer's Art Raises Dressmaking to the Highest Level," *NYT*, April 13, 1960, 42, Karinska clippings, NYPL-BR.

4. Quote by James Baughman in Shefter, *Capital of the American Century*, 124.

5. See Gerald Berkowitz, *New Broadways: Theatre Across America, Approaching a New Millennium* (New York: Rowan & Littlefield, 1982); Peter Novick, *Beyond Broadway* (New York: Hill & Wang, 1968); and Joseph Zeigler, *Regional Theatre: The Revolutionary Stage* (New York: Da Capo Press, 1977).

6. See Vincent Cannato, *The Ungovernable City: John Lindsay and His Struggle to Save New York* (New York: Basic Books, 2002); Robert Beauregard, *Voices of Decline: The Post-War Fate of U.S. Cities* (New York: Wiley-Blackwell, 1994); and Freeman, *Working-Class New York*.

7. For the characterization of Kook, see Simonson, *On Broadway Men Still Wear Hats*, 131–32.

8. For more on Kook's early career, see Henderson, *Mielziner*, 102–3; and "Maude Adams Invents Stage Lighting Device," *NYT*, October 15, 1931, 21.

9. Quoted in Henderson, *Mielziner*, 103.

10. "Lincoln Center Theater to Utilize an Electronic Lighting System," *NYT*, September 6, 1963, 34.

11. "Experts in the Spotlight: How They Solve Stage Lighting Problems on Broadway," *NYT*, March 30, 1958, X3.

12. "Lincoln Center Theater to Utilize . . .," *NYT*, September 6, 1963, 34.

13. For Kook and Mielziner's consulting across the country, see Henderson, *Mielziner*, 274.

14. "For 'Chorus Line,' a Moon Shot of Broadway Lighting," *NYT*, September 17, 1975, 40.

15. The journalist John Gunther in 1947, as quoted in Berkowitz, *New Broadways*, 1.

16. See introduction in Zeigler, *Regional Theatre*.

17. Quotes from Zeigler, *Regional Theatre*, 17; and Berkowitz, *New Broadways*, 68–73.

18. Details were culled from Berkowitz, *New Broadways*, 70–73; as well as http://www.alleytheatre.org, accessed March 23, 2007.

19. November 25, 1965, program for Kalita Humphreys Theatre, clippings folder "1955–79," Dallas Theatre Center, NYPL-BR.

20. *Tulane Drama Review*, fall 1965, clippings folder "1955–79," Dallas Theatre Center, NYPL-BR. In the 1980s the expanded and renovated center employed even more theater professionals.

21. See Theatre Communications Group interview with Fichandler, http://www.tcg.org/publications/at/2001/zelda.cfm, accessed March 13, 2009.

22. Berkowitz, *New Broadways*, 70–72.

23. See Martin Mayer, *Bricks, Mortar, and the Performing Arts: Report of the 20th Century Fund Task Force* (New York: 20th Century Fund, 1970), 1.

24. Details of the Guthrie's founding were culled from Berkowitz, *New Broadways*, 75; as well as the Guthrie's online history at http://www.guthrietheater.org/about_the_guthrie/theater_history, accessed March 14, 2009. For the quote on "national weight," see Zeigler, *Regional Theatre*, 4.

25. For descriptions of the Guthrie shops, see Mike Steele, "Guthrie Has Its Own Do-It-Yourself Shop," *Minneapolis Star Tribune*, October 14, 1988, E01.

26. Milwaukee details can be found in "Our 1st 20 Years: 1954–74 . . . ," Milwaukee Rep. folder, NYPL-BR. For the Houston anecdote, see http://www.alleytheatre.org, "History," "A Home of Our Own," accessed March 14, 2009.

27. See chap. 1 of Zeigler, *Regional Theatre*, for an analysis of the Guthrie's singularity.

28. Howard Taubman, "Theater: New Minnesota Playhouse," *NYT*, May 9, 1963, 41.

29. Headlines are from *Seattle Post-Intelligencer*, February 17 and June 16, 1963, Seattle Rep clippings, folder "1960–69," NYPL-BR. Characterizations of Vaughan and Wright are from Douglas Q. Barnett, http://www.historylink.org/, Essay 9058: "The Seattle Repertory Theatre Affair," accessed March 14, 2009.

30. "Birth of a Theatre," *Playbill*, September 1965, Seattle Rep clippings, folder "1960–69," NYPL-BR.

31. Ibid.

32. Quotes and factual material are from "Arts," *Women's Wear Daily*, November 23, 1983; "A City That Staged a Fair and Got Culture," *Wall Street Journal*, March 9, 1979; and *Seattle Centerstage* #15, 1977/78, Seattle Rep clippings, NYPL-BR.

33. *Variety*, March 9, 1966, 1.

34. Atlanta details are from *Players* 43, no. 2 (December 1967–January 1968), Theatre Atlanta clippings, NYPL-BR.

35. 1991 *Encore* program, Oregon Shakespeare Festival clippings, NYPL-BR.

36. *Players* 43, no. 2 (December 1967–January 1968), 7, Milwaukee Rep clippings, NYPL-BR.

37. Berkowitz, *New Broadways*, 97–98, cites *Effect of Gamma Rays* coming from Houston in 1968 and *Streamers* coming from New Haven in 1976. For analysis of the "long line" of shows transferring after *The Great White Hope*, see Adler, *On Broadway*, 5.

38. Originally printed in the *Tulane Drama Review* and widely quoted since. For more from Gregory, see his Theatre Communications Group interview, http://www.tcg.org/publications/at/Mar05/gregory.cfm, accessed March 15, 2009.

39. Magnum was also let go because, according to the 1974 artistic director, "Mrs. Magnum was cast as leading lady in a few too many plays"; see "Our 1st 20 Years: 1954–74 . . . ," Milwaukee Rep clippings, NYPL-BR.

40. See *Simon's Theatrical Directory*, 1955, 1963, 1966, 1970, and 1975 editions.

41. "Straw Hat Revue Opening Delayed to Friday Because Scenery Isn't Union-Made," *New York Herald Tribune*, September 25, 1939, "Scenery: Construction" clippings, NYPL-BR: "[I]t was discovered that the scenery used by the revue during its engagement in Bushkill, Pa., did not bear the union label. After conferring with the Stagehands' Union, Local 1, the management agreed to order a complete new production. Night and day shifts will be used to complete the work."

42. For quote and voting details, see letter from Andy Clores, January 29, 1970, folder 1, "Corr.," box 4, NYU-W65.

43. Berkowitz, *New Broadways*, 35; and Samuel Leiter, *Ten Seasons: New York Theatre in the Seventies* (New York: Greenwood Press, 1986), 25, both begin their analyses of Off Broadway with the Atkinson review. Characterizations of Atkinson and his bow ties are drawn from Atkinson obituary, *NYT*, January 15, 1984, 1; and review of *Summer and Smoke*, "At the Theatre," *NYT*, April 25, 1952, 19.

44. Berkowitz, *New Broadways*, 31–35, does an excellent survey of non-Broadway theater prior to 1952.

45. See Stephen Langley, *Producers on Producing* (New York: Drama Book Specialists, 1976), "Commentary by Theodore Mann," 113–16.

46. See Berkowitz, *New Broadways*, 34. The deal also raised the number of seats producers were allowed to have while paying reduced Off-Broadway wages, from 299 seats or fewer to 499 or fewer.

47. Only in the late 1970s and early 1980s did Off-Broadway producers begin to work with nonunion scene shops in the five boroughs. See "Major Non-Union Shops

Serving New York," *Theatre Crafts*, November 1986, "Scenery: Construction" clippings, NYPL-BR.

48. To this day commercial theater spaces with 99 seats or fewer count as "Off-Off Broadway," those with more than 99 but fewer than 499 are "Off Broadway," and anything over 500 seats is fair game for Broadway's unions. For copious detail on these distinctions, see Leiter, *Ten Seasons*, chaps. 1–3.

49. The scandals in question were known as the Lefkowitz hearings and will be discussed in Chapter 6.

50. Edgar B. Young, *Lincoln Center: The Building of an Institution* (New York: New York University Press, 1980), 7.

51. Mayer, *Bricks, Mortar, and the Performing Arts*, 20.

52. Ibid.

53. Young, *Lincoln Center*, 307.

54. "Largest Costumers Announce a Merger," *NYT*, November 21, 1962, 24.

55. A Van Horn rental facility appears on W. 47th St. in the 1960 Yellow Pages, NYPL-MRR.

56. Jacobs, *The Death and Life of Great American Cities*, 167.

Chapter 6

1. "Every Day a Little Death" is a song from the 1973 Broadway musical *A Little Night Music*. Climate information is from "Weather," *NYT*, March 11, 1980, A1. Information on shows of that evening is from http://www.ibdb.com, accessed June 1, 2009.

2. "3 Seized in Slaying," *NYT*, March 13, 1980, B6; "Victim Is Identified in Dismemberment," *NYT*, March 14, 1980, B3.

3. Press release dated October 16, 1979, detailing the Mellon Grant, folder "1970–79," Seattle Rep clippings, NYPL-BR; cover advertising with "Broadway's Pal Joey" language from *Repartee* magazine, April/May 1980, folder "1980–85," Seattle Rep clippings, NYPL-BR.

4. A 1901 map of Times Square bordellos appears in Timothy Gilfoyle, *City of Eros: New York City, Prostitution, and the Commercialization of Sex, 1790–1920* (New York: Norton, 1994), 208.

5. See "Olympia Ready to Open," *NYT*, November 24, 1895, 13; and "Police Call in Olympia," *NYT*, November 26, 1895, 1.

6. Van Hoogstraten, *Lost Broadway Theatres*, 39, cites 1920 as the last year for theater at the Olympia. For this project I have defined "theater craft" as broadly as possible, to include all of the nonperforming professionals involved in crafting, producing, selling, and marketing finished theatrical products.

7. Though the two buildings were connected, the tower extended back so far that its main entrance actually sat on 46th St. See "New Lyceum a Model of Comfort," *NYT*, September 27, 1903, 26.

8. See Elizabeth Blackmar, "Uptown Real Estate and the Creation of Times Square," in William Taylor, ed., *Inventing Times Square: Commerce and Culture at the Crossroads of the World* (Baltimore: Johns Hopkins University Press, 1996), 64.

9. This space is currently the Shubert Archive, a vital depository of theatrical records. The author's research trips to this archive in 2004 were a major inspiration for this book.

10. "New Lyceum a Model of Comfort," 26. See Henderson, *The City and the Theatre*, 266–67, for a description of the "warren of spaces."

11. Manhattan *Business Listings*, 1903, NYPL-MRR.

12. Pons's credits were gleaned from his obituary, *NYT*, January 30, 1959, 27. After his passing, Helene was still an active costumer, and she was interviewed by WQXR radio in 1966. See "Today on WQXR," *NYT*, September 23, 1966, 74.

13. See Van Hoogstraten, *Lost Broadway Theatres*, 39, for a full history of the building.

14. Firm names were collected from Manhattan *Business Listings*, 1940, NYPL-MRR.

15. In the records of NYPL-MRR, the peripatetic Pons shop is a case in point. *Business Listings* for 1929 show it at 112 W. 44th, the same building where Barbara Karinska was. In 1940 it was at 125 W. 45th, while 1950 listings show it at 8 W. 56th. In the listings for 1960, after George passed, Helene Pons appears at 254 W. 56th, the last known address of the shop.

16. Tracy C. Davis coined this excellent, useful phrase in *The Economics of the British Stage*.

17. See Campbell, *The Golden Years of Broadcasting*, 242. He cites 1954 as the beginning of the segment.

18. The argument of this paragraph is grounded in the theories proposed by the urbanist Jane Jacobs in her iconic 1961 book, *The Death and Life of Great American Cities*.

19. Chronicled at http://www.nysonglines.com/45st.htm, accessed January 10, 2010, but not verified through archival research.

20. Letter from Dick Jones regarding Emma Z. Swan, January 25, 2001, sent after Mr. Jones learned that the Museum of the City of New York was paying tribute to costume workers. See Dazian's clippings, MCNY-TC.

21. Joan Roberts in-person interview with the author, Rockeville Centre, NY, September 2006; Celeste Holm story chronicled in Frommer and Frommer, *It Happened on Broadway*, 101.

22. See Toni Bentley, *Costumes by Karinska* (New York: Harry N. Abrams, 1995). Even as an elderly woman, Karinska prided herself on doing her own fabric shopping. As a 1968 interviewer related, "[N]ow at 81 . . . she is most likely to run around and do most of the shopping for fabrics"; see "Life Begins at 40," *NYT*, September 4, 1968, 50.

23. Gladstone was on West 47th, while Maharam was on West 46th; see *Yellow Pages*, 1950, NYPL-MRR.

24. In 1929 the owners of the building counted Manus Music Company, the music instructors Winter & Caffrey, Cosmopolitan Opera Co., Consolidated Theatrical Enterprises, Frank A. Miller's Entertainment Lyceum, and the agents A. B. Hunter, Ted Rosenthal, and Edwin Sheres as tenants; see *Business Listings*, 1929, NYPL-MRR.

25. "Midtown Jeweler Shot in Robbery," *NYT*, March 9, 1968, 59.

26. "Gunmen Rob . . . Garage in Midtown," *NYT*, May 28, 1963, 18; "Holdup Suspect, 18, Seized . . . ," *NYT*, July 11, 1965, 57.

27. See "Four Held in Pistol-Whipping Linked to 35 Burglaries," *NYT*, June 6, 1964, 20; "Suspect in Feb. 3rd Slaying of Book Designer Is Seized," *NYT*, April 9, 1967, 51; and "Bank Guard Here Shoots Man Suspected of Robbery," *NYT*, April 20, 1968, 36.

28. "Muggings Disturb *Borstal Boy* Cast," *NYT*, July 16, 1970, 42.

29. "Jersey Youth Slain Near Times Square," *NYT*, December 27, 1971, 16; mob killing from "Reputed Gallo Family Associate Convicted . . . ," *NYT*, May 11, 1973, 40. For more on the Mafia, see Sagalyn, *Times Square Roulette*, 47.

30. It is also possible that new reporters at the *Times* showed more interest in covering midtown crime than their predecessors did, but the author has not encountered evidence suggesting that such a shift occurred.

31. "9 Peep Shows Are Raided in Times Square Area," *NYT*, August 11, 1971, 21; "Hotel in Times Square Closed in Cleanup Campaign," *NYT*, August 28, 1972, 55.

32. In *The Death and Life of Great American Cities*, Jane Jacobs famously argues that strangers unknowingly perform a "street ballet" of safety on city sidewalks. See also Mayor's Office report from Lindsay, "Confidential Subject Files," folder 182: "Prostitution," box 15, New York City Municipal Archives (hereafter NYC-MA).

33. The survival of Fanny Violino's hats is particularly poignant when one considers the caustic, somewhat nostalgic dialogue of the 1970 musical *Company*. During her iconic song "Here's to the Ladies Who Lunch," the character of Joanne asked audiences at the Alvin Theater on 52nd Street, "[D]oes anyone still wear a hat?" which implied that few did. All the while Fanny Violino continued to craft precisely these items in her shop only five blocks away.

34. Chenko created the bear costumes of the 1958 musical *Goldilocks*; see *Playbill* for this show, NYPL-BR.

35. The addresses of adult and criminal businesses are listed in a Lindsay administration report, "Confidential Subject Files," folder 182: "Prostitution," box 15, NYC-MA. Most sites also appear on the maps printed for Gail Sheehy's 1972 exposé in *New York* magazine, featured in Sagalyn, *Times Square Roulette*, 44.

36. For ticket sellers, see Business Listings, 1929, NYPL-MRR: Central tickets at 810 8th Ave., Johnies at 308 W. 49th, and Lords Milenthal at 304 W. 49th. For the Federal Theatre Project at Ringle's, see "July 1936 Schedules, Fed. Music Dept.-NYC 9B-5," folder 6, Administrative Files, box 967, LOC-FTP.

37. The bookstores in question were at 801 and 809 8th Ave. See Mayor's Office report from Lindsay, "Confidential Subject Files," folder 182: "Prostitution," box 15, NYC-MA.

38. *Business Listings*, 1903: Hurtig & Simon and Reich at 147 W. 42nd, Brooks and Klaw & Erlanger at 214 W. 42nd, NYPL-MRR.

39. *Business Listings*, 1929, "Tickets," NYPL-MRR: Circle Tkt. Office at 1475 Broadway; Wilson & Coleman tickets at 1465 Broadway; Managers Tkt. Svc. at 229 W. 42nd; David Mandel at 227 W. 42nd; Broadway Theatre Tkt. Co. at 218 W. 42nd; Theatre Tkt. Library at 212 W. 42nd; Everins at 206 W. 42nd; Louis Cohn's at 204 W. 42nd; Oscar Alexander at 200 W. 42nd; Tyson Co. Inc. at 151 W. 42nd; Tyson & Co. at 148 W. 42nd.

40. Academic works such as Daniel Makagon, *Where the Ball Drops: Days and Nights in Times Square* (Minneapolis: University of Minnesota Press, 2004), provide gritty details from a sociological perspective, while trade titles add to the historical record with detailed descriptions, interviews, and anecdotes. See especially Marc Eliot, *Down 42nd Street: Sex, Money, Culture, and Politics at the Crossroads of the World* (New York: Warner Books, 2001); and Anthony Bianco, *Ghosts of 42nd Street* (New York: William Morrow, 2004).

41. Henderson, *The City and the Theatre* , 187–88.

42. Taylor, *Inventing Times Square*, xxv.

43. Quoted in Brooks McNamara's essay, "The Entertainment District at the End of the 1930s," in Taylor, *Inventing Times Square,* 190.

44. When city leaders clamped down on pornographic shops, some landlords had to go to great lengths to disguise their involvement. For details on this and for the history of properties being "milked," see Sagalyn, *Times Square Roulette*, 45–47.

45. For more on actors' reluctance to embrace their trade as "labor," see Sean P. Holmes, "All the World's a Stage! The Actors' Strike of 1919," Journal of American History 91 (March 2005): 1291–1317; and McArthur, *Actors and American Culture.*

46. A notable exception in the 1940s, 1950s, and 1960s was *Playbill,* which occasionally featured backstage workers and was handed out by ushers to all theatergoers.

47. "5 Theatre Aides Accused by Jury," *NYT*, May 19, 1964, 1.

48. Ibid.

49. "2 Producers of Mythical Musical Held," *NYT*, April 27, 1949, 32, "Stage: Financing," clippings, 1940–49, NYPL-BR.

50. See John F. Wharton, "A Fresh Look at Theatre Tickets," a report of Legitimate Theatre Exploratory Commission, 1966, "Production—Financing," clippings, NYPL-BR.

51. "Lindsay Wows Em in Broadway Debut That's Simply Boff," *NYT,* March 24, 1973, 22.

52. See Cannato, *The Ungovernable City,* chap. 15, "Assessing the Lindsay Years."

53. "Cleaning Up Hell's Bedroom," *New York* magazine, November 13, 1972, 50–66; "The Landlords of Hell's Bedroom," *New York* magazine, January 20, 1972, 67–80. See also Cannato, *The Ungovernable City.*

54. John V. Lindsay, "Let's Quit Squandering Land," *Realty*, December 13, 1966, Lindsay clippings, NYC-MA.

55. Sagalyn, *Times Square Roulette*, 55. Sagalyn notes that it was the first specialized, nonhistoric zoning district in the city.

56. For wrecking crew details, see "Plazas Planned for Astor's Site," *NYT*, January 5, 1967, 37.

57. Marilyn Stasio, "Now Playing on Broadway, the Big Squeeze," *NYT*, July 9, 1989, H5.

58. Details about these studios appear in ibid.; and in Jennifer Dunning, "A Legendary Dance Studio That's Still Kicking," *NYT*, June 15, 1989, C15. Peter Marinos, who appeared in several Broadway shows during the 1970s and 1980s, confirmed Stasio's assertion that rehearsal studios were a "precious commodity." In an in-person oral history interview with the author at his Upper West Side apartment on January 24, 2011, Marinos also confirmed that *Evita*'s producers used the Minskoff studios for Equity chorus auditions in 1979.

59. William Robbins, "Revival Comes to Broadway," *NYT*, January 20, 1968, 31.

60. Milton Esterow, "City Proposes More Theaters to Revitalize Midtown District," *NYT*, October 1, 1967, 1.

61. Walter Kerr, "Not a Championship Season: Can Broadway Move?," *NYT*, June 3, 1973, 272.

62. Joseph P. Fried, "Manhattan Plaza Wins Approval as Housing for Performing Artists," *NYT*, February 4, 1977, 37; John Wark, "Performers Queuing Up—to Audition for an Apartment," *NYT*, July 10, 1977, 200.

63. For details of who moved in, see the documentary *Miracle on 42nd Street* (Bahr Productions, expected release 2014), featuring interviews with Angela Lansbury and others. See also "Neighbors Helping Neighbors," CBS broadcast on Manhattan Plaza, May 13, 1991. For rehearsal room details, see Joseph P. Fried, "Manhattan Plaza Plan Gains," *NYT*, January 4, 1977, L1.

64. Sagalyn, *Times Square Roulette*, 59.

65. Ibid., 53–54.

66. Unidentified newspaper clipping, November 23, 1983, Seattle Rep clippings, NYPL-BR.

Chapter 7

1. The lyrics in the chapter title come from the song "And the Money Kept Rolling In" in the musical *Evita*. After the British musicals *Oliver!*, *Stop the World—I Want to Get Off*, and *Roar of the Greasepaint, Smell of the Crowd* succeeded in the 1960s, U.S. theater journalists buzzed about a "British invasion." Lloyd Webber's *Jesus Christ Superstar* continued the trend in 1971, prior to *Evita*.

2. For details on sales, see "A London Hit Arrives—With a Controversial New Heroine," *NYT*, September 23, 1979, D1.

3. An excellent example comes from 1915, when British costumer Lucile outfitted Broadway star Irene Castle. See Schweitzer, *When Broadway Was the Runway*, 168.

4. In his letters to Theatre Projects Lighting Ltd., Prince expressed frustration over delayed delivery. See folder "Correspondence—Misc.," boxes 28,235, 28,236, and 28,237, Harold Prince Collection, NYPL-BR.

5. For vocal cords as "raw hamburger meat" due to strain, see Patti LuPone, *Patti LuPone: A Memoir* (New York: Three Rivers Press, 2011), 116. This was confirmed and fleshed out in detail by Peter Marinos, an original cast member, during an oral history interview at his apartment on the Upper West Side, January 21, 2011.

6. Peter Marinos interview, January 21, 2011; LuPone, *A Memoir*, 108–9.

7. Audition schedules were discovered in folder "H2S-Miscellaneous," box 44C, Bob Fosse & Gwen Verdon Collection, Music Division Special Collections, Library of Congress (hereafter LOC-FV). Based on the flexibility of Fosse's audition schedule within several "go-to" theaters, it seems unlikely that he was being charged much, if anything, to use them. In the copious financial records available in the LOC-FV collection, there is no evidence of such payments.

8. Afternoon auditions at both theaters are documented in folder 3, "Pippin-Casting," box 25B, LOC-FV.

9. For *Little Me* at Variety Arts, see folder marked "Little Me Auditions," box 44C, and for *Pippin* at Studio 58, see "Casting Folder 4," box 25B, both in LOC-FV. For the stagehands' strike, see letter from Michael Shurtleff Casting to Fosse, September 26, 1975, folder "Corr. Stuart Ostrow, Michael Shurtleff, Bob Fosse 1971–77," box 25B, LOC-FV.

10. Documentation of auditions at "Minskoff Rehearsal Studio #4" on June 8, 1977, is available in "Casting Folder 4," box 25B, LOC-FV.

11. Gatekeeper history details are from an oral history interview with IATSE stagehand Michael Corbett at the New Amsterdam Theatre, February 25, 2011. When invited to trail the musical *Big* in 1995, the writer Barbara Isenberg got intimate access to the scenery and described it as follows: "[T]he 3-sided units, each 14-ft. tall and weighing maybe 1/2 a ton, will move along tracks that can be jammed with something as small as a ballpoint pen"; see Barbara Isenberg, *Making It Big: The Diary of a Broadway Musical* (New York: Limelight Editions, 1996), 55.

12. LuPone, *A Memoir*, 113.

13. Peter Marinos interview, January 21, 2011.

14. See Ted Chapin, *Everything Was Possible: The Birth of the Musical Follies* (New York: Applause Books, 2005), 3.

15. "Allied Studios Inc.," 1970 *Yellow Pages*, "Theatrical Equipment & Supplies," NYPL-MRR.

16. For 890 Broadway, see "Now Playing on Broadway, the Big Squeeze," *NYT*, July 9, 1989, H5.

17. All details come from an oral history interview with William Ivey Long at his Tribeca workshop, May 9, 2011.

18. Peter Marinos interview, January 21, 2011.

19. William Ivey Long interview, May 9, 2011.

20. A rider in the Hersey contract reads: "first-class round-trip travel and transportation expenses, when he is required by the Manager to travel outside of England in connection with the services hereunder"; see folder 6: "Evita—contracts misc," box 28,235, Harold Prince Collection, New York Public Library (hereafter NYPL-HP).

226. Details on the show's mural and the Martin Gottfried quote on "fabulous imagery" are chronicled in Carol Ilsen, *Harold Prince: From Pajama Game to Phantom of the Opera and Beyond* (New York: UMI Research Press, 1989), 265, 274.

22. Before Channing, leading lady Anna Maria Alberghetti is said to have worn one for the 1961 musical *Carnival.* Sound expert Bill Merrill noted this in a letter to the editor," *NYT*, June 30, 1996, H27.

23. Ilsen, *Harold Prince*, chap. 16, "Evita."

24. Larry Fuller is quoted in Foster Hirsch, *Harold Prince and the American Musical Theatre* (Cambridge: Cambridge University Press, 1989), 165.

25. Letter from Harry McCune Sound Service, Inc., San Francisco, April 13, 1979, folder 6: "Evita—contracts misc," box 28,235, NYPL-HP.

26. Letters between Prince and the Stigwood group detail long-standing concerns about sound. See folder 2: "Evita: Correspondence," box 28,236, NYPL-HP.

27. Frank Rich, "Stage View," *NYT*, February 21, 1982, D4.

28. Contract between Howard Haines and Theatre Techniques Associates, October 20, 1980, folder 6: "Evita—contracts misc," box 28,235, NYPL-HP.

29. For a feature on these machines, see "For 'Chorus Line,' a Moon Shot of Broadway Lighting," *NYT*, September 17, 1975, 40.

30. Letter from contractor Bran Ferren to production manager Howard Haines, October 19, 1979, folder 6: "Evita—contracts misc," box 28,235, NYPL-HP.

31. Mitchell's investments sometimes appear under the slightly disguised heading "R. M. Theatricals," in folder 6: "Evita—contracts misc," box 28,235, NYPL-HP.

32. Stroock appears in several of Leo Shull's *Angels* booklets. In Prince's investor lists from the 1960s and early 1970s (NYPL-HP), many names appear repeatedly for shows such as *Flora, the Red Menace; It's a Bird, It's a Plane . . .; Cabaret; Zorba; Company;* and *Follies.*

33. It is interesting that Columbus, Ohio, was also featured in Chapter 1 as the site to Mathias Armbruster's scenery and backdrop painting business in the 1870s and 1880s. The scenery credit for Theatre Magic in Columbus appears in the 1983 *Playbill* for *Cats.*

34. *Les Misérables* costume details are from interview with William Ivey Long, May 9, 2011. *Jerome Robbins' Broadway* shoe details are from "Now Playing on Broadway, the Big Squeeze," *NYT*, July 9, 1898, H5. *Show Boat* scenery details are from the 1993 *Playbill. Medea* scenery details are from an interview with IATSE stagehand Michael Corbett, February 21, 2011. *Dirty Rotten Scoundrels* details are from a phone interview with Neal Mazzella of Hudson Scenic by the author, fall 2005.

35. See Adler, *On Broadway*, 20. For "entertainment conglomerates" as producers, see also Maurya Wickstrom, *Performing Consumers: Global Capital and Its Theatrical Seductions* (New York: Routledge, 2006), 8–9.

36. See Elizabeth Wollman, *The Theater Will Rock* (Ann Arbor: University of Michigan Press, 2009), 103.

37. See Michael McKinnie, *City Stages: Theatre and Urban Space in a Global City* (Toronto: University of Toronto Press, 2013), chap. 1, on "theatrical" downtown Toronto and displays of urban affluence.

38. See Wickstrom, *Performing Consumers*, 66.

39. Robert Long and Larry Opitz, "Giving Them the Business: Broadway's Union Scene Shops," *Theatre Crafts* (March 1986): 72, in "Scenery: Construction," NYPL-BR.

40. Details of the studios and Cora Cahan quote in Jesse McKinley, "Bookings Greet New 42nd Street Studios," *NYT*, June 14, 2000, E3.

41. "For Troupes in Need of Soaring Space, Sharing Is the Real Estate Buzzword," *NYT*, August 28, 1999, B16.

Index

Page numbers in italics indicate images.

Acknowledgments

TO BRING THIS project to fruition, I relied on invaluable assistance from many wonderful people. I would never have taken the scholar's path were it not for the strong and supportive mentorship I received from Marysa Navarro and Gene Garthwaite many years ago at Dartmouth College. They pushed me to do my best work as a researcher and writer, and I thank them for showing me how to be an historian. At Columbia University, Alan Brinkley was an equally indispensable resource, and I thank him for his insights regarding the potential of this research. When the *Blue-Collar Broadway* project was in its infancy, Elizabeth Blackmar provided thoughtful, heartfelt advice about choosing a book topic that one can love for many years, and for this I will be forever grateful. Many thanks as well to Owen Gutfreund for savvy advice about publishing, academic conferences, and the urban history angle of this project.

For inspiring my passion for teaching, learning about, and writing about cities, I am delighted to thank Kenneth T. Jackson. Without his infectious enthusiasm for urban history, I doubt that my most exciting research discoveries about Times Square or Broadway would have ever come to pass. Some of my fondest memories of learning about New York City history come from his utterly relatable and engrossing lectures, from attending many world-class walking tours, and from riding along on the legendary midnight bike ride. I must thank Nancy Friedland of Butler Library at Columbia for so generously helping me shape my ideas for publication. For many years of camaraderie in Butler, I thank a great cohort of friends, colleagues, roommates, and fellow tour guides, including but not limited to Nancy Kwak, Monica Gisolfi, Rona Holub, Jeffrey Trask, Reiko Hillyer, Toru Umezaki, Ted Wilkinson, James Downs, Sarah Gregg, Jung Pak, Jennifer Tammi, Seth Kamil, Ben Martin, Victoria Cain, Josh Wolff, Alex

Cummings, Niki Hemmer, Daniel Freund, Julia Golia, Zaheer Ali, Jenna Feltey Alden, and Christopher Klemek.

I thank Ellen Schrecker and Hadassa Kosak at Yeshiva University for so generously helping me to connect this research to my teaching. This project also benefited greatly from the vibrant scholarly community of the New School and the rich archival holdings of the New-York Historical Society, where I worked as a Bernard and Irene B. Schwartz Fellow. I thank the entire Committee on Historical Studies at the New School and the archival team at N-YHS, especially Jean Ashton, for investing in me and in this book. During these same years, it was my pleasure and privilege to connect with Timothy Gilfoyle at the offices of the *Journal of Urban History*, who not only gave me an excellent opportunity to publish my ideas but also provided sound insights into the research questions I had concerning Times Square. Mark H. Rose and Richard Greenwald were tremendously generous conference colleagues during this process, and I thank them for taking me under their wing and helping me connect to invaluable people and ideas.

Over the course of my research, I encountered many talented archivists who went out of their way to find me relevant materials and were patient with my requests for "one more folder" as closing time neared. In particular, I thank Jeremy Megraw of the New York Public Library's Billy Rose Theatre Collection; Walter Zvonchenko and Jasminn Winters of the Library of Congress; Sylvia Wang, Maryann Chach, and Mark Swartz of the Shubert Archive; and Gail Malmgreen and Kevyen Barr of the NYU Tamiment Library. Beyond the archives, this project was built upon many vital oral history interviews. For their time and thoughtful reflections, I thank interview subjects William Ivey Long, Peter Marinos, Michael Corbett, Gary Stevens, Neil Mazzella, and Joan Roberts.

Most recently, as this project reached its final stages, I benefited from a wonderfully supportive team at New Jersey City University. I owe a deep debt of gratitude to history department colleagues Rosemary Thurston, Jose Morales, Jason Martinek, Rosamond Hooper-Hamersley, Carmela Karnoutsos, and John Bragg for their camaraderie throughout this entire process. Outside of my department, I am grateful to Bill Montgomery for help with Geographic Information Systems, to Ellen Quinn for connecting me to the illustration software and experts I needed, and to Manuel Barreiro for his excellent illustration skills. I also thank visionary NJCU leaders Barbara Feldman, Joanne Bruno, and Sue Henderson for their support of this project.

In regard to my editor Bob Lockhart, I cannot thank him enough for steering this massive project with such thoughtfulness over many years. Bob was there from nearly the beginning of this book, as its scope became much wider and its questions more profound. I have fond memories of conversing over pulled-pork sandwiches about the kind of book that this could become, and I am grateful to him for his patience and vision. I am also very thankful for Erica Ginsburg's keen eye and support.

To my families, both in California and in New York/New Jersey, I thank you for putting up with the exhausting rhythms of academic publishing, in which "the book" is never quite done. To my partner, Keith Slusser, I extend my deepest thanks for sharing his life with me, for creating a home in which I am encouraged to be my best self, and for believing me when I promised that at the end of the tunnel, past the rewrites, research, and revisions, all of the long hours on this book would pay off.

CPSIA information can be obtained at www.ICGtesting.com
Printed in the USA
LVOW10*0856190715

446784LV00002B/16/P